WIT...

No lo...
B...
Sale of this ... ...rary

OMNIVM LVX CIVIVM

BOSTON
PUBLIC
LIBRARY

THE BLAZE OF NOON

THE BLAZE OF NOON

A Reading of *Samson Agonistes*

BY

ANTHONY LOW

COLUMBIA UNIVERSITY PRESS

New York and London 1974

The Andrew W. Mellon Foundation, through a special grant, has assisted the Press in publishing this volume.

Library of Congress Cataloging in Publication Data

Low, Anthony, 1935–
    The blaze of noon.

    Includes bibliographical references.
    1. Milton, John, 1608–1674. Samson Agonistes.
I. Title.
PR3566.L6   1974   821'.4   74–1484
ISBN 0–231–03842–9

Copyright © 1974 Columbia University Press
Printed in the United States of America

FOR PAULINE

PREFACE

Setting aside the tragedies of Shakespeare, which are unique, *Samson Agonistes* is unequaled by any other English tragedy in the strength of its emotions, the authority of its action, the quality of its verse, or in sheer total density. It is worthy to stand beside those writers with whom Milton dared comparison: Aeschylus, Sophocles, and Euripides. The more one reads it, the more it comes alive, while most other non-Shakespearean plays begin to seem poor and thin under such scrutiny. Yet *Samson* has never had quite the recognition it deserves. Most Miltonists know its worth, but few other critics have written on it, writers on English drama seldom give it its due, and ordinary intelligent readers, though they usually respond to it with enthusiasm if they meet with it in an academic course, seldom seek it out voluntarily. Yet like *Paradise Lost, Samson Agonistes* is a work that will fully repay any effort a modern reader is willing to give to it.

The reasons for this relative neglect of the play are mostly fortuitous. It will not fit into academic courses on the drama. It was not

intended for the stage, it comes too late to be included with the
Elizabethan or Stuart plays, it is a fish out of water among Restoration comedies, and it is the work of a primarily non-dramatic writer.
Besides, it ignores most of the precedents of Elizabethan tragedy and
(except perhaps for Shelley) it has no worthy English descendants.
Like *Paradise Lost,* it is too big to fit conveniently into its proper
niche in literary history. Finally, until this century not even Miltonists have given *Samson* the kind of criticism it deserves. Fortunately,
this no longer is true: the play is now getting the kind of critical
attention that has done so much recently to illuminate *Paradise Lost*
for the common reader. A wider understanding should result from
this criticism. If this book contributes to such an end, it will have
accomplished most of its purpose.

My intention in this study is to say something useful both to professional Milton scholars and teachers and to Milton's ordinary
readers. The last is a smaller class than it should be, but a choice
one. I have made the explorations and the technicalities as lucid and
free from jargon as I can, while at the same time avoiding more than
the necessary recapitulation of what has been well said elsewhere. I
have also written and revised these chapters, during the course of
the past seven years, in order to understand better my own reactions
to the play and to put them in some order—though such a task is
never satisfactorily completed. The book's present form is partly the
result of an emerging necessity, not entirely foreseen when the work
began. I have avoided going through *Samson* relentlessly scene by
scene, proceeding instead by a series of excursions into various
aspects which I think important or illuminating, occasionally coming
back to the same point from a different angle. I believe this method
has advantages which make it worth following: particularly the opportunity to pursue in depth topics which are not restricted to one
part of the play. *Samson* lends itself to this kind of treatment, because
it is both very complex and very simple. By the end of the book, these
excursions will be found to converge into a unified reading.

I have included a substantial number of citations in the notes
(though it would be easy to add many more) and provided line references throughout for the verse. Both practices clutter the text; but
the citations will be useful for some readers, as well as suggesting

some of my indebtedness to other Miltonists, while the line references facilitate reference to the play. Moreover, because *Samson* is not
a static but a dynamic work, it is important to know where in the play
a phrase or a passage appears. I hope, however, that those readers not
interested in such technicalities will ignore them. There is nothing
in the notes essential to the argument, and it is easy to train one's
eye to skip over line references without seeing them.

Parts of Chapters 3, 4, and 9 were previously published, in sub-
stantially different form, as essays, in *PMLA* (1969), *Texas Studies in
Literature and Language* (1969, copyright University of Texas Press),
and *Huntington Library Quarterly* (1971). I have revised them for the
book in the light of what I have learned or thought through since they
appeared. I wish to thank the editors for permission to reprint. I also
thank Columbia University Press for use of *The Works of John Milton*
(cited in the notes as *Works*) which is my authority throughout for
Milton's prose and poetry.

I owe a special debt to Douglas Bush, with whom I studied Milton
while I was at Harvard — though later I wrote my thesis under him on
quite a different subject. I have received research grants from Seattle
University and the Graduate School of New York University. My
friends Murray Prosky and A. J. Magill helped in the earlier stages
with advice and much-needed encouragement, while David H.
Greene and James W. Tuttleton read through the nearly completed
manuscript. William F. Bernhardt at Columbia University Press
steered the book through several potential difficulties. Isaac Asimov
suggested the title. Several readers whom I cannot name assisted me.
C. A. Patrides, John M. Steadman, and J. Max Patrick gave generous
and plentiful advice that led to many revisions in the typescript.
What errors remain are my own.

Finally, my wife, to whom this book is dedicated, has sustained me
as Milton thought an ideal wife should, by her presence and companionship, by her intelligent Yeatsian abstention from things
academic, and by her efforts to keep me human in spite of the long
immersion in books and in words.

New York University and Dark Harbor, Maine   A. L.
1973

CONTENTS

THE BLAZE OF NOON

1
INTRODUCTION

Of Milton's three major works, only *Paradise Lost* has had the relatively uninterrupted approval of both critics and ordinary readers. *Paradise Regained,* after centuries of neglect or disapproval, is currently enjoying a revival among Milton scholars, yet the poem remains an acquired taste, for which one must earn a liking. Until recently, the opposite has more happily been true of *Samson Agonistes.* Although it might have had more readers if the critics had treated it better, *Samson* has met from the beginning with spontaneous admiration from those who have read it. At the same time, it has had little but censure and disapproval from its critics. Only within recent years have the professional investigators and taste makers caught up with or partly explained the natural enthusiasm that *Samson* has aroused, as often as not against its readers' own better judgment.

In one of the few references to the play in the eighteenth century, Francis Atterbury wrote to Alexander Pope (1722) that *Samson* is "Written in the very Spirit of the Ancients," and could with but little trouble (presumably putting it into heroic couplets) be turned "into a perfect Model and Standard of Tragic Poetry, always allowing for its being a Story taken out of the Bible which is an Objection that at this time of day, I know is not to be got over."[1] Atterbury admired the play, but against his critical principles, and he obliquely raised for the first time a presupposition that was later to cause critics great difficulty: that the Bible and Greek tragedy will not mix.

Samuel Johnson, in several influential essays, raised two other objections that were to haunt the critics: that the play often lacks proper decorum, and that is has no chain of causation or "middle" in the Aristotelian sense, and therefore does not move forward dramatically.[2] Johnson testifies to another purpose, however, when he writes in the *Life of Milton* that the play has been "too much admired." He cannot be speaking of published estimates, which hardly existed at this time. The natural presumption is that he was referring to contemporary readers of the play. Although *Samson Agonistes* violates several Neoclassical canons of style and structure, what little evidence there is suggests that it was popular among those who knew no better, and also among those who could not help liking it in spite of its supposed faults.

The nineteenth century too produced little formal criticism of the play, but the evidence of spontaneous liking coupled with critical disapprobation is again clear. Macauley, Wordsworth, and Landor all admired its sublimity and passion, but at the same time echoed or expanded on Johnson's critical strictures. Coleridge resented the slight implied to Shakespeare by Milton's rejection of Elizabethan structure and conventions and his condemnation of the Elizabethan practice of mingling comic and tragic. Nevertheless, he still considered *Samson* the finest imitation of Greek drama ever written. James Russell Lowell, oddly enough, showed himself to be more independent in his judgment. In an essay on Swinburne he repeated the now-standard remark that *Samson* is the best re-creation in English

[1]Letter to Pope, 15 June 1772, in *Milton: The Critical Heritage,* ed. John T. Shawcross (London: Routledge & Kegan Paul, 1970), p. 243.

[2]There are brief comments in the *Life of Milton*; on the lack of a middle, see *The Rambler,* No. 139 (16 July 1751); on anachronisms, harsh prosody, indecorous diction, see *The Rambler,* No. 140 (20 July 1751).

of Greek tragedy, both in substance and in manner, but he also added
that it is "the most masterly piece of English versification."[3] Lowell
was thus the first critic before Gerard Manley Hopkins to admire
Milton's verse technique in the play. Hopkins found precedents in
Samson Agonistes for his own metrical experiments, and thus Milton
became an important forerunner of modern poetry. Hopkins praised
Milton's verse technique highly in letters to his friend Bridges. Since
Hopkins' own verse and letters were not published for some time,
his opinion had no immediate influence, but his insights bore fruit in
Bridges' book on Milton's prosody.[4] Although Bridges' technical
analysis of the verse is partly outmoded, his appreciation of Milton's
metrical virtuosity has had considerable weight.

The twentieth century has made up for the reticence of earlier
periods. Since 1900, scholars have paid more attention to *Samson
Agonistes* than to any of Milton's other works except *Paradise Lost*. It
cannot be said that all the problems have been solved, but some of the
long-standing objections have finally, one hopes, been laid to rest.
There are still difficulties in coming to grips with the play, however.
Thus some recent critics have called *Samson* a great drama, while
others insist that it is an extended lyric with no dramatic interest.
Even to call it a play has been thought heretical. Its rhythms and its
verse techniques have been praised not only by critics but by poets,
while other poets and critics have condemned them as stiff and
wooden. The choruses have been described alternatively as sublime
or as comic. Recently, it has been argued that Samson, Manoa, and
the Chorus, instead of arriving through purgation at some vision of
the truth, as most critics had thought, end the play in a state of wrong-
headed ignorance. There is no closer agreement about the central
question of the play's spirit or meaning. *Samson* has been interpreted
as autobiography, as political allegory, as philosophical discourse, as
Greek or Hebrew tragedy, as religious drama, as a Christian or a
Puritan morality play, or as a combination of any two or three of these
things at once.

[3]Lowell, "Swinburne's Tragedies" (1866), in *Literary Essays,* 11 (Boston:
Houghton Mifflin, 1890), 133–34.

[4]Robert Bridges, *Milton's Prosody* (London: Oxford Univ. Press, 1901).

Such disagreement among the critics is not surprising, nor is it reprehensible. Much of the work on *Samson* has been stimulating and fruitful for any reader or critic who wants to read the play for himself. Although, for example, William Riley Parker's insistence on Greek spirit and structure conflicts with F. Michael Krouse's claims for a tradition of Christian exegesis (as Parker reveals in his stern review of Krouse's book), and both disagree with the unfortunately more diffuse arguments for Hebrew spirit and style, none of these approaches can be ignored. As one might expect, *Samson* studies have obeyed the rule that most criticism must necessarily be partial. As usual, therefore, the intelligent reader must make his own synthesis, based mainly on his informed response to the play.

That the reader must make a synthesis in the case of *Samson* is not surprising, because Milton was himself a synthesizer, who had the ability to take an enormous diversity of material and make it his own. Thus, for example, we shall see that *Samson* makes use of the basic five-act Greek structure, and also of the traditional five stages of Christian regeneration: conviction of sin, contrition, confession, departure from evil, conversion to good. The play stresses both active heroism like that of the Greek warriors and passive suffering like that of the Christian saints — or a combination of activity and suffering that might characterize Greek hero, Christian saint, or Hebrew patriarch, judge, or prophet. At the highest level, the literatures of the Greeks, Hebrews, and Christians are far from incompatible. In spite of their obvious differences, the visions toward which they strive have much in common.

2

Concerning the date *Samson* was written, currently a matter of debate, I shall have more to say in the concluding chapter. Although *Samson* was published after *Paradise Lost,* and was traditionally thought to be Milton's last poetical work, several prominent critics have recently attempted to date it earlier: in the early 1660's, or even back to the 1640's. No solid evidence has yet been offered for dating it before *Paradise Lost,* although one may readily grant that Milton had thought about the subject (among many others), and that perhaps he had done some preliminary work on it, before 1660. Attempts based on internal evidence, such as word frequency or prosody, to date the play either early or late have so far been inconclusive. Arguments that the play is badly written, however—awkward, even unfinished—show remarkable critical insensitivity. In this respect the many unprofessional readers who have enjoyed the play are a better guide. Similarly, arguments that *Samson* is too bitter or pessimistic for Milton's serene late years ignore half its spirit: for it rises out of defeat and despair to the heights of triumphant faith. Indeed, as with *Lycidas* and *Paradise Lost,* the greater the depth, the greater the ultimate height. Every reading of *Samson Agonistes* has left me more convinced that it is, in its present form, Milton's last work in poetry. Since there is no absolute proof of this, I have avoided relying on chronology in my arguments. But I hope by the final chapter of this study to have added to the weight of probabilities that favor a late dating.

The best guide to the structure and the basic dramatic techniques that Milton employed in *Samson Agonistes* is William Riley Parker. Parker has shown in detail that Milton derived his structure and techniques not from one Greek tragedian or another, or from one play or another, but from a systematic and deep familiarity with nearly all the Greek tragedies.[5] Acquaintance with the Greek tragedians was unusual at the time: Seneca had been far more influential on Elizabethan drama. Milton mentions Aeschylus, Sophocles, and Euripides in his preface, though he may have known Aeschylus less well than the others.[6] He was also thoroughly familiar with Aristotle's critical works and knew the later developments in tragic theory by the great Italian Renaissance critics.

Some of the devices that Milton borrowed from the Greeks are mentioned in his preface. Among them are the use of a Chorus and a prologue, the observance of unity of tragic spirit, and the limitation

[5]Parker, *Milton's Debt to Greek Tragedy in Samson Agonistes* (Baltimore: Johns Hopkins, 1937).

[6]See J. C. Maxwell, "Milton's Knowledge of Aeschylus: The Argument from Parallel Passages," *Review of English Studies,* 3 (1952), 366–71.

of the action to twenty-four hours. In fact, a number of unities are observed in the play: unity of time, from dawn to noon; unity of place, before the prison; unity of action; and what may be called unity of plot and spirit—that is, the elimination of the comic characters and the subplots and overplots that characterize Elizabethan and Stuart tragedy. A major effect of this classical severity is to increase the play's emotional pressure and intensity. Finally, as with the Greeks, all violent action takes place off stage and is recollected or reported to the audience by the characters, especially by that typically Greek personage, the Messenger.

Like the Greek tragedies, *Samson* has a kind of inevitability. This is not, as Parker argued, precisely Greek fate. Nevertheless, Samson will as surely pull down the temple and die as Eve will eat the apple in *Paradise Lost*. Paradoxically, however, both these Miltonic characters act freely. In a sense, character is fate, while what lies beyond the characters' control in the events that impinge on them is not Greek fate but the free will of others or the subtle guidance of divine providence. In *Samson*, unlike *Paradise Lost*, Milton's God never appears directly. His Providence is usually hidden, only to be seen in retrospect, attaining its ends through the free actions, even the perversities, of men and nations. Nevertheless, it is God and not fate that rules over the universe of the play.

Although Milton tells his readers in his preface that *Samson* is not divided into acts or scenes, Parker has suggested that Milton imitated the basic structural plan of the Greek tragedies.[7] Making use of Parker's findings, and realizing that precise lineation is made difficult by brief transitional passages that join the episodes, one may tabulate the play's divisions roughly as follows:

prologos, 1-114, Samson's soliloquy
parodos (Chorus' entry song), 115-75, Chorus
1 epeisodion (episode), 176-292, Samson and Chorus
1 stasimon (chorus), 293-329, Chorus
2 epeisodion, 330-651, Samson and Manoa
2 stasimon, 652-724, Chorus
3 epeisodion, 725-1009, Samson and Dalila

[7]Parker, pp. 14–17. I have slightly changed the lineation.

3 stasimon, 1010-61, Chorus
4 epeisodion, 1062-1267, Samson and Harapha
4 stasimon, 1268-1307, Chorus
5 epeisodion, 1308-1426, Samson and Public Officer
5 stasimon, 1427-44, Chorus
exodos (exit song), 1445-1758; Manoa, Messenger, Chorus
including
kommos (dirge), 1660-1758, Manoa, Chorus, and Semichoruses.

Thus the play may be divided into an introductory part, which includes the prologue and the Chorus' entry; a body, of five episodes and related choruses, and an exodos, or exit of the Chorus and other characters, which concludes with a joint dirge.

There is no doubt that this is a useful description of the play's structure. As recent analyses of *Paradise Lost* have suggested, however, Milton need not have limited himself to a single structural form. One may well perceive several other structures underlying the play. It is suggestive that the fourth and fifth episodes are much briefer than the others, while one might think that the temple catastrophe ought not be relegated to the exodos, but rather should be considered part of the main body. Parker is again helpful: he suggests an alternative tabulation of the play's divisions:[8]

Samson alone and with the Chorus, 1-329
Samson and Manoa, 330-724
Samson and Dalila, 725-1061
Samson and the two instruments of force, 1062-1444
Samson in the temple, 1445-1758

Other plans could be suggested, but these two outlines appear to be the most helpful. There is no need to obey one's natural impulse to choose between them. As in nearly every other area of the play, the structure is characterized by harmonious integration of diversity.[9]

[8]Parker, pp. 60–64, again with slight modifications.

[9]Many Renaissance works have complex, overlapping structural schemes: for example, *The Faerie Queene* or Shakespeare's Sonnets. On the latter, and on the nature of such complex structures, see Stephen Booth, *An Essay on Shakespeare's Sonnets* (New Haven: Yale Univ. Press, 1969).

3

It is my intention in this study to consider all those aspects of *Samson* or its background that will significantly help a reader to approach the play with an informed understanding. At the same time, we shall proceed by a series of excursions toward an examination of the central tragic and religious meanings of the play. Although we shall come to qualify the words, *Samson* may best be seen as a Christian tragedy. Both Christian and tragic elements have previously been touched on by Milton's critics, but usually separately and often with the aim of excluding one element or the other from consideration.[10] The treatment of *Samson* as a religious, or ultimately a Christian, tragedy will seem oxymoronic to some readers, since it is commonly denied that such a thing can exist.[11] In particular, the promise of life after death is supposed to make a tragic vision of life impossible, and the introduction of this promise into a play is thus thought to rob the hero's destruction of all its tragic force. Since there is no agreement exactly what tragedy, or the tragic, is, this assertion is difficult to refute. Indeed, there is no harm in admitting that it may generally be true. Milton, however, solved the difficult problem of mixing the tragic with the Christian in *Samson Agonistes*. He did so by using a technique that can be traced through several of his earlier works, especially

[10]On the Christianization of the Samson story, see F. Michael Krouse, *Milton's Samson and the Christian Tradition* (Princeton: Princeton Univ. Press, 1949); on typology, see William Madsen, *From Shadowy Types to Truth* (New Haven: Yale Univ. Press, 1968); on Christian regeneration see Marcia Landy, "Character Portrayal in *Samson Agonistes*," *Texas Studies in Literature and Language,* 7 (1965), 239–53, and George M. Muldrow, *Milton and the Drama of the Soul* (The Hague: Mouton, 1970); see also Barbara K. Lewalski, "*Samson Agonistes* and the 'Tragedy' of the Apocalypse," *PMLA,* 85 (1970), 1050–62. The Greek tragic side of *Samson* is well summed up in a single study: Parker's *Milton's Debt to Greek Tragedy in Samson Agonistes.*

[11]Two critics have pled against this common view: A. S. P. Woodhouse, "Tragic Effect in *Samson Agonistes*," *Univ. of Toronto Quarterly,* 28 (1959), 205–22; and Robert H. Goldsmith, "Triumph and Tragedy in *Samson Agonistes*," *Renaissance Papers* (1968), pp. 77–84. See also Woodhouse's fine restatement in *The Heavenly Muse* (Toronto: Univ. of Toronto Press, 1972).

Lycidas, "Methought I saw my late espoused Saint," and certain parts of *Paradise Lost*: that is, the concealment or masking of the Christian theme by some classical or non-Christian analogue. In this way, the world and human life can be viewed experientially, at the same time that the Christian solution is shadowed forth and prepared for, either to be openly revealed as in *Lycidas,* or else to be implicitly projected as in *Samson.*

Milton's resolution of the basic problem of Christian tragedy will become clearer in subsequent chapters, but a few preliminary difficulties may be touched on here. The first is whether Samson can rightly be called a Christian play in any sense. The Christian element in it is implicit, embedded in the action, the imagery, and the characters. Explicit hints are few and ambiguous, in no way violating the historical decorum (the anachronisms Dr. Johnson found are insignificant). What I intend to show, however, is that what Milton accomplished could have been achieved in no other way. The Christian element is *necessarily* implicit, but a perception of that element is central to a full understanding of the play.

The argument must convince or fail on its own merits, but some preliminary support may be claimed for it here. First, Milton was a deeply dedicated Christian who considered his artistic achievements to be closely connected with his divinely allotted purpose in life, and who addressed an audience whom he also thought of as Christian. Considering this, it is difficult to see how he could have justified to himself a play that was purely Greek or Hebrew in spirit. He and his audience were used to reading not only the Old Testament, but also the classics from a Christian point of view. Milton was no naive reader of the Greek and Latin writers like those in the Middle Ages who dressed Achilles in the armor of chivalry; but neither was he by habit a purist unwilling to translate or adapt whatever he read to his own views and purposes. His inveterate habit, in every significant poem that he wrote, was to remake what he found to his own liking, whether a genre, a style, or an idea. Just as in *Paradise Lost* he Christianized the epic and described a higher heroism than Homer or Virgil, so in *Samson Agonistes* he could be expected to Christianize tragedy: but in both cases to bend and refashion what he found, not to break it.

Added to this argument, a number of critics have convincingly demonstrated the presence of various Christian elements in the play. *Krouse* has shown that at the time Milton wrote the play the Samson tradition had received a thorough reinterpretation at the hands of Christian exegetes and earlier Christian poets. Landy, Muldrow, and others have shown that Samson's inner growth, now thought to be an essential part of the action and to account for that "middle" which Johnson found missing, resembles the process of Christian conversion and regeneration. Still others have suggested that Samson's heroism is more nearly Christian than Greek, that he is more a martyr or saint than an active hero. There is no room to examine these arguments in detail here, though most will be discussed later; but taken together, they are persuasive. That there is a major Christian element in the play is plausible; one intention of this study is to show that it is not inconsistent with the Greek and Hebrew elements other critics have found.

An incidental difficulty in treating the play as Christian, which is neither a literary nor a critical problem yet should be frankly faced, is that some readers are offended by the possibility. There is little that can be done about this, except to ask for suspension of disbelief. Among Milton's axioms were these: that Christian doctrine is truth; that, as Muldrow shows, human character development has an inescapable religious dimension; that the Christian God is at the very basis of reality. Readers who cannot accept this dimension in Milton ignore it at the cost of distorting what they read. One need not accept Milton's beliefs as true; one ought, however, in some way to suspend disbelief, to read sympathetically as allegory or myth what cannot be accepted as literal.

The other side of the problem of Christian tragedy is the belief on the part of many Miltonists that *Samson* is not a tragedy, indeed not even a drama. That it is not a tragedy is a conclusion arrived at from the theory that tragedy and religion are incompatible, and that Milton's major concern is dogma or doctrine. That it is not a drama is derived either from Milton's remark in the preface about not intending *Samson* for the stage, or from Samuel Johnson's remark about the work's lack of a middle. Indeed, more attention has been paid to this last difficulty than to any other aspect of the play. A few critics have seconded Johnson, but most have attempted to refute him. Although sleeping dogs will probably never lie, the general outcome of the critical encounter is the theory that the meetings between Samson and the other characters develop his inner state, and thereby lead him progressively from initial despair or near despair to readiness for his concluding action in the temple of Dagon. This may not be a chain of causation quite like what Aristotle described in the *Poetics,* but it is a reasonable variation, in tune with the other internalizations that have characterized the evolution of Western literature. *Samson* actually involves a double chain of causation that moves the hero toward the catastrophe, both strengthening him and preparing him to act, and at the same time developing his inward spirit. Thus the play has the kind of internal causality and inevitability that we expect of tragedy. At the same time, as a Christian tragedy, Samson's will is free.

As Una Ellis-Fermor points out, few great religious dramas have been written,[12] nor are there many great tragedies. Milton accomplished in *Samson Agonistes* something remarkable, a worthy parallel to what he achieved in *Paradise Lost.* If the play is narrower in scope than the epic, it is more intense. But the combination of religion and tragedy is not so unprecedented as some modern critics would suggest. Aeschylus and Sophocles also achieved a fusion of the human and the divine. Tragedy examines life experientially, while religion imposes an explanation on it, yet certainly religion can be lived while tragedy too has its theoretical side. They ask, and sometimes answer, many of the same questions: the nature and purpose of the world; the nature of man and his relation to God, to the world, and to other men; the reason for suffering, evil, and death. Euripides turned tragedy away from its marriage to formal religion. His example was followed by such later tragedians as Shakespeare and Racine, though in none of these cases is the separation absolute. The possibility of fusion remained. Marlowe approached it in *Doctor Faustus,* and it might be argued that Racine achieved it in his two last plays. But only *Samson Agonistes* succeeds in summing up the Christian drama of regeneration and sacrifice, yet at the same time fulfills the basic patterns of

[12]Ellis-Fermor, *"Samson Agonistes* and Religious Drama," *The Frontiers of Drama* (London: Methuen, 1945; rev. 1964).

genuine tragedy — and that in a poetry, both style and vision, of which only the mature Milton was capable. Thus Milton soared once more into the Christian realm "Above th' *Aonian* Mount," but at the same time recreated for his own time genuine tragedy in the spirit of the Greek playwrights. What but such a Christian tragedy could satisfy Milton's "great task Master" or be "doctrinal and exemplary to a Nation" — even to so small an audience as remained to Milton after the Restoration?

In the following chapters, after approaching the play by way of three of Milton's earlier poems, we shall examine various aspects of *Samson Agonistes*. In one degree or another, all the discussions will turn about the central theme of *Samson* as a religious tragedy, or the play's combination of the human and the divine. Sir Thomas Browne described man as the "great amphibium," half in this world, half in the next. Few English poets have realized more intensely than Milton the beauty or the tragedy of the material world; few have set their eyes so continually on God and the next world. Milton could inhabit both worlds at once because he naturally thought of them as one. The tragedy of this world, the divine comedy of the next, are both equally real to him, and both are vividly conveyed in his major poems. The vision that can produce a religious tragedy is simple and unified. The method of conveying it, as we shall see, is in some respects complex and indirect. As Frank Kermode has suggested in a brilliant essay,[13] perhaps indirection and complexity are the necessary instruments of poetry in a fallen world, if the reader is to be led convincingly up to the poet's vision of ultimate truth.

[13]Kermode, "Adam Unparadised," *The Living Milton,* ed. Kermode (London: Routledge & Kegan Paul, 1960).

2
THE FUSION OF CHRISTIAN
AND CLASSICAL

Milton grew up in an age when writers were likely to be as familiar with the literature of Greece and Rome as with that of their own country; when young boys learned the rudiments of grammar, logic, and rhetoric in Latin; and when poets plundered Ovid and Virgil not only for their gods and goddesses, but for their genres, structures, styles, themes, images, and tropes.[1] From Spenser to Milton, classical allusion was indispensable to poetry. The relative avoidance of the pantheon by Donne and the Metaphysicals was an uncharacteristic piece of self-denial (though productive for them and congenial to modern taste) that, as Carew foresaw, hardly survived the poet who decreed the exile. Because the classical gods and classical myths were

[1]See Donald L. Clark, *Milton at St. Paul's School* (New York: Columbia Univ. Press, 1947); Douglas Bush, *Mythology and the Renaissance Tradition in English Poetry,* rev. ed. (New York: Norton, 1963); John R. Mulder, *The Temple of the Mind* (New York: Pegasus, 1969).

so popular — both at court and among the people, as the masques and pageants of the times demonstrate — their use in poetry was naturally abused by lesser poets merely to "stuffe their lines, and swell the windy Page."[2] But all significant artistic trends have been imitated and abused. The crux in this case is whether or not, in Renaissance terms, the larger decorum is observed;[3] or in Coleridgean terms, whether the allusion is successfully fused into (or seems to grow out of) the poem as a whole, and thus is organically significant. Milton nearly always uses classical allusion organically and not merely as appendage or ornament, showing the ability to do so very early in the "Nativity Ode" and even in some of the academic poetry. In "Elegia Quinta" he moves about in the classical world with an ease and freedom that many a more mature poet might envy.

The Greek and Roman classics are a pervasive ingredient in Milton's poems, serving a number of purposes. One function, however, is increasingly important in his poetic development: the use of classical allusion as a mask or veil for Christian truth. This way of using the classical gods was a venerable one — in fact, it was one of the original excuses for retaining the old pagan myths in a new Christian world. In the Renaissance especially, ancient religion was interpreted allegorically in order to bring it into some semblance of conformity with revealed truth. There are, of course, only a few veiled (and anachronistic) allusions to the classics in *Samson Agonistes*; but the patient reader will find that Milton's handling of classical allusion in his earlier poems offers a useful key to understanding a major technique in the play. So it is necessary to approach *Samson* indirectly by way of *Lycidas,* Sonnet 23, and *Paradise Lost.* It is hoped, however, that the discussion will also be of interest on its own merits.

1

In *Lycidas,* Milton does something with classical allusion more significant than anything he had attempted before. Apollo and Jove, the

[2]Thomas Carew, "An Elegy upon ... Dr. John Donne," *The Poems,* ed. Rhodes Dunlap (Oxford: Clarendon Press, 1949).

[3]See Thomas Kranidas, *The Fierce Equation* (The Hague: Mouton, 1965).

Fury, the nymphs, and Orpheus become essential parts of the poem's structure and of its central strategy. The nymphs act as mediating links between Nature, with its human sympathies and its participation in the mortality resulting from the fall, and Man, who no longer enjoys quite the unbroken connection with the lower orders that was his birthright in Genesis. Orpheus is the type of the poet-priest, the order-bringer and harmonizer of chaos or unruly passions.[4] As such, he is closely linked as a symbol with both Lycidas and the poem's narrator. But it is the role of Apollo, Jove, and the Fury that most concerns us here. Rosemond Tuve has suggested that Milton uses Apollo rather than, say, Christ the Good Shepherd to answer the first great outburst of questioning and doubt in the poem because he wishes at this point to use "indirection" or "a more figurative functioning in the language."[5] Miss Tuve's insight deserves expansion. (While discussing *Lycidas* and the other poems, I shall speak for convenience as if Milton made a number of conscious technical decisions. The argument is not affected by the possibility that his strategy was partly, or at times wholly, unconscious.)

"All-judging *Jove*," to whose tribunal Apollo refers the problem of apparent injustice raised by the narrator, is the traditional mask for God the Father. His power, his justice are the attributes that are stressed in the passage on earthly and heavenly fame. He has also appeared earlier, in the invocation, where his name solemnizes the origin of poetry and its power to challenge the humanly "unacceptable."[6] Jove had so often stood for God the Father in Renaissance poetry that Milton could count on his readers making this connection automatically. Nevertheless, although Jove is God's analogue, the identity is not complete.

[4]See Caroline Mayerson, "The Orpheus Image in *Lycidas,*" *PMLA,* 54 (1949), 189–207.

[5]Tuve, *Images and Themes in Five Poems by Milton* (Cambridge: Harvard Univ. Press, 1957), pp. 75–76. See also Douglas Bush, *English Literature in the Earlier Seventeenth Century,* rev. ed. (Oxford: Clarendon Press, 1962), pp. 386–87; Michael West, "The *Consolatio* in Milton's Funeral Elegies," *Huntington Library Quarterly,* 34 (1971), 233–49; and H. R. Swardson, *Poetry and the Fountain of Light* (Columbia: Univ. of Missouri Press, 1962).

[6]Tuve, p. 73

Apollo, who appears at the moment of crisis to answer the narrator's doubts, is the god of light, intellect, healing, and harmonizing song—of all that is "Apollonian." Mediating between the human poet and Jove, he is the type of God the Son. This identification is reinforced near the end of the poem, when the setting and rising of the sun (Apollo) is used to suggest Christ's death and resurrection. This image, led up to most carefully, finally dominates *Lycidas,* embodying the movement up from death to eternal life:

> For *Lycidas* your sorrow is not dead,
> Sunk though he be beneath the watry floar,
> So sinks the day-star in the Ocean bed,
> And yet anon repairs his drooping head,
> And tricks his beams, and with new spangled Ore,
> Flames in the forehead of the morning sky:
> So *Lycidas* sunk low, but mounted high,
> Through the dear might of him that walk'd the waves. . . .[7]

The use of Apollo to represent Christ would not have been as automatically understood by Milton's first readers as the connection between Jove and the Father, but the symbolism gradually grows clear. *Lycidas* is not, in any case, a poem to be understood at the first reading.

Milton uses Jove and Apollo in the first parts of the poem, rather than the Father and the Son, because they are fictions.[8] Apollo can

---

[7]All Milton quotations are from *The Works of John Milton,* ed. Frank Patterson, et al. (New York: Columbia Univ. Press, 1931–40), hereafter cited as *Works.* The text of *Samson* is that of the first edition (1671), except that I have silently expanded "&." The original spelling and punctuation, though in a very few instances confusing, are helpful guides to pronunciation and rhythm, and probably come close to Milton's intentions.

[8]Lovers of the classics are surprised when Milton attacks the classical deities in *Paradise Lost* and *Paradise Regained,* but he never thought of them as real. They are great fictions, archetypes or symbols, shadowy inventions that can nevertheless be used to express truths. When full expression of the truth is served by reminders that these figures are "empty dreams," Milton does not hesitate to do what his poem requires.

I am aware that in speaking here (and elsewhere) of Milton's probable purpose I am committing the "intentional fallacy." It is impossible, however, to avoid without distortion the question of intention, when the artist is as conscious and deliberate a poetic craftsman as Milton. I have left out some of the

respond to Milton's doubts, provide the reader with a preliminary reassurance, without breaking too quickly or too facilely through the veil of earthly experience to the truth beyond. It is, after all, this very truth which is in doubt, and which must, therefore, be sought with difficulty and in the terms of this world. Possibly Milton always knew what the answer would be; but he wished to take his reader through the doubts he himself felt, not to present him with dogmatic solutions. If an overused term can be used here in a general sense, one might say that Milton wished to treat the subject of *Lycidas* existentially. But Milton did not want his poem to remain in the material world: his problem was gradually and convincingly to transcend it, taking his reader along with him. This he accomplished, in large part, by the device of the classical mask; by a progression from the answer given by Apollo, to the diatribe of St. Peter, disguised as a river god and periphrastically named, to Christ, emerging from the imagery of sun god and river god to reveal unmasked the final response to all earthly injustice: resurrection and eternal life.

To some readers, this conclusion seems a weakness. John Arthos expresses well an objection that many of my students have also made:

> The analogy at the end between the rising of the sun out of the sea and Christ's ascent into Heaven, the reference also to the resurrection of Edward King, is so finely and sensitively reticent, even humbly reticent, that one accepts it as a way of affirming faith. The obvious inadequacy of the argument is not concealed, and there is no effort to lead one to suppose that this is in any sense a reasoned proof. But even so, the appeal, at this point, to "the dear might of him that walked the waves," is an appeal that comes at the end of the poem, separate from the argument. . . . This is the conclusion the argument pointed to, but the gap is obvious, and the comfort fails.[9]

Milton himself believed that a gap must exist between heaven and

---

hedging words and qualifiers that might modify the discussion for the sake of readability; but careful readers will know that I am not privy to Milton's mind, rather merely projecting his possible intentions or artistic decisions from the nature of the poetry.

[9]John Arthos, *Dante, Michelangelo and Milton* (London: Routledge & Kegan Paul, 1963), p. 94.

earth until, after the Last Judgment, the promise of Revelation is fulfilled and they are made anew (see the "Nativity Ode"). He could
attempt to bridge the gap, as he would later attempt to do in *Paradise
Lost,* but he could not remove it. Nevertheless, he does prepare for
the solution in *Lycidas* by approaching it from the realm of experience, through gods who are human inventions but at the same time
who shadow forth the divine. In the resurrection image are intri-
cately fused most of the thematic strands developed earlier, now revealed explicitly in the transition from human speculation to divine
revelation.[10]

The "blind *Fury*" is likewise ultimately seen as a mask for one of
the faces of the Christian God. She seems at first to stand for disorder
and evil, for destruction and death, as an enemy of Apollo and his
human servants. She is, however, only a projection of the narrator's
doubts and fears as to the conduct of the universe, born from his fear
of irrational death and compounded from the Furies and the Fates of
Greek myth. But in reality neither Furies nor Fates have any part in
running Milton's universe, nor are they to be seen in the heaven that
opens at the end of *Lycidas.* Instead, Milton's blind Fury is finally
understood to be a mask for God's inscrutable providence, distorted
for the moment by appearances and by the speaker's doubt. There
can be no question at the end of the poem that Milton's God is as
firmly in control as he is later in *Paradise Lost:* "Necessitie and
Chance / Approach not mee, and what I will is Fate" (VII.172-73).
Why introduce a fictional Fury if God is really in charge of events?
Because Milton thus enables himself to attack God's ways to men
with a ferocity that would not otherwise be possible. The intensity
of his hatred for the seemingly pointless in human existence, represented by the premature death of Lycidas, cannot be directed (at least
by Milton) toward the Christian God. At the thought of God, all
doubts fade, become trivial and meaningless. Yet they must be fully
and sincerely expressed before they can be legitimately answered.
Milton's solution is again a figure built up from classical mythology.

[10]The most obvious of Milton's preparations earlier in *Lycidas* for this passage
is the water imagery. See Robert P. Adams, Wayne Shumaker, Cleanth
Brooks, and John Hardy in *Milton's Lycidas,* ed. C. A. Patrides (New York:
Holt, Rinehart & Winston, 1961).

Only by indirection can he do justice to both realms of experience—both to the questions and to the final answer. For the answer to all the bitter questions in *Lycidas*—as to those in *Paradise Lost* and *Samson Agonistes*—is one: God, the Truth, who by his very nature once understood, simply by his existence, makes all doubts cease, and all injustices become, finally, justice.

2

Milton continues to experiment with the use of classical allusion as a veil or mask in *Epitaphium Damonis*—though in this poem it persists right into the conclusion, no longer as a veil but as a deliberately "undecorous" element in the final unbounded joy:

> Ipse caput nitidum cinctus rutilante corona,
> Letáque frondentis gestans umbracula palmæ
> Æternum perages immortales hymenæos;
> Cantus ubi, choreisque furit lyra mista beatis,
> Festa Sionæo bacchantur et Orgìa Thyrso.

("Your radiant head shall be bound with a glittering crown and, with shadowing branches of the joyous palm in your hands, you shall for ever enact the immortal marriage, where hymns and the ecstatic sound of the lyre mingle with the choric dances of the blessed, and festal throngs revel under the thyrsus of Zion.")[11] More useful to the present discussion, however, is the technique Milton uses in his last sonnet, "Methought I saw my late espoused Saint." For here, on a small scale, Milton successfully achieves what he will accomplish more significantly in *Samson Agonistes*: the perfect balance and union of the Christian with the tragic. This sonnet includes within its few lines not only the full Christian promise—the radiant vision of his late wife in heaven—but also the basic human predicament, foreshadowed in the ambivalent death of Alcestis and realized in the death and loss of his wife.

A first reading of "Methought I saw" may lead to some puzzlement. Is the poem finally happy or sad? Does the poet finally regain his

[11]Translation from *The Complete Poetical Works of John Milton,* ed. Douglas Bush (Boston: Houghton Mifflin, 1965).

wife, or lose her? The Christian vision is quite explicit. His wife appears as a "Saint," enjoying life after death in heaven. She is vested in white, symbolizing both purity and triumph. Although Milton cannot see her face, love and goodness shine from her very body: she combines the divine love of the saints with the personal love of a wife for her husband. The speaker is confident he will join her in heaven: "yet once more I trust to have / Full sight of her in Heaven without restraint." Then joy will be complete, as all losses and restraints fall away, and they are reunited once more. But this blissful state, though foreshadowed in the speaker's vision or dream, is in the future. It is not a present reality, only a promise: "I *trust* to have. . . ." The word "trust" is ambivalent, suggesting both absolute surety and at the same time a lack of any present satisfaction. The same ambiguity characterizes the entire vision: "*Methought* I saw. . . ." Has she appeared to him in a dream, in a vision, in some higher actuality—or in an illusion?

The first quatrain, with the rescue of Alcestis, seems at first to have a positive emotional tenor. Hercules conquers death, husband and wife are made "glad." But the quatrain, with "grave" at the strategic end of the second line, concludes with an emphasis on death and debilitation: Alcestis is "Rescu'd from death by force though pale and faint." The monosyllables (as in the sonnet's final line) seem to draw out the process, to make it difficult, to show the great power of death as it reluctantly releases its victim. Hercules has rescued one woman for a time, but death loses none of its ultimate power; and early readers of Milton's sonnet knew well that Admetus, Alcestis, and Hercules himself would all die: Hercules, who now challenges and apparently defeats death, dies at the last both painfully and tragically. As Milton had once written, in a juvenile elegy on the death of the vice-chancellor of Cambridge:

> Si destinatam pellere dextera
> Mortem valeret, non ferus Hercules
> Nessi venenatus cruore
> Æmathiâ jacuisset Oetâ

("If man's right arm had the strength to ward off appointed death, fierce Hercules would not have been laid low on Emathian Oeta by

Nessus' poisonous blood.")[12] The sense of desolation and loss, which thus forms such an undercurrent in the first quatrain, is more directly conveyed by the sonnet's conclusion, coming as a sudden reversal of the poem's mounting joy, just as the reunion is about to reach its fulfillment:

> But O as to embrace me she enclin'd
> I wak'd, she fled, and day brought back my night.

The poem's last word, concluding a series of last words in nearly every line that are either strongly positive or strongly negative, is "night."

Thus the sonnet seems finally to be tragic rather than joyful, to recognize that separation and death have the last word. But still another dimension is concealed in the rescue of Alcestis by Hercules. For Hercules, in the view of Renaissance interpreters of the classics, is a type or foreshadowing – an imperfect anticipation – of Christ. He is the son of the king of the gods and a human mother, as Christ is the son of God the Father and Mary, and it is thus that Milton presents him in the poem, in a phrase that consists of both classical periphrasis and typological emphasis: "*Joves* great Son." Hercules, like Christ, did great deeds, spending his life assisting others as he does Admetus; but unlike Christ his death is not victorious but tragic. He does more than any other classical hero to battle the forces of darkness, in a life that chooses virtue and duty over pleasure; but finally he is defeated. Behind the figure of Hercules in "Methought I saw," however, is the figure of Christ. He is the true conqueror of death, the missing element that can reconcile the poem's strong sense of death and loss with its promise of future bliss. But he cannot appear directly, any more than he can appear in the early stages of *Lycidas,* for in doing so he would destroy the strong consciousness of mortality that gives the sonnet its great power. Only by concealing the Christian paradigm behind classical myth does Milton achieve the balance between life and death, gain and loss, grave and heaven, which does justice to his feelings.

"Methought I saw" makes use of a Hebrew as well as a Greek ana-

[12] "Anno aetatis 16. In obitum Procancellarii medici," ll. 9–12; translation by Bush, *The Complete Poetical Works.*

logue, which is of particular interest in relation to *Samson*. The second quatrain of the sonnet reads as follows:

> Mine as whom washt from spot of child-bed taint,
>   Purification in the old Law did save,
>   And such, as yet once more I trust to have
>   Full sight of her in Heaven without restraint,
> Came vested all in white, pure as her mind. (5-9)

Because of his attitude toward the rituals and sacramentals of the Anglican Church, Milton cannot be referring to the ceremony known as "churching." The reference is to Leviticus xii.2-5, and the purification after childbirth prescribed in the Mosaic law. Milton did not believe this law to have any applicability after the inauguration of the covenant of faith by Christ. The ceremonial purification of the "old Law" is, however, a type or foreshadowing of the Christian dispensation. It evokes old, legalistic conceptions of birth, impurity, and purification, while Christianity introduces a new conception of birth: birth of the spirit into eternal life; and a new conception of purification: not the ritual washing of the body or the clothes, but purification of the soul itself by Christ. Milton reminds us that it is his wife's "mind" that is pure, but he partly conceals this triumph under ritual, metaphor, and type. As Hercules brings into the poem vividly realized images of mortality and the power of death, purification by the old law introduces other elements of human weakness and mortality: the "spot of child-bed taint" that intrudes on the joyful vision, as a reminder of the curse of Eve:

> Thy sorrow I will greatly multiplie
> By thy Conception; Children thou shalt bring
> In sorrow forth. . . . (*Paradise Lost* X.193-95)

The sonnet's narrator, of course, suffers equally from the penalty of being human and mortal; he needs, as much as his wife, to be rescued from darkness and death. Thus the references to Hercules and the Jewish purification ritual convey the deeply-felt reality of man's plight, while at the same time implicitly revealing its solution.

3

Milton continues to make use of the classical in *Paradise Lost,* but, as one would expect, the method of the epic is far more varied and complex than that of the earlier poems. To the classical epic and to Aristotle *Paradise Lost* owes its basic form. Just as basically, it relies on the *Iliad,* the *Odyssey,* the *Aeneid,* and their successors for contrast between Christian and pagan muses, and between true and false heroic ideals. Milton demolishes the classical ideal of heroism in warfare in the invocations and in the War in Heaven, where two days of fighting produce only ludicrous confusion and the destruction of the heavenly landscape.[13] Satan is associated with Turnus, with Achilles, with Odysseus. He and his followers seek military honor, glory, and renown; they march and countermarch; they play Greek-style games to keep fit; but all their splendor and activity prove meaningless. The Messiah represents Milton's ideal in the poem: although his is not the role of the poem's central hero, he is the model of true heroism in *Paradise Lost.* He conquers Satan and his followers at their own chosen métier, warfare; but his greatest deeds, which express his true nature, are creative rather than destructive. The creation of the universe, the making and remaking of Man, heroic self-sacrifice and selfless love are his chief accomplishments.

To warfare as a subject of the epic the Italians added a second subject: love. Spenser writes in the proem to Book I of *The Faerie Queene,* "Fierce wars and faithful loves shall moralize my song." Like heroic warfare, heroic love is anatomized and dismissed in *Paradise Lost.* Satan is the courtly lover of the poem when he seduces Eve, who is quickly infected by the disease and passes it in turn to Adam. "O glorious trial of exceeding Love, / Illustrious evidence, example high!" (IX.961-62) she cries, as she persuades him to join her in self-destruction. Adam is an "example," an *exemplum,* of a kind of love;

[13]On Milton's critique of classical heroism, see Davis P. Harding, *The Club of Hercules* (Urbana: Univ. of Illinois Press, 1962); and John M. Steadman, *Milton and the Renaissance Hero* (Oxford: Clarendon Press, 1967); on the war in heaven, see especially Arnold Stein, *Answerable Style* (Seattle: Univ. of Washington Press, 1967), pp. 17-37.

but, of course, he here exemplifies a false ideal. The true exemplar is again the Son, who represents genuine selfless love. The love that Adam and Eve display at this point in the poem is not only human, as opposed to divine: it is false, as opposed to true. Their human love before Eve's fall, and after their repentance, reflects the love embodied in the Son; but the romantic love that leads to Adam's fall is a false ideal, in which they resemble such tragic figures as Dido, or Tristan and Iseult.[14]

Milton does not introduce warfare and courtly love into *Paradise Lost* merely to dismiss them, however. The poem is not primarily a satire. Satan's military heroism appears, from the perspective of God's throne, ridiculous; but, paradoxically, at the same time it gives him an aura of tragic greatness. The same is true of the fallen love of Adam and Eve. When they stand before the Son in judgment, Adam's behavior seems weak, shameful, and foolish: "Was shee thy God, that her thou didst obey / Before his voice[?]" (X.145-46). But no human reader can fail to be impressed by the genuine tragedy of their behavior or of Adam's difficult choice. Indeed, many critics have been seduced into unreserved approval of their actions. Milton addresses himself in *Paradise Lost* to a "fit audience . . . though few" (VII.31), that is, among other things, to readers who agree with him theologically (or at least can suspend their disbelief), but who also have human sympathies and human understanding. For *Paradise Lost* has a double vision: divine comedy and human tragedy; and it achieves this vision partly through the use of heroic warfare and heroic love.

This paradox underlay the lengthy controversy over whether Satan is a hero, or is admirable. From the ultimate, divine perspective he is a comic fool, ridiculous for even thinking of challenging God. He is not really the opponent of God in the poem's present action, but succeeds only in making war against Eve, whom he attacks deceitfully, willing to lick the dust at her feet in order to do her harm,

[14]For further discussion of Milton's treatment of love in *Paradise Lost,* see my "Milton's God: Authority in *Paradise Lost,*" *Milton Studies,* 4 (1972), 19–38; John M. Steadman, *Milton and the Renaissance Hero,* pp. 108–36; Ernest S. Gohn, "The Christian Ethic of *Paradise Lost* and *Samson Agonistes,*" *Studia Neophilologica,* 34 (1962), 243–68.

though she has never harmed him. But even in this action Satan is not totally unheroic, for he resembles the Odysseus of many wiles and disguises, preferring strategy to brute force,[15] and he has a vast if ignoble end in view. He appears far more heroic in Hell, however, where no sensitive reader can fail to respond with a part of himself to the picture he presents — even though it is ultimately only a picture and not a reality. When we hear that Satan "durst defie th' Omnipotent to Arms" (I.49), our logical part sees the futility of such an action, but our illogical part admires him. When he speaks of "the unconquerable Will, / And study of revenge, immortal hate, / And courage never to submit or yield" (I.106-08), we both question a purpose based on hatred and vengeance and admire the stubborn intransigence of his will. When he concludes his address to his legions wallowing in the burning lake, all critics and readers have admired his concluding line: "Awake, arise, or be forever fall'n" (I.330). The words ring splendidly. But should not the phrase "forever fall'n" echo ironically in our ears? For whatever activity Satan's followers may rouse themselves to, regardless of whether they raise themselves from their prone positions to resume their warfare against God, they must remain, for eternity, "forever fall'n."

As the Blind Fury works in *Lycidas* to allow Milton to question divine providence, and as Hercules in "Methought I saw" allows him to give death its due, so the mask of military heroism in *Paradise Lost* — strength, courage, indomitable perseverance in defeat — helps prevent the poem from becoming a one-dimensional theological treatise. Satan and the dark forces which he represents must be given their due, for they are weighty realities in human history, and, like death or the appearance of meaninglessness in the conduct of the world's affairs, cannot be lightly dismissed. Satan raises himself only to fall, exalts himself and is humbled. This is the pattern both of the tragic hero and of the butt of satire, and Satan is both at once. So too are Nimrod the first tyrant and his subordinate builders of Babel, or the architect of Pandemonium, or the Egyptian founders of "great *Alcairo*" (I.718), or the Assyrian builders of Babylon. All raise mighty

[15] On Satan and Odysseus see John M. Steadman, *Milton's Epic Characters* (Chapel Hill: Univ. of North Carolina Press, 1968), pp. 194–208.

works or mighty deeds in the face of Heaven, and all are doomed to a fall, both tragic and comic.[16]

Among the more valuable properties of poetry is that it can say more than one thing at a time. In the Invocation to Book IX, Milton declares openly and scornfully that he prefers to sing the better fortitude of patience and heroic martyrdom, rather than "to dissect / With long and tedious havoc fabl'd Knights / In Battels feign'd" (29-31). He earlier begins to prepare for this redirection of the epic by such devices as comparing Satan and his troops to famous earthly armies. Logically, such comparisons belittle all earthly human military endeavors. Illogically, however, they help to cover Satan with the cloak of tragic grandeur; for who can help but be moved by a passage like that in which Milton compares the fallen angels with

> all who since, Baptiz'd or Infidel
> Jousted in *Aspramont* or *Montalban,*
> *Damasco,* or *Marocco,* or *Trebisond,*
> Or whom *Biserta* sent from *Afric* shore
> When *Charlemain* with all his Peerage fell
> By *Fontarabbia.*   (I.582-87)

Baptized or infidel, on the friendly or enemy side, it hardly matters; in comparison with the great events Milton describes their battles are no more significant than the wars between the cranes and pygmies. Yet even in the total defeat arranged by Milton, Charlemagne's death with all his peers takes on tragic magnificence. What matter if warfare accomplish nothing? As the tragedians have discovered, there can be more to admire in useless defeat than in victory. Milton takes full advantage of this paradox in his delineation of Satan as noble warrior and foolish leader in a lost cause.

What Milton does in *Paradise Lost* with the heroism of war resembles rather closely what he does with the heroism of love. After both have fallen, Adam and Eve sink to simple lust, thus managing to make a happy and lawful relationship into something guilty and illicit. But between the fall of Eve and the fall of Adam, the poem is dominated not by lust, but by romantic love. Adam may fall because he is

---

[16] See my "The Image of the Tower in *Paradise Lost,*" *Studies in English Literature,* 10 (1970), 171-81.

"fondly overcome with Femal charm" (IX.999), but that "charm" is more than simple physical attraction. It is, rather, the heroic ideal of "all for love" and "the world well lost." And that, as Shakespeare shows, is an ideal to which, though our intellects question it, our sympathies are drawn. Indeed, so many critics have been attracted to the love between Adam and Eve during the course of the fall, that they have rejected Milton's simultaneous critique of it, and invented the myth that Milton did it all by accident, and that his instincts were better than he knew.

From the viewpoint of Heaven and of Milton's God upon his throne, the love between Adam and Eve after her fall is no true love at all. It is selfish, for it puts their desires above their duty to their creator, to their progeny, and to the universe of lower creatures which they rule. It is sinful, according to St. Augustine's definition of sin, for it puts the subordinate good above an ultimate good. More, it is ridiculous and even comical, for in attempting to put a relative good in place of the absolute, it tries to deny the very basis of reality in Milton's universe. Love, beauty, goodness, bare existence are contingent upon God in *Paradise Lost*. Unless human love is in harmony with divine love, it will be bound to turn, as it does, to lust and then to hate. The relationship between Adam and Eve descends from Adam's desperate attempt to preserve at all costs the bond that joins them inevitably, but by God's grace for a time only, to hatred and discord. Thus the gulf of "distance and distaste" (IX.9) which they open between themselves and God soon opens between them. From recrimination, they proceed to absolute separation. "Out of my sight, thou Serpent" (X.867) Adam cries to Eve when she tries to approach him. Even in the lower orders, separation and hatred are now the rule:

> but Discord first
> Daughter of Sin, among th' irrational,
> Death introduc'd through fierce antipathie:
> Beast now with Beast gan war, and Fowle with Fowle,
> And Fish with Fish; to graze the Herb all leaving,
> Devourd each other. . . .   (X.707-12)

So the world moves from love to hate, from harmony to discord, from union to separation; and so it will proceed until the final day of "respiration to the just" (XII.540) — save for the counter-influence of divine intervention in human history. Milton's God first reverses the general trend when Adam and Eve are regenerated, and thus enabled to rebuild their love for God and for each other. When their feelings for each other cease to be set against love of God, they can grow once more into a deep and abiding love, which will strengthen them in their life-long exile until they return to God through death.

C. S. Lewis points out the foolishness, lies, and deceit in Eve's conduct after her fall.[17] She first thinks to keep Godhead to herself and so to be "more equal" (IX.823) than Adam. Then it occurs to her that she may die after all, and Adam marry another Eve, "A death to think" (IX.830). So she resolves that Adam shall eat the fruit too, and share her fate. The essence of this intention, as Lewis points out, is murder. She returns to Adam, telling him that she has missed him and felt great "agonie of love" (IX.858) during their separation, though, in fact, during her temptation and fall, and for a good while afterward, she has completely forgotten about him. Having told him this lie, she then proceeds to play the part of the serpent, to seduce Adam as Satan has seduced her. She uses every method of persuasion at her disposal; Adam accedes; and so the fall is completed.

These, baldly, are the facts of Eve's behavior; but it would be wrong to think that she acts with full, deliberate, Machiavellian deceit. Rather she plays a double role, and is at the same time a sinful temptress and a tragic victim of her own uncontrollable emotions. She has, in fact, become with Adam an exemplar of "heroic love." The very thought of murder is couched in the language of love's sacrifice:

> *Adam* shall share with me in bliss or woe:
> So dear I love him, that with him all deaths
> I could endure, without him live no life. (IX.831-33)

The irony is that it is Adam whom she is offering to sacrifice for love, not herself; but almost certainly it is an irony of which she is unaware. In the same way, when she tells him "Thee I have misst, and thought it long, depriv'd / Thy presence, agonie of love till now / Not felt" (IX.857-59), she is as much deceived as deceiving. No doubt she is playing the orator, but also no doubt she feels a genuine agony

---

[17] Lewis, *A Preface to Paradise Lost,* rev. ed. (New York: Oxford Univ. Press, 1961), pp. 125–28.

which she thinks to be love. She may even believe her own words when she tells Adam that she has eaten the fruit and sought Godhead chiefly for his sake, and would despise it without him (IX.878-79). Although this assertion is directly contrary to what has happened, she has fallen into the Satanic habit of changing the past in order to bring it into conformity with present thoughts and feelings.

Adam's reaction is astonishment and speechlessness. He recognizes immediately the nature and the basic implications of what Eve has done. Now the poem pivots on his choice: to stand, or to join her in the fall. His decision is also immediate, and it is, basically, the decision of a heroic lover: he is determined to join Eve in death.

> Certain my resolution is to Die;
> How can I live without thee, how forgoe
> Thy sweet Converse and Love so dearly joyn'd,
> To live again in these wilde Woods forlorn?
>   . . . no no, I feel
> The Link of Nature draw me: Flesh of Flesh,
> Bone of my Bone thou art, and from thy State
> Mine never shall be parted, bliss or woe.
>   (IX.907-10, 913-16)

Adam goes on to rationalize his decision, but he finally comes back to the same theme: the "Bond of Nature" (IX.956), which draws him to her more strongly than any other consideration. Adam's decision can be faulted, but only on the basis that he attempts to put a high value, human love, above a higher value, divine love. In short, he literally sacrifices the world for love, and because he puts Eve before all else, she becomes in effect his God.

Eve, having won Adam over, now begins a paean of praise for his conduct. She too is caught up in heroic love:

> O glorious trial of exceeding Love,
> Illustrious evidence, example high!
> Ingaging me to emulate. . . .
> To undergoe with mee one Guilt, one Crime,
> If any be, of tasting this fair Fruit,
> Whose vertue, for of good still good proceeds,
> Direct, or by occasion hath presented
> This happie trial of thy Love, which else
> So eminently never had bin known. (IX.961-63, 971-76)

If the effect of the fruit be good, then the two will soar up together like gods; if bad, it will still have proved Adam's great love, his willingness to die for her. This last sentiment, one realizes, is a parody of the *felix culpa,* the happy sin of Adam which results in the incarnation of the Son. Indeed, Eve's whole speech is a parody: for the "trial" which Adam undergoes and the sacrifice he makes undoubtedly are to be compared unfavorably with the trial and sacrifice that prove the love of the Son. Eve's words echo the Father's, when he praises his Son for his great love, and exalts him in return for his voluntary humiliation and self-sacrifice. "O glorious trial of exceeding Love, / Illustrious evidence, example high!" The words would better apply to the Son after he has volunteered to die than to Adam as he resolves to bring death into the world, making the decision which, in fact, seals the need for the Son's sacrifice. The Second Adam, not the first, is the "example" who is worthy of emulation.

Thus, given the nature of Milton's universe, the sentiments of Adam and Eve are painfully specious and parodic, and their desire to cling together will merely drive them apart. Nevertheless, no balanced reader can fail either to be attracted to their magnificent and stirring words, or to sympathize with the tragic humanity of their feelings and actions. As the panoply of heroic warfare throws the cloak of glamor over Satan and gives his underhanded actions a desperate ambivalence, so heroic love blurs and partly conceals the sordid nature of what Adam and Eve are engaging themselves to: the betrayal of God and the destruction of a world. After the fall has begun, and before repentance and reconciliation can partly turn the tide, genuine love between Adam and Eve is impossible. But sex or lust would be insufficient motives in themselves to draw Adam into complicity, or to engage the reader's sympathy. The solution is heroic love, whose powerful language and bewildering confusion of emotions — admirable yet foolish, all-excusing yet guilty, selfless yet selfish — are exactly what is needed to give the poem richness at this crucial juncture, and to prevent a breakdown in the double vision of comedy and tragedy, the balance between the human and the divine. The sin of Adam and Eve must be understood, both theologically — what did it actually involve, what were its results? — and humanly — what did they feel, why did they do it? So once again Milton uses the technique of the veil, covering truth with fiction, in order to hold off at this stage the absolute light of eternity, and thus to preserve the human, experiential viewpoint.

4

What Milton does — in a variety of ways — in *Lycidas,* in "Methought I saw," and in *Paradise Lost,* he does again in *Samson Agonistes.* (In *Paradise Regained,* he abandons the veil and exposes everything to the white light of eternity, thus losing all but acclimated readers.) *Samson Agonistes* is Greek in form; its story is Hebrew; it is both Greek and Hebrew in spirit.[18] It contains no important anachronisms or overtly Christian allusions. Yet the Greek and the Hebrew in *Samson* are finally only veils for a deeply Christian meaning. Why else would the Christian poet, inspired as he thought by the Christian God, address Christian readers? Certainly not with a purist intention of re-creating the dead past — an accomplishment Milton would have considered vain and pointless. Rather, he uses Greek and Hebrew elements in order to temper his vision of the ultimate truth. Samson is a type of Christ, and a paradigm of the Christian hero, fallen for a while but finally victorious. But he is also a man, unable to see beyond this world, though he raises himself above it by blind faith, drawn by the guidance of his God. His humanity is preserved because, although Samson acts out the part of Christ, he does so not only imperfectly, but unknowingly, lacking a full consciousness of the nature and potency of his vicarious sacrifice, and lacking a knowledge of Christian life after death.

The matter of life after death is important: it offers us one of the

---

[18]The Greek element is discussed by William Riley Parker, *Milton's Debt to Greek Tragedy in Samson Agonistes* (Baltimore: Johns Hopkins, 1937); for the Hebrew see Richard C. Jebb, "*Samson Agonistes* and the Hellenic Drama," *Proceedings of the British Academy,* 3 (1908), 341-48; Ann Gossman, "Milton's Samson as the Tragic Hero Purified by Trial," *JEGP,* 61 (1962), 528–41, and "Samson, Job, and the 'Exercise of Saints,'" *English Studies,* 45 (1964), 212–24; and Samuel S. Stollman, "Milton's Samson and the Jewish Tradition," *Milton Studies,* 3 (1971), 185–200.

keys to Milton's approach. As critics have often pointed out, the after-
life is a conception which is ultimately incompatible with tragedy:
for how can a death leading to such a reward (or punishment) be
tragic?[19] Under certain conditions, however, life after death need not
be incompatible with tragedy: the main condition being that the after-
life not be brought too much to the fore. In the sonnet "Methought I
saw," a tragic awareness of death and loss is possible because heaven
is treated only as a promise, a bliss to be trusted in but not immediately experienced: and so, from a human point of view, not *certain*. In
Samson Agonistes, all overt references to the promise are avoided. It is
a possibility that neither Samson nor any of the other characters even
think about; it lies outside the realm of the play. On the other hand,
Milton undoubtedly believed that Samson had earned a place in
heaven by his final obedience and reconciliation with God, and he
wrote for an audience that would believe so too. The parallels between Samson's career and Christ's—and the differences—would not
escape Milton's ideal reader. Nor would he miss the opportunities
the play provides for reading in a Christian meaning: Manoa's words,
for example, on ordering the disposal of Samson's body, "Home to his
Fathers house" (1733); or the idea of resurrection which is implied in
the phoenix image (1697-1707). Neither of these passages refers
overtly to another life, of course, but both suggest it to a reader who
knows more than the characters in the play.

Samson's tragedy is that he lives before Christ, and so before the
Christian promise becomes explicit. He points toward that promise,
but the full significance of his life can be understood—like the story
of Abraham and Isaac, or of Moses leading his people out of Egypt—
only after Christ has fulfilled it. Such was the universal belief of
biblical exegesis in Milton's time. Therefore, Samson must act

[19]A commonplace, occasionally questioned but generally accepted. A typical
and influential study is George Steiner, *The Death of Tragedy* (New York:
Alfred Knopf, 1963). One cannot do justice to Steiner's theory here, since
only *Samson* is at issue, but I should say that tragedy can be called dead only
if it is narrowly defined, and that its "death"—or rather transformation—is
more properly laid at the door of secularism than Christianity. At the crux of
the argument are the great tragedies of Shakespeare, whose spirit has escaped
the agreement of critics.

blindly, freely committing himself to the guidance of God in a course which he cannot fully understand, unless he sees something of the truth in his final moments. This much is in the spirit of the Greek tragedies, in which the hero is caught between the axiom of surety that the gods are good and just, and the experience of a fate that is painfully unjust and wrong. (Such at least is the characteristic theme of Aeschylus and Sophocles; about Euripides there is little agreement.) Samson dies in a fallen world, in a manner contrary to his expectation of military victory over the Philistines, and unaware of his final reward. The reader, also living in a fallen world, shares Samson's experience of suffering and death. Although he is conscious of the nature of Samson's ultimate triumph to a degree which Samson himself cannot enjoy during the play, suffering and death remain.

Undergraduate readers of Milton — and one suspects not a few critics — think that faith was easier for Milton than it is for us. Milton lived in an age of faith; we live in an age of doubt. This, of course, is not true. The seventeenth century was as much an age of doubt and change as our own — as readers of Donne, Shakespeare, Montaigne, Hobbes, Descartes, Marlowe, Chapman, or Webster will realize. If Milton attained and held to an unshakable faith, it was only through a lifetime of questioning. It is well known that he took nothing "on faith" in the sense of accepting the word of others. His was rather the course of Donne's ideal seeker in *Satire III*:

> On a huge hill,
> Cragged and steep, Truth stands, and he that will
> Reach her, about must, and about must go;
> And what the hill's suddenness resists, win so;
> Yet strive so, that before age, death's twilight,
> Thy soul rest, for none can work in that night.

Milton did not move simply from doubt to faith. In one sense, he never lost his faith; in another, he never ceased to question the axioms on which it rested. The whole *Christian Doctrine* was Milton's attempt to examine thoroughly and think through the nature of his beliefs: it was a "methodical tractate" that would be "useful in establishing my faith or assisting my memory. I deemed it therefore safest and most advisable to compile for myself, by my own labor and study, some original treatise which should always be at hand, derived solely from the word of God itself."[20] Not for Milton the comfort of custom, tradition, or authority in the matter of religious belief.

After *Lycidas,* all Milton's poems are affirmations; but they are affirmations that assert a final vision when "wrauth shall be no more / Thenceforth, but in thy presence Joy entire" (*Paradise Lost* III.264-65), yet allow full weight to the blind Fury and to Satan, Sin, and Death. *Lycidas* returns the reader, after his glimpse of the beatific vision, to daily life in the world: "To morrow to fresh Woods, and Pastures new." *Paradise Lost,* as it progresses, increasingly returns to the vision of the end of things:

> The Womans seed, obscurely then foretold,
> Now amplier known thy Saviour and thy Lord,
> Last in the Clouds from Heav'n to be reveald
> In glory of the Father, to dissolve
> *Satan* with his perverted World, then raise
> From the conflagrant mass, purg'd and refin'd,
> New Heav'ns, new Earth, Ages of endless date
> Founded in righteousness and peace and love
> To bring forth fruits Joy and eternal Bliss.
>
> (XII.543-51)

Nevertheless, at the conclusion of *Paradise Lost* Adam and Eve must still face life in the world, carrying out the promise but going into exile. Thus they are placed in the same position as the author and the reader. Man cannot evade his burden. He may firmly expect a happy outcome, but his faith will not permit him to escape exile, trial, suffering, loss, and death.

Samson is a Judge of Israel, elected by God, declared by Saint Paul to be a Saint of God. But he is also human, like us, and lives in our world. The Greek and the Hebrew are the veils that make Samson human. Yet to say that they are veils is not to say that they are unimportant. On the contrary: they are the very stuff out of which the play is made. In *Paradise Lost,* the narrator continually insists that everything classical is false and illusory, yet without the classical the poem would not be anything like the *Paradise Lost* we know. Warfare and

[20]*Works,* XIV, 7.

heroic love are also shown to be illusory, yet without them the poem would be a mere skeleton. Although the Hebrew and the Greek are, in their different ways, typological for the Christian in *Samson Agonistes,* they are at the same time the very structure, texture, and essence of the drama. They make it human and this-worldly, they mediate and incarnate the divine in experience the reader can share. They permit the balance of time and eternity, human experience and ultimate faith, whose fusion is at the center of the play.

3
TRAGIC PATTERNS

In this century, critical opinion has emphasized almost unanimously that in *Samson Agonistes* Milton has cleaned up the originally disreputable folk hero of the Book of Judges and made him presentable to his readers.[1] The Samson of Judges was a "brawny barbarian" or "sanctified barbarian,"[2] a "rambunctious tribal hero" chiefly notable for "his wenching and his brawlings,"[3] "muscle-bound" and "earthy,"[4]

---

[1] The point has been made by dozens of critics, including nearly everyone who has touched on the relationship of *Samson Agonistes* to Judges. For fuller citation, see my "Tragic Patterns in *Samson Agonistes,*" *Texas Studies in Literature and Language,* 11 (1969), 915, n. 1.

[2] Douglas Bush, ed., *The Complete Poetical Works of John Milton* (Boston: Houghton Mifflin, 1965), p. 514; A. S. P. Woodhouse, "Tragic Effect in *Samson Agonistes,*" *Univ. of Toronto Quarterly,* 28 (1959), 208.

[3] Watson Kirkconnell, *That Invincible Samson* (Toronto: Univ. of Toronto Press, 1964), p. 146.

[4] A. B. Chambers, "Wisdom and Fortitude in *Samson Agonistes,*" *PMLA,* 78 (1963), 315; E. Wright, "Samson as the Fallen Champion in 'Samson Agonistes,'" *Notes and Queries,* N. S. 7 (1960), 223.

a "primitive ruffian of a half-savage legend . . . hairy sun symbol . . . repulsive to those who do not read his story with sanctified inattention."[5] Milton's Samson, on the contrary, is "a man of sensitive conscience, integrity, and piety," a "Saint," or even a "Protestant-Stoic."[6] The terms used to contrast the two Samsons often reveal an uncommon intensity of feeling, almost as if there were a contest to find the most apt denigratory phrase. Certainly, there are considerable differences between the Samson of Judges and Milton's Samson, whether Milton originated them or derived them from the earlier developments of Christian exegesis.[7] And certainly the now almost universal recognition of the integrity and intellectual strength of Milton's Samson is preferable to a belief that he shares the disreputability of his forerunner.[8] But—leaving aside what amounts to considerable distortion of the Book of Judges—because Milton's critics have been diverted to this contrast, they have given insufficient attention to an important element in the play, which has been stressed only by those out of sympathy with *Samson*. For although in comparison with Judges Milton's Samson may seem respectable, this should not obscure the significance of his still disreputable appearance. He is dressed in rags, diseased, dirty, the

[5]Don Cameron Allen, *The Harmonious Vision* (Baltimore: Johns Hopkins, 1954), p. 82.

[6]Bush, *Complete Poetical Works,* p. 514; F. Michael Krouse, *Milton's Samson and the Christian Tradition* (Princeton: Princeton Univ. Press, 1949), passim; E. M. W. Tillyard, *The Miltonic Setting* (London: Chatto & Windus, 1938), pp. 86, 88.

[7]On the development of the Samson story and the differences between Milton and Judges, see Krouse, and also Chauncey B. Tinker, *"Samson Agonistes," Tragic Themes in Western Literature,* ed. Cleanth Brooks (New Haven: Yale Univ. Press, 1955), pp. 59–76. The only Miltonist with a good word for the Samson of Judges is Evert M. Clark, "Milton's Conception of Samson," *Univ. of Texas Studies in English,* 8 (1928), 88–99. For some reason Miltonists have accepted uncritically the pronouncements of the recent "demythologizing" school of exegesis, though one might expect literary scholars to better appreciate the role of "myth" and "fiction" than theologians.

[8]As argued by earlier critics such as James Waddell Tupper, "The Dramatic Structure of·*Samson Agonistes,"* *PMLA,* 25 (1920), 375–89.

wielder of an ass's jawbone even at the height of his prosperity, and the companion of slaves and asses in the depths of his misery.

A balanced appraisal of *Samson* must keep these elements in mind, not only noticing the differences between Milton and the Bible, but also coming to terms with Samson as he actually is. Closer attention to these relatively neglected elements proves useful in adding to one's understanding of the play. Samson's less attractive physical attributes help to contrast the outer man with the inner, the physical with the spiritual;[9] they serve as a correlative to his mental suffering; and they are also essential to delineating his character and the nature of his heroism. They prove to be vital to the tragic effect, or catharsis, which the Preface reveals to be among Milton's major concerns in the play. In this chapter, therefore, we will examine Samson's less respectable characteristics and relate them both to his heroism and to the central action. It will be seen that Samson, noble, heroic, and spiritual as he is, also exhibits a series of negative characteristics integral to the action that contribute significantly to the tragic effect and Christian meaning. In brief, Samson, though a hero, is also delineated as an outcast, as a scapegoat, and as a kind of monster.

1

Almost everyone immediately notices the essential isolation of the hero of *Samson Agonistes*. This isolation has sometimes been explained autobiographically. Samson is Milton, deserted on the collapse of the Puritan movement, fallen on evil days and compassed round by the Royalist sons of Belial. In one recent staged version of the play, the actors even dressed in Seventeenth-Century costume. This parallel — if we accept the traditional dating of the play — accounts for the emotional richness Milton gives the isolation theme. Samson is not Milton, however, regardless of how much he may reflect Milton's experience. To push autobiographical theories further, as their responsible exponents recognize, is to depart from

[9] See George Williamson, *Milton & Others* (Chicago: Univ. of Chicago Press, 1965), p. 87.

the play itself.[10] Samson's isolation has also been explained as basically Protestant, deriving from the stress on man alone with his God, without the support of a priesthood or of human mediation. Tillyard suggests that Samson retreats into "the Protestant-Stoic citadel; utterly isolated"; then he sallies forth at the play's conclusion, thus transcending the limitations of Protestantism.[11] A similar proposal is made by Steadman; he suggests that Samson must isolate himself from action and fight the battle within his own mind because he reflects a Calvinist predisposition to stress faith over works; then, just as works stem from faith, Samson's decisive action finally issues from this interior struggle.[12] Each of these interpretations offers us a valuable insight into the play. It would be wrong, however, to draw from these observations the conclusion that *Samson* is a restrictively Protestant work. It has been influenced by Protestant thinking, undoubtedly; but it is not narrowly dogmatic. As in the case of *Paradise Lost,* Milton took care to make his poem broadly Christian.

The pattern of withdrawal followed by recommitment, or of contemplation followed by action, is common in the works of this period. It characterizes *Paradise Regained,* whose main subject is Christ's withdrawal into the desert and into his own mind, a withdrawal that enables him, at the end of the poem, to "enter, and begin to save mankind" (IV.635). The same might be called the subject

[10] See James Holly Hanford, *"Samson Agonistes* and Milton in Old Age," *Studies in Shakespeare, Milton and Donne* by Members of the English Dept. of the Univ. of Michigan (New York, 1925), pp. 178–79; and A. S. P. Woodhouse, *"Samson Agonistes* and Milton's Experience," *Transactions of the Royal Society of Canada,* 3rd Ser., Vol. 43, Sec. 2 (1949), 169–75.

[11] Tillyard, *The Miltonic Setting,* pp. 86, 88.

[12] John M. Steadman, "'Faithful Champion': The Theological Basis of Milton's Hero of Faith," in *Milton: Modern Essays in Criticism,* ed. Arthur E. Barker (New York: Oxford Univ. Press, 1965), pp. 467–83. Still another explanation is given by Kenneth Fell, "From Myth to Martyrdom: Towards a View of Milton's *Samson Agonistes,"* *English Studies,* 34 (1953), 146; he thinks Samson's isolation is a vestige of the solar imagery in Judges, stemming from mythical origins that equate Samson with the sun, for "the sun always worked alone."

of Marvell's poetry, especially of "Upon Appleton House." But this
is not simply a peculiarly Protestant pattern. In Catholicism one can
point to the great popularity at this time of the thirty-day Ignatian
retreat, a withdrawal into self that was followed by re-entry into life
with a new, active sense of commitment. In very practical terms, the
Ignatian retreat was the source of much of the energy of the Catholic
Counter-Reformation. Beyond this, it will be evident that withdrawal before action is in fact a basic human pattern, an archetypal
motif, so widespread in literature and so characteristic of real life
that citation is hardly necessary.

Accompanying Samson's withdrawal is his isolation. He towers
like an Aeschylean hero above the other characters and stands apart
from them, severe and forbidding. Indeed, it is by a technical method
borrowed from Aeschylus, the limitation of the number of characters
on stage, that Milton achieves much of this effect.[13] The Danites
play two roles, as character and as chorus. If this distinction is made,
it will be seen that through most of the play there are only two
characters on stage at one time: Samson alone, Samson and the
Chorus, Samson and Manoa, Samson and Dalila, Samson and Harapha,
Samson and the Public Officer. Until the climax, Samson is at one
side of every interchange, and when he leaves the stage, he is the
only subject of the conversation. The emphasis on him is relentless;
no other relationship is allowed to dissipate our attention. It might
be interesting, for example, to learn what Manoa and Dalila have to
say to each other, but this is a distraction that Milton will not
permit us.

Although Samson is constantly seen talking with the other characters, which implies a degree of sociability and a constantly double
focus, in fact the attention focuses almost entirely on him. He remains one of Milton's characteristically lonely heroes. He is like
Enoch in *Paradise Lost*, jeered at by his people, or like Abdiel among
the followers of Satan; and he is isolated for the same reason: because he holds his ground against odds and remains the faithful

---

[13] Cf. William Riley Parker, *Milton's Debt to Greek Tragedy in Samson
Agonistes* (Baltimore: Johns Hopkins, 1937), pp. 117–18; and Bush, *Complete Poetical Works*, p. 513.

"Servant of God" even more firmly after he thinks he has lost everything. He has wavered from this stand before the play begins, and he
has paid and is paying heavily for his sin. For this reason his position
is now even more difficult than Abdiel's, since he cannot take comfort
in never having fallen. But though at first without hope, he refuses
to give in to the pressures of his friends and society.

As a Nazarite, Samson has been set aside by God, "solemnly
elected" (678) from the time of his conception. Specially chosen
for his role, his strength and his closeness to God set him apart
from friend and foe alike. Although he is the enemy of the Philistines,
he is also betrayed and deserted by the Hebrews. Samson still has a
few friends and well-wishers left when the play opens, his father and
the chorus of Danites, but even those friends play the unwitting role
of Job's comforters. They can do little to console him. Their comment
and advice usually have the opposite effect from what they intend,
and the more they express their concern and their good intentions,
the more Samson is made to realize his complete isolation. None
of them understands the true nature of his greatness. One way of
looking at the play, in fact, is to say that it recounts Samson's progressive separation from all humanity. As Martin E. Mueller points
out, "Samson deliberately severs his connexions with his fellow-
men; when he leaves the stage he has done with Manoa, Dalila, and
the Danites."[14] The separation is deliberate because Samson acts
freely; but it is also necessary because of the position he finds
himself in.

The progressive isolation of the hero is characteristic of all the
greatest tragedies. One thinks of Job, Prometheus, Oedipus, Macbeth,
Faustus. Indeed, one may say that part of the very essence of tragedy
is for the hero to be or to become isolated, for he is different from
other men. Even when the difference consists in nobility, the hero
is usually, like Samson, forbidding, stern, aloof, too caught up in his
destiny or his larger concerns to be capable of normal human relations. Hamlet has no time or part of himself to offer to Ophelia,
Coriolanus rejects Virgilia, Faustus is parted from his friends the

[14]Mueller, "Pathos and Katharsis in Samson Agonistes," ELH, 21 (1964),
156–57.

Scholars; there is an inability, tragic in itself, to be involved in anything but the central tragic fate which overwhelms everything else.

Samson's isolation, like that of many other tragic heroes, is simultaneously admirable and pitiable; admirable in religious terms, or in the light of eternity, but tragic in human terms and in the light of ordinary relationships. The reason for this ambivalence is the irony that his very closeness to God is responsible for his distance from men. Not even the comfort and reassurance of a special providential plan can entirely compensate for his loss of human friendship and understanding, except, possibly, in the last moments of his life. The ironic two-sidedness of Samson's isolation, the fact that nearness to God must entail separation from men in a fallen world, is not an incidental effect in the play, for it connects intimately with the development of the plot.

Reference to a passage from A. S. P. Woodhouse's acute interpretation of *Samson* suggests how the ambivalence characteristic of Samson's isolation can be related to the central action of the play: "What Milton has done in respect of the action we have seen: he has made the way of repentance and restoration, the way back to God, also the way that leads inevitably to the catastrophe, and has thus achieved at a stroke the only kind of irony that is at once compatible with a Christian outlook and as potent as any to be found in tragedy anywhere."[15] The isolation of Samson is a necessary component in Milton's development of the ironic action, with its double significance, that Woodhouse describes. Like the construction of Milton's plot, and in conformity with it, Samson's character and his relation to humanity and to God help explain how the play can be both tragic and Christian, catastrophic and triumphant. One of the action's major ironies is thus enriched by the circumstance that Samson's closeness to God outlaws him, makes him an outcast from his fellow men, puts him beyond the understanding even of his father and his few would-be friends. This separation is progressively unfolded in the play, in preparation for the culminating moment when Samson pauses in the Temple of Dagon, revolving in his mind

---

[15] Woodhouse, "Tragic Effect in *Samson Agonistes*," *Univ. of Toronto Quarterly*, 28 (1959), 220–21.

what he is about to do. One man against the Philistine nation, he is also isolated from his friends. In his last moments he is entirely alone with God. Here and in his death the twofold movement toward God and away from man reaches its completion.

2

Although Samson's isolation from his own people is due mainly to his virtues—his nobility, courage, unwillingness to endure slavish subjection to the Philistines, his strength (which although real is also a symbol of spiritual distinction and divine favor), above all his adherence to God's will—yet he is also separated from humanity by a series of very different characteristics. These are his blindness, his rags, his working at the mill among animals, and his impaired condition whether physical or spiritual. As the Chorus points out, Samson's uniqueness has two faces:

> As signal now in low dejected state,
> As earst in highest, behold him where he lies.
>
> (338-39)

The Chorus partly errs, however—as we will see further in the next chapter—by separating these two kinds of uniqueness in time. Samson, in his present abject condition, is inwardly reaching new heights. Like many other statements in the play, this is an ironical half-truth.

Both the Chorus and Manoa are deeply disturbed by Samson's physical condition. Their first reaction is shock at the very sight of him:

> This, this is he; softly a while,
> Let us not break in upon him;
> O change beyond report, thought, or belief!
> See how he lies at random, carelessly diffus'd,
> With languish't head unpropt,
> As one past hope, abandon'd,
> And by himself given over;

> In slavish habit, ill-fitted weeds
> O're worn and soild;
> Or do my eyes misrepresent? Can this be hee,
> That Heroic, that Renown'd,
> Irresistible *Samson?* (115-26)

Thus Samson's friends the Danites react on first seeing him; and quite similar is the reaction of Manoa his father:

> O miserable change! is this the man,
> That invincible *Samson,* far renown'd,
> The dread of *Israel*'s foes . . . ?
>
> (340-42)

Manoa and the Chorus feel chiefly pity and sorrow at the change they see in him, this "change beyond report, thought, or belief." But another reaction is also possible. Harapha, also noticing Samson's degraded appearance, speaks of it in terms less sympathetic:

> To combat with a blind man I disdain,
> And thou hast need much washing to be toucht.
>
> (1106-07)

This comment has a great effect in arousing Samson and preparing him for the action he will soon take, as the critics have noticed; but, leaving aside Harapha's unpleasant tone, what he says is true. Harapha's reaction is disgust rather than pity, but what he and Manoa see is not actually very different. Elsewhere, Manoa says that Samson is in a "miserable loathsom plight" (480). That is, while his plight is miserable, in terms of normal human reactions it is loathsome as well. The word, a strong one, may refer primarily to Samson's circumstances rather than his person, as in the "loathsom prison-house" of line 922; but inevitably it reflects on Samson as well, whose slavish and degraded appearance reflects his shameful task at the mill, his apparent loss of a free man's integrity.

Milton has not toned down the biblical description of Samson's degradation in order to make his hero outwardly more respectable and decorous. Quite the opposite: he has emphasized it. He spares no details; while in Judges the entire prison episode is presented in a few powerful but restrained words: "But the Philistines took him, and put out his eyes, and brought him down to Gaza, and bound him with fetters of brass; and he did grind in the prison house. Howbeit the hair of his head began to grow again after he was shaven." The difference between this account and Milton's can be laid to several causes. First, the exegetical tradition and previous literary versions of the story had increasingly stressed and elaborated the last stages of Samson's life. Second, having chosen these events as the subject of his play, Milton was guided by his dramatic sense and by the principles of *copia*—abundance or rhetorical expansion of his subject. Emphasis on this part of Samson's life did not, however, require Milton to put so heavy a stress on negative elements. Reference to Samson's filth, degradation, smell, to his vermin and rags, might have been held to a minimum, or even eliminated by a lesser playwright as anti-heroic.

Samuel Johnson, although he was speaking mainly of the diction, was struck by Milton's apparent indifference in *Samson Agonistes* to poetic elevation or the conventions of tragic drama. He writes: "All allusions to low and trivial objects, with which contempt is usually associated, are doubtless unsuitable to a species of composition which ought always to be awful, though not always magnificent."[16] That is, the hero may lose his prosperity and face adversities that strip away his worldly pomp, but he must not be allowed to lose his effect of awing the audience. Johnson's remarks—to which he gives as great a scope as to his better-known complaint that *Samson* lacks a middle—do not illustrate the presuppositions of his age only. That many earlier critics would have agreed with him is suggested by Sir John Harington's protest against carping critics in his "Briefe Apologie of Poetrie" prefacing his translation of *Orlando Furioso:* "Yea sure there be some that will not sticke to call *Hercules* himselfe a dastard, because forsooth he fought with a club and not at the rapyer and dagger."[17] One can imagine what these critics, if not

[16] *The Rambler,* No. 140 (20 July 1751), in *The British Essayists,* ed. E. Chalmers, 21 (London, 1808), 184–85.

[17] G. Gregory Smith, ed., *Elizabethan Critical Essays* (London: Oxford Univ. Press, 1904), II, 194. Hercules and Samson were traditional analogues in the Renaissance.

overawed by biblical authority, would have thought about an ass's jawbone as a gentleman's weapon.

If *Samson Agonistes* is elevated and heroic, and I am sure most readers would feel that it is, then its elevation does not depend on the exclusion of "low and trivial" elements in its hero. Milton was never one to stand on ceremony, or to be concerned with appearances for their own sake. It was, of course, necessary to stress the *painfulness* of Samson's plight, and to have him undergo great suffering; but that is something different from shame and degradation and the dwelling on unwholesome details that could easily have been eliminated. Yet in spite of his stress on interior events and on the growth of Samson's mind and spirit, Milton insists, with imagery or with direct description, on detailing almost every aspect of Samson's physical degradation.

Samson's physical appearance contrasts with his spiritual nobility, and thus reinforces it. But his appearance has another function: it interacts with his isolation. It separates him from other men, and symbolizes the separation. As Harapha unkindly points out, his closest comrades in the prison are "Slaves and Asses" (1162). Even his friends are from the very first put off by his appearance, as we have noticed. Although they are sympathetic, even drawn to him more strongly by his suffering, nevertheless his appearance leads them to misjudge him. They cannot advance beyond their initial impressions, until the revelation of Samson's nature in the catastrophe forces a revaluation on them. The reader, if he is alert, senses a gradual and impressive growth in Samson, because he is allowed some insight into Samson's mental processes; but Manoa and the Chorus, because they are guided mainly by their eyes and their first impressions, continue to misjudge him. His dirt, his rags, his careless posture, and most of all his blindness, make Manoa and the Chorus assume that God has abandoned his champion, that Samson is no longer a hero and will never be one again. He is to be pitied and helped, ransomed and cared for, rather than looked up to or followed as a national leader. It is Manoa's unquestioning assumption of this attitude that so disturbs Samson, and that lies at the root of the misunderstanding that separates them more and more as Samson grows inwardly.

Manoa cannot see his son as a hero. If God is ever to make use of him again, it will only be by a miraculous return to the past—by the restoration of Samson's eyesight and, by implication, his former heroic appearance (581-89, 1503). Samson, oppressed and momentarily overcome by their vision, draws upon their feelings and amplifies them when he paints the picture of what his future will be in his father's house, if ever he lets their patronizing pity get the best of him:

> Now blind, disheartn'd, sham'd, dishonour'd, quell'd,
> To what can I be useful, wherein serve
> My Nation, and the work from Heav'n impos'd,
> But to sit idle on the houshold hearth,
> A burdenous drone; to visitants a gaze,
> Or pitied object, these redundant locks
> Robustious to no purpose clustring down,
> Vain monument of strength; till length of years
> And sedentary numness craze my limbs
> To a contemptible old age obscure.
> Here rather let me drudge and earn my bread,
> Till vermin or the draff of servil food
> Consume me, and oft-invocated death
> Hast'n the welcom end of all my pains.
>
> (563-76)

This nightmare picture of an alternative future, although Samson paints it, actually stems from the feelings about him expressed by his father and friends. He momentarily accepts their vision, transforms it with his own sense of its disparity from his divine mission, extends it to its furthest limits, and then rejects it. This is their idea of the future, not his.

We have seen that although Samson's isolation and separation from others grows during the play, it began in the past, at the moment of his conception, when he was set aside to carry out the divine purpose. In the same way, although Samson's degradation is completed in prison, there are "unheroic" elements in his past as well. At the very height of his former glory, the battle of Ramath-lechi, about which his friends fondly reminisce, Milton pointedly contrasts his deeds with chivalric or gentlemanly ideals. He is described as a man

> whom unarm'd
> No strength of man, or fiercest wild beast could withstand;
> Who tore the Lion, as the Lion tears the Kid,
> Ran on embattelld Armies clad in Iron,
> And weaponless himself,
> Made Arms ridiculous, useless the forgery
> Of brazen shield and spear, the hammer'd Cuirass,
> *Chalybean* temper'd steel, and frock of mail
> Adamantean Proof;
> But safest he who stood aloof,
> When insupportably his foot advanc't,
> In scorn of thir proud arms and warlike tools,
> Spurn'd them to death by Troops. The bold *Ascalonite*
> Fled from his Lion ramp, old Warriors turn'd
> Thir plated backs under his heel;
> Or grovling soild thir crested helmets in the dust.
> Then with what trivial weapon came to hand,
> The Jaw of a dead Ass, his sword of bone,
> A thousand fore-skins fell, the flower of *Palestin*
> In *Ramath-lechi* famous to this day . . . (126-45).

Samson is renowned, heroic, irresistible, at the height of his pride; yet the unheroic or "barbaric" elements of Judges are retained and in fact emphasized: the ass's jawbone becomes even more inglorious by the accidental nature of its picking up, by Milton's epithet "trivial," and by the contemptuous reference to the "dead Ass" from which it came; to this is added from an earlier episode in Judges the bare hands tearing the lion and the association with "fiercest wild beasts." Samson becomes a "foot," a "heel," himself now a ramping lion like the one he killed. These details, or ones like them, are familiar in the Samson tradition, but Milton, who proved himself again and again capable of handling tradition with whatever freedom he chose, could have eliminated them, or at least tried to "make the best" of them. Instead, he retained and transformed them, reveled in them, and emphasized the contrast with chivalric heroism even further by adding a long contemptuous catalogue of useless weaponry and armor. Climaxing this are the two pictures of old warriors

forced to turn their "plated backs" under his heel, in a kind of en-
forced cowardice, and the final shame of the symbols of military
pride, as the Philistines' "crested helmets" are forced to grovel and
soil themselves in the dust. At the same time, however, even as
Milton dismisses these symbols of honor and glory, he manages to
appropriate all their favorable associations to Samson, so that the
magnificence of brazen shield and spear and adamantean armor seems
to transfer itself to him. He achieves this effect partly by the ambiguity with which he introduces the catalogue of arms: Samson "ran
on embattelld Armies clad in Iron." At first reading, it seems to be
Samson who is clad in iron. But the transfer is accomplished mainly
by the subtle illogic of poetry, which can say one thing and accomplish another, in this case much like the passages in *Paradise Lost*
in which Milton ridicules war and its rituals but at the same time
reflects glory on Satan as a mighty warrior. The main effect of the
passage in *Samson,* however, is to condemn popular chivalric ideals.
Milton has not eliminated the barbaric element at all: he has subsumed it into his ideal of heroism and made it seem admirable.

Even before his downfall, then, Samson was not the common kind
of hero. Although the Danites reminisce about his glorious youth
and his moments of splendid heroism, this heroism, even if we label
it Hebraic as opposed to Hellenic or Chivalric in our attempts to
explain it, still is not the popular human ideal. That ideal, symbolized
by the knightly weapons that the Philistines always carry into battle,
is further embodied in Harapha, who is a caricature of chivalry, of
the desire for honor and glory, and of the false heroism of the
Romances. Harapha, with his "glorious arms / Which greatest
Heroes have in battel worn" (1130-31), his helmet, brigandine,
habergeon, vant-brace, greaves, and gauntlet, spear and shield
(1119-22), represents the kind of hero people want—and indeed he
is the Philistines' champion, though under pressure he proves to be
hollow. Samson, on the contrary, was not popular with his people
even at the peak of his career. Milton makes no mention of his twenty
years as an honored judge over Israel (Judges 15.22), presumably in
order to emphasize his unpopularity and essential isolation. He is
not the kind of leader whom the Jews want: for he will neither be
expedient in his dealings with the Philistines, leaving the Jews to
their comfortable slavery, nor will he lead them against the Philistines

as a proper hero should, with the romantic appurtenances of sword, shield, and glistening armor.

One need only recall the systematic coupling of romantic chivalry and worldly honor with Satan in *Paradise Lost* to realize what Milton intends. Satan draws his followers to him by the clever use of the trappings of chivalric leadership, from the War in Heaven to the military maneuvers in Hell. In Heaven he is "armd in Adamant and Gold" (VI.110), topped by a "proud Crest" (VI.191), imitating with his entourage the splendor of God himself. In Hell he and his followers put on a military show that is one of the most magnificent pieces of visual or symbolic rhetoric in literature, in the passage that begins with the unfurling of his imperial ensign by the Cherub Azazel, and ends with the clashing of swords on shields by his enthusiastic followers (I.531-98, 663-69). It is this passage that Milton modulates in order to draw in King Arthur, the jousters of Aspramont and Montalban, and Charlemagne, and thus to undercut man's chivalric ideals. While Harapha is in this tradition, Samson, the champion of God, refuses to make any such concession to popular taste. Speaking of the failure of the Jews to support him, he says:

> I on th' other side
> Us'd no ambition to commend my deeds,
> The deeds themselves, though mute, spoke loud
> the dooer. . . . (246-48)

Samson refuses to prostitute himself to popular wishes, to go around canvassing for support; not words or the manipulation of appearances, but deeds, must be allowed to speak for him.

Although Samson is God's champion, he is not a knightly figure or a gentleman. J. W. Tupper is correct, if insensitive to the spirit of the play, when he writes that "it is not a knight of God but a prize fighter who declares he will

> with one buffet lay thy structure low,
> Or swing thee in the air, then dash thee down,
> To the hazard of thy brains and shattered sides." [18]

Samson is scornful here of knightly sensibilities — although perhaps he speaks as he does partly in order to goad Harapha into fighting

---

[18] Tupper, "The Dramatic Structure of *Samson Agonistes*," pp. 385–86.

with him. Samson is no knight; he is a man, stripped of the usual heroic accidentals in much the same way that Adam in *Paradise Lost* is the more kingly because he lacks the outward props:

> Mean while our Primitive great Sire, to meet
> His god-like Guest, walks forth, without more train
> Accompani'd then with his own compleat
> Perfections, in himself was all his state,
> More solemn then the tedious pomp that waits
> On Princes, when thir rich Retinue long
> Of Horses led, and Grooms besmeard with Gold
> Dazles the croud, and sets them all agape. (V.350-57)

Samson need not dress himself up in a human convention, for he is sufficiently a man to do without such support.

To suggest that Samson embodies chivalric heroism or Renaissance courtesy, as a few critics have done, or that he has been "improved" by the development of the western heroic ideal, is misleading. He is much closer to the original "barbarian" of Judges than that. He represents Milton's ideal of Christian heroism, but he is not "civilized." The obvious analogues to Samson with respect to his heroism are the Hebraic heroes: the prophets, judges, and great men of the Old Testament. Samson's physical appearance before the prison, his earlier scorn for arms and armor, recall figures like Jeremiah, Isaiah, or John the Baptist. Woe to those in Judah who trust in horses and chariots, and not the Lord their God, cries Isaiah (31.1-3). In this context, Samson's rags and his very dirt are appropriate. When John the Baptist asks the crowd whether they expected a prophet "clothed in soft raiment," his question is rhetorical, at the most a reminder of what prophets look like. Another close parallel to Samson is Moses. He begins life as a prince, well-dressed, well liked by the Egyptian court; but everything is stripped away when he takes up his mission and becomes a true hero. These other figures in the Bible are suggestive analogues, not sources; but one can see their kind of heroism in Milton's Samson. It would be going too far, however, to say that his heroism is only Hebraic, for he resembles several of the greatest Greek and Elizabethan heroes as well. The Oedipus of Sophocles' last play, one imagines, had no need of external trappings to reflect his natural aura of authority – nor had Lear.

One final element in Samson's degradation, not so far mentioned, Milton has added both to Judges and to his other sources. This is the suggestion that Samson is diseased and ulcerated, suffering from "wounds immedicable" (620). In part, this disease may be physical: Samson is blind, covered with vermin, and threatened with malnutrition from eating the "draff of servil food" (574). (It might be noted that many of the victims of religious persecution in sixteenth- and seventeenth-century England sickened and died because of the conditions they were subjected to while in prison.) Samson's disease is mainly spiritual, however, the result of sin or the stinging of conscience. Certainly disease imagery is a major element in the play, and its constant recurrence gives each instance a more than local meaning. Its significance grows, in much the same way that recurrent image clusters grow in Shakespearean plays, or in Milton's own *Paradise Lost,* taking on a richly symbolic meaning through repetition and complex interconnection.[19] Instances of disease imagery occur in lines 183-86, 480, 571-75, 579, 599-601, 617-32, and 697-704. In addition, words like "balm" (186, 651), "ease" (17, 18, 72), "unwholsom" (9), or "healing" (605) unobtrusively contribute to the motif, together with numerous related references to Samson's filth, subjection, or shameful condition.

The disease imagery has often been noticed. It can symbolize the perils of despair, the spiritual fruits of sin, the shameful condition of slavery. It contrasts with Samson's former healthy state and underlines his suffering. It cannot be said entirely to oppose the physical to the spiritual, because Samson is impaired in both respects. Several critics have suggested that Milton's intention was to apply catharsis not only to the audience but also to Samson, to purge him of his

[19] On Shakespeare, see Caroline Spurgeon, *Shakespeare's Imagery* (Cambridge: Cambridge Univ. Press, 1935), and Wolfgang Clemen, *The Development of Shakespeare's Imagery* (New York: Hill & Wang, 1962). The main study of Milton's imagery, Theodore Banks, *Milton's Imagery* (New York: Columbia Univ. Press, 1950), is little more than a catalogue, but for one running image, see my "The Image of the Tower in *Paradise Lost,*" *Studies in English Literature,* 10 (1970), 171–81.

spiritual ills by a kind of homeopathic medicine.[20] Each character in the play helps to cure Samson of his spiritual malaise by displaying and externalizing the same spiritual ill himself. Thus, for example, Manoa externalizes Samson's despairing accusations against providence and so cures him of the practice, Dalila pleads weakness and provocation by others and thus purges Samson of these errors, Harapha displays an inflated pride like Samson's before his downfall. Probably, when Milton referred to purgation in his preface, he had in mind mainly the traditional Aristotelian doctrine of purgation of the audience or reader, modified by taking purgation in a medical sense.[21] The two effects are not necessarily incompatible, however, and it can well be argued that the purgation of the reader is mediated through the purgation of Manoa and the Chorus, who in turn are affected mainly by the example of Samson.

Although Samson's disabilities, whether mental or physical, cause him great suffering and pain, he dwells even more on their shamefulness and repulsiveness. The worst thing about his blindness is that it makes him appear a fool. Occasionally he does not mention pain at all, as in his vision of the future when a "sedentary numness"

[20] Hanford, "*Samson Agonistes* and Milton in Old Age"; Mueller, "*Pathos and Katharsis in Samson Agonistes*"; Georgia Christopher, "Homeopathic Physic and Natural Renovation in *Samson Agonistes*," ELH, 37 (1970), 361–73; Raymond B. Waddington, "Melancholy Against Melancholy: *Samson Agonistes* as Renaissance Tragedy," *Calm of Mind*, ed. Joseph Anthony Wittreich, Jr. (Cleveland: Press of Case Western Reserve Univ., 1971), pp. 259–87.

[21] What Milton meant by catharsis is difficult, though many historians of tragedy credit the preface of *Samson* with breaking new ground. See Mueller, Christopher, and Waddington, cited above in note 20; also Paul R. Sellin, "Sources of Milton's Catharsis: A Reconsideration," *JEGP*, 40 (1961), 712–30; Martin E. Mueller, "Sixteenth-Century Italian Criticism and Milton's Theory of Catharsis," *Studies in English Literature*, 6 (1966), 139–50; Sherman Hawkins, "Samson's Catharsis," *Milton Studies*, 2 (1970), 211–30; John M. Steadman, "'Passions Well Imitated': Rhetoric and Poetics in the Preface to *Samson Agonistes*," *Calm of Mind*, ed. Wittreich, pp. 175–207. Another study that throws light on Milton's use of poetry as medicine is David M. Miller, "From Delusion to Illumination: A Larger Structure for *L'Allegro-Il Penseroso*," *PMLA*, 86 (1971), 32–37.

will "craze" his limbs, and he will sink into "contemptible old age obscure" (571-72). He often stresses his shameful and unheroic appearance. Even in the passage where he complains about the sharpness of his thoughts, the emphasis is as much on repulsive appearance as on pain. Both are unbearable:

> My griefs not only pain me
> As a lingring disease,
> But finding no redress, ferment and rage,
> Nor less then wounds immedicable
> Ranckle, and fester, and gangrene,
> To black mortification. (617-22).

The disease imagery, by its ugliness, is coupled with his sense that he has been shamed and made inglorious, is "sung and proverbd for a Fool" (203). His fear of mockery, his sensitivity to appearance, are the reactions of a man who knows that he is cut off, rejected, different from other men. Before his fall he could take pride in the difference; after it he feels shame. Thus the disease imagery, like the rags and the other disagreeable things about him, is connected with his loneliness and isolation.

There are two parallels to Samson in his diseased state. One is Job, who, though sinless, suffers from similar pain and degradation. The other is Philoctetes. Unlike these two, Samson's disease is mainly mental, his shame more abstract; but there is some reflection in his physical appearance. Since the parallel with Job, a major Old-Testament type of the "suffering servant," has been discussed elsewhere, I will merely point out that Job is another example of the stripped hero, the "bare forked animal" that is man without decoration or pretention. The parallel with Philoctetes, though briefly noticed, has received less attention.[22] The incurable wound of the Greek bowman is usually interpreted, among other things, as the mark of the outcast or the man set apart. Because the wound is so

[22]Brief mention of Philoctetes was made by Richard Cumberland, *The Observer*, No. 76 (1788) and by A. W. Verity in his introduction to *Samson Agonistes* (Cambridge: Cambridge Univ. Press, 1892), p. liv. Cumberland calls both heroes "most abject." Parker, *Milton's Debt to Greek Tragedy*, oddly does not note the parallel.

repulsive and smells so bad, the Greeks cannot stand his company
and exile him to an uninhabited island. But in Philoctetes, as in the
fallen Samson, repulsiveness is coupled with more-than-human
capabilities. In one case, the greatness is signified by the irresistible
bow that will bring down the city of Troy; in the other by Samson's
miraculous strength, that will destroy the Philistines in their temple.
The Jews and the Greeks both have to come to terms with the
heroes that have been given to them, though neither hero is initially
welcomed by his people. Perhaps, as Edmund Wilson suggests in an
interesting essay, the wound and the bow are necessary concom-
itants.[23] Or one may go further, and suggest that they may even be
two sides of the same coin — just as Samson's separation from man is
the other and inescapable side of his nearness to God. Both a
repellant quality and greatness set heroes apart from other men. And
greatness, especially when it refuses to clothe itself in the expected
garb, as it so often does, is fearful, even monstrous, in the eyes of
ordinary men.

3

In addition to his isolation and his "repulsiveness," which we have
seen to be closely connected, there is a third characteristic, or rather
a third way, of describing Samson's relations to men and to God. His
role in the play resembles at many points that of a scapegoat or
sacrifice. The motif is emphasized by a background of constant
reference to ritual sacrifice: the burnt offering made by Samson's
parents when the angel foretold his birth (26), the Philistines'
sacrifice which will be offered to Dagon (436), Manoa's suggestion
that a ransomed Samson propitiate God with future offerings (519),
the sacrifices and games that the Public Officer demands Samson
participate in (1312), and finally, the Philistines gathered in the
Temple in the last moments before the catastrophe, when "Feast
and noon grew high, and Sacrifice / Had fill'd thir hearts with mirth,

[23] Wilson, *The Wound and the Bow* (New York: Oxford Univ. Press, 1965),
pp. 223–42.

high chear, and wine" (1612-13). Samson, of course, proves to be the last ironic sacrifice; but he has played the scapegoat all along. The Jews, his people, turn against him and deliver him bound to his enemies as a scapegoat is expelled from a tribe, in order to avert vengeance and rid themselves of a focus of danger. Dalila delivers him up a second time in order, among other things, to fulfill her duty to religion and state. These are the actions of people who act deceitfully and wrongly. But God's providence (with Samson's concurrence) brings about his final sacrifice, this time as a victim in the service of truth.

Although Samson is the chosen of God, he is God's chosen holocaust as well as his champion. Through the workings of providence, the two apparently contradictory roles are one. The flames in which the prophesying angel ascends to heaven foreshadow Samson's end as well as his beginning.[24] The Phoenix emblem symbolizes the death and resurrection, or the triumph in defeat, of a sacrificial victim. Other details, which fit naturally enough into the literal action so they may escape our notice, also gain significance in this context. After Samson has finally separated himself from man and been accepted by God, he is led unresisting to the sacrifice. He is given new clothes to wear (1317, 1616), natural enough in the circumstances but also appropriate to a sacrificial ritual. He offers himself up after prayer, at a religious festival, in a temple, but is transformed in an instant from Dagon's victim to Jehovah's. At the same time the Philistines, who have come to offer sacrifice of bulls and goats to a false god, are themselves unwittingly offered up to the true God in a merited, ironic reversal.

The motif of sacrifice is central to most tragedy. It is a commonplace (though disputed) to trace the roots of Greek drama back to Dionysian religious rituals in which a scapegoat is offered to the god. The scapegoat or sacrificial victim becomes the tragic hero as ritual becomes drama, and as the sacrifice becomes symbolic instead of real. It is unimportant for present purposes whether or not this transformation ever really took place. Probably, if it did, the matter was more complex than it once seemed. What is important, however,

[24]Roger B. Wilkenfeld, "Act and Emblem: The Conclusion of *Samson Agonistes*," *ELH*, 32 (1965), 163-64.

is the resemblance that many critics have noticed between the drama
and ritual or myth. The tragic hero is a great man, larger than life;
he falls, or rather rises, into *hybris;* he is increasingly depersonalized
and isolated from those around him; he turns, in their eyes, into a
monster and an outcast; finally, he is killed or exiled, as a scapegoat,
and in this way order is restored to society or state. John Holloway,
in a provocative study, has described a similar pattern in Shakespearean tragedy.[25] The theory loses persuasiveness when it is so
briefly summarized. To some extent, too, it has been discredited by
sweeping over-application in the hands of critics who see all literature in terms of ritual and myth — or even "monomyth." Nevertheless, temperately considered, it throws light on *Samson Agonistes.* As
a solitary outcast, as a kind of "monster" (in this specialized sense)
in the eyes of those around him, and as a victim, Samson fits the
pattern.

Parallel to this ancient and archetypal pattern of ritual sacrifice
is another, that is basically similar: the Christian ideal of the way of
humiliation and self-sacrifice, of which the primary exemplar is
Christ. Milton speaks of this pattern toward the end of *Paradise Lost:*

> with good
> Still overcoming evil, and by small
> Accomplishing great things, by things deemd weak
> Subverting worldly strong, and worldly wise
> By simply meek; that suffering for Truths sake
> Is fortitude to highest victorie,
> And to the faithful Death the Gate of Life.
> (XII.565-71)

The Son is the pattern of the scapegoat who takes on himself the
sins of man, "Giving to death, and dying to redeeme" (III.299). This
principle of the subversion of the worldly powerful and of evil by
self-sacrifice accounts not only for Samson's suffering, but for his
degradation and humiliation. The stoic endurance of mere pain is
not enough: Samson must also be shamed and despised. Like the
Psalmist, he must say: "But I am a worm, and no man; a reproach of

[25] Holloway, *The Story of the Night* (Lincoln: Univ. of Nebraska Press, 1961).

men, and despised of the people. All they that see me laugh me to scorn: they shoot out the lip, they shake the head, saying, He trusted on the Lord that he would deliver him: let him deliver him" (Ps. 22.6-8). Samson, echoing this, says that he has

> Inferiour to the vilest now become
> Of man or worm; the vilest here excel me,
> They creep, yet see, I dark in light expos'd
> To daily fraud, contempt, abuse and wrong,
> Within doors, or without, still as a fool,
> In power of others, never in my own;
> Scarce half I seem to live, dead more then half.
>
> (73-79)

Psalm 22 has traditionally been interpreted as a prophecy of Christ's passion and death. The Hebraic treatment of humiliation, artistically if not theologically, is hard to distinguish from the Christian. St. Paul, in several well-known passages, stresses that the crucifixion seems shameful and foolish as well as painful: "Christ hath redeemed us from the curse of the law, being made a curse for us: for it is written, Cursed is every one that hangeth on a tree" (Gal. 3.13, cf. Dt. 21.23). "But God hath chosen the foolish things of the world to confound the wise; and God hath chosen the weak things of the world to confound the things which are mighty; And base things of the world, and things which are despised, hath God chosen, yea, and things which are not, to bring to nought things that are" (I Cor. 1.27-28).

There is danger in going directly to the Christian analogue, for one may lose sight of the tragic significance of this pattern. It is important to see that the pattern of rejection from humanity and of sacrifice is characteristic alike of Christian and non-Christian tragedies. It has a deep emotional appeal, answering to something basic in human nature. Holloway, in his study of Shakespeare, tentatively suggests that the "sacrifice rhythm" of tragedy is "the principle ordering its representation of life"; that tragedy embeds "the essential movement of that ritual in life's common fabric"; that it *"ritualize[s] reality"*[26] — as, indeed, most art does. By ritualiz-

[26] Holloway, pp. 153-54.

ing or ordering something dark and fearful, tragedy satisfies its audience, provides it with catharsis. The hero is pitied and feared. We pity Samson as a victim at the same time that we fear him as something more than human, as a "monster" and outcast who condemns our common ideals or pretensions. He is indisputably fearful. One would not like to meet him socially as he sits before the prison, or even to approach him too closely. His suffering purges him of his guilt and shows him the path he must take, and this spectacle—both of the suffering and of the ultimate triumph—arouses in the other characters of the play the two emotions Aristotle considered central to tragedy. Pity is the dominant feeling of Manoa and the Danites, fear of Dalila and Harapha; the messenger expresses both. These characters, and especially Manoa and the Chorus, involve the audience simultaneously in a movement of sympathy and one of repulsion. To say that Samson is the source of purgative fear is a departure from orthodoxy. Perhaps it would be more accurate to push the process back a step further, and to say that the reader is meant to feel the proper kind of terror at the inexplicable workings of divine providence—which, however, still work themselves out mainly through Samson, steadily preparing him for the catastrophe.

Samson Agonistes follows a common tragic pattern: the hero, looked on as something monstrous or unacceptable, is killed or exiled, or as in Samson's case is forced by his character, by religious or moral necessity, or by circumstances, into a position where death is inevitable. This pattern is also Christian. It is related to Milton's often-repeated ideal of Christian heroism, of plain heroic magnitude of mind, of the single just man rejected by his fellows, or of the suffering of the saints. With unadorned heroism, Samson defeats worldly greatness: physically, with no other weapons than his bare hands, spiritually, with nothing but the divinely-inspired strength of his will. He sets his plainness and determination against human strength and glory. The Chorus, when it describes the kind of man God chooses to deliver his people, describes Samson:

> He all thir Ammunition
> And feats of War defeats
> With plain Heroic magnitude of mind
> And celestial vigour arm'd,

> Thir Armories and Magazins contemns,
> Renders them useless. . . . (1277-82)

Throughout the play man unadorned is set against man armed with
the trappings of war and of pride. The Miltonic ectype of the unadorned hero is the Christ of *Paradise Regained,* who sets the example *par excellence* of "deeds / Above Heroic, though in secret
done, / And unrecorded" (I.14-16). But the tragic effect of *Samson*
is not lost in the Christian or cancelled out by the sense of triumph.
There remains a "reality of suffering which neither the assurance of
God's special favors . . . nor . . . resolute insistence on the final triumph of his righteousness can blot out."[27] Once more then, at the
most basic level, the same pattern fulfills the requirements of both
tragic and Christian drama.

Although Samson is pitiable and fearful, a man who is degraded,
dirty, and outcast, nevertheless he remains great, noble, and heroic.
He is both abject and splendid at the same time. The negative elements, far from detracting from his greatness or merely contrasting
with it, actually add to it. We think no less of Oedipus, Job, or
Lear because they are set apart from common values and the ordinary
preoccupations of life. Rather we think more of them. Divested of all
accidental qualities, they are reduced to their essential selves. "Lear"
is as honorable a title as "King Lear," and Oedipus helps to define
what the Greeks meant by kingship. Manoa, when he speaks the
eulogy for Samson, can think of no greater or more appropriate
praise than this:

> *Samson* hath quit himself
> Like *Samson.* . . . (1709-10)

As a man, he is something greater than a king, a knight, a leader,
or a judge. *He has become himself.* The idea that Milton's Samson is
foolish, ignoble, stronger in muscle than in mind or spirit, has long
been discredited, though presumably a few critics will never be
lacking to raise the point once more.[28] As Arnold Stein among

---

[27] Hanford, *Samson Agonistes* and Milton in Old Age," p. 184.

[28] Evert M. Clark, "Milton's Conception of Samson," gives a history of earlier
critical disparagement of Milton's Samson, with a refutation.

others has shown, Samson's intellectual capabilities are discriminating and powerful.[29] Yet Milton has retained or even added to many of the barbaric attributes of the biblical Samson. They make his hero not less but more heroic. By a more vital principle of decorum than Samuel Johnson was willing to allow, things normally not thought heroic deepen and humanize, even elevate, Samson's character. If he had been drawn as a straightforwardly civilized and refined hero, a Renaissance gentleman, as a few critics assume, he would have verged on the priggish, or become an empty abstraction like Addison's Cato. Milton plainly has successfully avoided this danger. His Samson has gained in intellect, but he has not lost his physical presence. He has not only human weaknesses, but human strengths. He combines intellectual vitality and nobility of spirit with the starkness of a biblical prophet. But his heroism cannot be reduced to any one class or tradition. His analogues, with like qualities of essential greatness, are the heroes of three traditions: Job, Oedipus, and Lear.

[29] Stein, *Heroic Knowledge* (Minneapolis: Univ. of Minnesota Press, 1957), pp. 137–202. Recently, critical attacks on the intelligence and sensitivity of Manoa and the Chorus (see Chapter 6 below) have shown some signs of extending themselves to Samson. It may be that the whole question of Samson's intelligence will have to be argued over again.

4

IRONY:
REVERSAL AND SYNTHESIS

The range and extent of the irony in *Samson Agonistes* have seldom been equaled outside of Greek drama; indeed, one might claim that Milton approaches even Sophocles in this respect. Like the Greeks, Milton bases his action on a familiar story with a well-known outcome — the destruction of the temple resulting in Samson's death — thus replacing suspense with ironic foreshadowings, prophecies, and misunderstandings. Words, consciously or unconsciously, have double meanings; actions issue in unexpected results. Minor ironies abound, beginning with the title.[1] Major ironies, as in the plays of

---

[1] The title might be translated as "Samson Agonist," an epithet which may be understood by its surviving opposite, "antagonist." An *agon* is a struggle or an athletic contest, or by extension a spiritual conflict. Thus *agonistes* suggests athlete, combatant at public games, advocate, actor, champion, or by extension spiritual warrior or saint. There is considerable irony in the fact that the hero of an athletic contest should be blind, but — still more iron-

Sophocles, are integral with the action itself. According to E. M. W. Tillyard, "the essence of the plot in *Samson* is that nearly all the actions should lead whither they had not seemed to lead." Douglas Bush adds that "in the large ironic pattern, each of the first four 'acts' bring about a result contrary to that expected by the inter- locutor."[2] Secretly guiding and shaping the action is the hidden providence of God, which perfectly completes Samson's inner re- generation by means of his encounters with the Danites, Manoa, Dalila, Harapha, and the Public Officer. Contrary to the intention of some and the expectation of all his visitors, Samson in the end rises out of his near despair like the Phoenix from its ashes, to comply in an ironic fashion with the desire of the Philistine lords for entertainment.

1

The most prominent and familiar kind of irony in *Samson* is dra- matic or Sophoclean irony: that is, unexpected reversal in the action or of the characters' intentions. This irony, involving reversal, can be conveniently divided into four types for purposes of discussion: irony in the action or plot; irony in the development of important motifs, such as ransom or sacrifice; unconscious verbal irony in the statements of the characters; and conscious verbal irony.[3] I say that these divisions can be made "for purposes of discussion" because it will be evident that they cannot be so easily separated in their actual functioning in the play. Most of the verbal irony is intimately

ically—Samson proves the victor of both a spiritual and a physical combat. For further discussion, see F. Michael Krouse, *Milton's Samson and the Chris- tian Tradition* (Princeton: Princeton Univ. Press, 1949), pp. 109–33, and Paul R. Sellin, "Milton's Epithet *Agonistes,*" *Studies in English Literature,* 4 (1964), 137–62.

[2]Tillyard, *Milton* (London: Chatto & Windus, 1930), p. 343; Bush, *John Milton* (New York: Macmillan, 1964), p. 197.

[3]For a study of conscious and unconscious dramatic irony in the play see William Riley Parker, *Milton's Debt to Greek Tragedy in Samson Agonistes* (Baltimore: Johns Hopkins, 1937), pp. 157–67.

connected with the ironic reversals in the plot, and this is also true
of the major ironic motifs. But, of course, literary criticism must
resort to such artificial distinctions; afterward, the critic, or perhaps
better the reader, must reconcile them with the organic whole.

The first difficulty in speaking of ironies in the action of *Samson* is
that critics have not always agreed just what the action is. I will
contend, in the course of this chapter and — since the matter is
complex — in the rest of this book, that the action of *Samson Agonistes*
is in several ways double, but that through fusion or synthesis this
doubleness can finally be seen as single or unified. It is necessary
simply to state at this point what I hope to demonstrate more convincingly later in the argument. There is, first of all, a double action
which is exterior and interior: the play consists of a series of events
which prepare Samson, by his reactions to his visitors, to take the
action of pulling down the temple and thus to fulfill his role as
Israel's deliverer; and at the same time the visits result in his interior spiritual growth, from despair to a new kind of heroism.
Second, the action can be seen both as divinely guided — shaped by
the providence of God which works all along, though only revealed
at the close — and as natural or human, more and more under the
control of Samson's free choice and the imposition of his growing
will upon the other characters. Although on the surface Samson is a
peculiarly passive and helpless protagonist, who apparently sits in
one spot and is acted on by others, it is he who takes control and
shapes the play, while both friends and enemies are drawn into the
influence of his spiritual force, either to be destroyed or saved.

Each stage of this action involves a reversal. Samson is led on
stage for a day of rest from his labor in the prison, but, as he quickly
realizes, this respite can bring "ease to the body some, none to the
mind" (18). Thus his first relief from the consequences of his sin and
betrayal results in the leisure to realize fully and painfully just how
serious his sin was. Relief from his desperate plight leads him ironically toward greater suffering and despair. The Chorus next enters,
intending to show its friendship and to comfort and commiserate
with Samson. Instead, they increase his mental suffering and drive
home even further the realization of what he has done. The same is
true of Manoa's visit: comfort turns to exacerbation, and Manoa, who

hopes to ransom Samson, and thus to free him from his misery and his slavery, only succeeds in convincing him that this method of escape cannot be accepted. If Samson has hoped to escape from his captivity, he learns from Manoa that one way cannot be taken, for it entails spiritual surrender and recognition of the Philistine authority as lords over Israel. Dalila enters next, hoping to persuade Samson to return with her once more as her lover and husband; she only succeeds in closing this avenue of escape too, and in confirming Samson's freedom from his former "effeminacy" and "uxoriousness." Harapha comes to gloat and to confirm his own reputation for chivalric glory and honor; instead he is stripped of honor and forced into ignominious retreat. Samson, whom he had hoped to cow and to make his foil, is instead reinvigorated and prepared for further action. The Public Officer enters with the mission of bringing Samson to the Philistine festival, where he will surrender himself completely to the will of his conquerors and thus confirm their authority over him and his nation; instead, Samson resists, and refuses to come. The state, he argues, can exert force on him, but not authority. In still another reversal, however, Samson, having been rewarded for his constancy by a divine inspiration, abruptly agrees to go with the Public Officer. The play's final reversal is the sudden destruction of the Philistines at the very height of their pride and power.

The reversal of the action involves the constant frustration of all the characters' intentions, and of their respective plans for a materially successful outcome. Manoa and the Chorus wish material happiness, or at least a cessation of material suffering, for Samson: but this is not to be. Dalila, Harapha, the Public Officer, and the Philistine lords all want to use Samson variously for their material benefit or advantage: they fail too. There are further dimensions to the irony involved, however. Manoa and the Chorus are basically well-motivated and unselfish: they desire Samson's good, and in fact they receive it, though in a manner quite different from what they expect or intend. The Philistines, on the other hand, want to make use of Samson for their own various purposes; their motives are basically selfish; they fail completely. Still another related complexity: in the play weakness becomes power, shame becomes glory, near despair is necessary before happiness can be achieved, and in the most

general terms (with both tragic and religious relevance), the way up
is the way down.

2

Samson Agonistes is permeated with a number of what, for want of a
better word, may be called motifs. One might, making a musical
analogy, compare them to Wagnerian leitmotifs. Arnold Stein discusses the analogy of musical technique, especially of theme and
variation, in *Heroic Knowledge*.[4] The analogy is an extraordinarily
fruitful one; but what is chiefly of interest here is that most of the
recurrent themes or motifs in *Samson* are ironically developed. Thus
the important theme of "promise ruined" — of former glory and
present shame — is by the end of the play ironically reversed. The
former glory is seen as hybristic and inadequate, while present shame
becomes a means to a higher heroism and a more permanent and
lasting glory. Another major theme, Samson's blindness, is also
deeply ironic; but the matter is so complex and important that it
will be separately treated in the following chapter. Still another
theme suggested by Stein, Samson's "specially prescribed breeding,
'As of a person separate to God,'" we have seen in the previous
chapter to be ironically double. The motif of the temple ceremony,
introduced near the beginning of the play and increasingly important as the play progresses toward the catastrophe, is also highly
ironic. The rites of Dagon are the reason for Samson's day of rest,
but in several ways they are also the cause of his spiritual suffering:
because they give him leisure for self-analysis, and also because they
mark a triumph of Dagon over God for which Samson is largely
responsible. The rites are introduced, at least, as a triumph of the
Philistines and Dagon over the Israelites and Jehovah, but this is
reversed too. The catastrophe, which takes place at the ceremony,
resolves and completes all these reversals.

Another recurrent theme is imprisonment. Increasingly, Samson

[4]Stein, *Heroic Knowledge* (Minneapolis: Univ. of Minnesota Press, 1957),
pp. 137–39 ff. Quotations from Stein in the rest of the paragraph are also
from pp. 137–39.

realizes that imprisonment in the Philistine jail is preferable to
imprisonment to his own sinful pride and spiritual blindness, or to
the blandishments of Dalila and the enthrallment of her love. In the
light of his new understanding, the jail becomes for him, relative
to his former state, a "house of Liberty" (949). The irony in each of
these themes, it will be seen, is similar, and is related to the ironic
action. Schematically, the movement is from false prosperity, to adversity, to genuine but tragic triumph. That, at least, is the arc of
Samson and his friends. The Philistines describe an opposite arc:
when the fortunes of Samson drop, theirs rise; when Samson and
Israel finally triumph, Philistia is brought low. The metaphor of
rising and falling, though less literally developed than it is in *Paradise
Lost,* is similar, and as in *Paradise Lost* the forces of good move first
down, then up, since they conquer through defeat; while the forces
of evil move up, then down, because they are brought low by aspira-
tion and pride.[5]

Two final motifs may be mentioned: the theme of ransom and the
theme of sacrifice. Ransom has previously been discussed by the
critics, notably by T. S. K. Scott-Craig,[6] but it is important enough
to deserve a brief restatement. The idea of ransom is first introduced
by Manoa, who has come to visit Samson partly in order to inform
him of his intention to ransom him and thus to give him some hope:

> I already have made way
> To some *Philistian* Lords, with whom to treat
> About thy ransom. . . .   (481-83)

Samson rejects Manoa's proposal, preferring to remain in prison and
to work out the punishment for his crime. Manoa, however, is unwilling to listen to his son, and leaves intending to carry out his plan:

> I however
> Must not omit a Fathers timely care
> To prosecute the means of thy deliverance

[5] See my "The Image of the Tower in *Paradise Lost,*" *Studies in English Literature,* 10 (1970), 171–81.

[6] Scott-Craig, "Concerning Milton's Samson," *Renaissance News,* 5 (1952),
45–53; see also Ann Gossman, "Ransom in 'Samson Agonistes,'" *Renaissance
News,* 13 (1960), 11–15.

> By ransom or how else: mean while be calm,
> And healing words from these thy friends admit.
>
> (601-05)

Manoa's means for delivering Samson are not, of course, the ones
that prevail. Ultimately, Samson is ransomed by his triumphant
death, and he in turn is a ransom or an offering for his people, paying
the price that will enable them to be free — if they rise to the opportunity. Thus, as Scott-Craig observes, Samson is a type of Christ, who
is the ransom paid for the sins of men. Perhaps Manoa's near-sighted
though human and well-intentioned words are meant to contrast with
the divine Father, whose greater love is willing to permit the sacrifice
of his only son.

The theme of ransom grows increasingly more ironic, as Manoa
returns following his son's exit, full of hopes that the Philistine
lords will agree to let Samson go. In the very midst of these false
hopes, Manoa is interrupted by the first shout from the temple. As he
goes blindly and pathetically on, offering to give up his whole in-
heritance for a ransom, if that should prove necessary — if only he
can bring Samson home and tend his eyes — the second shout inter-
rupts him again. As Manoa instinctively begins to realize, almost at
once, it is the signal of Samson's death. So Manoa is brought to the
realization, at first bitter, then acquiesced in, that his plans were
fruitless:

> O all my hope's defeated
> To free him hence! but death who sets all free
> Hath paid his ransom now and full discharge.
>
> (1571-73)

Samson, in becoming a ransom for his people, is not following a
Christian pattern only, however. Ann Gossman suggests two non-
Christian parallels, Socrates and Hector, whose father Priam cor-
responds to Manoa.[7] But more immediately relevant, in becoming a
ransom Samson plays the part of the typical tragic hero, whose death

---

[7] Gossman, "Ransom in 'Samson Agonistes,'" pp. 12–15.

usually results in the purgation of some evil, or the restoration of society to a condition of order and normality.[8]

The motif of sacrifice was discussed in the previous chapter, and little more need be said about it here, except to reinforce the ironic nature of the reversals that take place. The Philistines offer a sacrifice to Dagon, which includes the humiliation of Samson; but Samson sacrifices the Philistines instead. At the same time, Samson, from being a sacrifice to the Philistine god, voluntarily offers himself as a sacrifice to the true God, but not in a way that anyone in the play expects. Sacrifice and ransom are interrelated, and to them one may also add Samson as the deliverer of his people, a theme which is also spoken about throughout the play and fulfilled in the final action. All three — ransom, sacrifice, deliverer — are Christian concepts; they are also long-standing Hebrew concepts; and, finally, they fit into the pattern of tragic ritual or drama.

3

Unconscious verbal irony is the most typically Sophoclean of the various kinds of irony Milton employs in the play, and as Parker points out in his useful discussion, such effective use of it is "rarely

[8] See Chapter 3 above and John Holloway, *The Story of the Night;* also A. C. Bradley, *Shakespearean Tragedy* (1904). Protestant theology stressed, in rather legalistic terms, that Christ was offered as a sacrifice or ransom to acquit man of his guilt before the bar of God's justice (a theory with roots in the Old Testament). Milton naturally followed this interpretation of the atonement in *Paradise Lost* and *Paradise Regained,* although in no simplistically legalistic way. He would have expected his readers to see the ultimate parallel between Samson's ransoming sacrifice and Christ's. A further discussion of the theological implications can be found in Scott-Craig's article, cited in note 6, and in C. A. Patrides, *Milton and the Christian Tradition* (Oxford: Clarendon Press, 1966), pp. 121–52. Some reservations to what I consider an overly harsh and rigorous view of Milton's theory of atonement on the part of many critics can be found in my "Milton's God: Authority in *Paradise Lost,*" *Milton Studies,* 4 (1972), 19–38.

found outside the tragedies of Sophocles."[9] This kind of irony, in which the speaker's words mean more to the audience than the speaker himself is aware of, depends on the foreknown outcome. Although we do not know just how Samson will arrive at the temple, and in what mental state—and much of the interest of the play lies in finding out—we know that arrive there he must. The great picture of Samson pulling down the temple is so familiar to us that we need scarcely to have read the Bible to know it well. Samson's very first words in the play mean more than he knows—"A Little onward lend thy guiding hand / To these dark steps"—and this is true of most of what both he and the other characters have to say. There is some degree of irony in nearly everything that is said, though some of the speeches are more obviously and predominantly ironic than others. Take, for example, Samson's words a few lines later:

> what if all foretold
> Had been fulfilld but through mine own default,
> Whom have I to complain of but my self? (44-46)

These are words of wisdom, but of course Samson is unaware that what has been foretold will yet be carried out, and by himself. So too with his similar realization that he cannot understand God's will in the matter:

> Suffices that to me strength is my bane,
> And proves the sourse of all my miseries. . . .
> (63-64)

Strength without wisdom has indeed been the source of his miseries; ironically, it will also be the means of his "bane" or death, but not at all as he expects. Toward the end of this same speech, Samson hears the approaching footsteps of the Danites, and concludes his soliloquy with these words:

> But who are these? for with joint pace I hear
> The tread of many feet stearing this way;
> Perhaps my enemies who come to stare
> At my affliction, and perhaps to insult,
> Thir daily practice to afflict me more.
> (110-14)

[9] Parker, *Milton's Debt to Greek Tragedy,* p. 160.

It is not his enemies, but his friends, who have come not to insult him but to comfort him; nevertheless, these well-meaning friends will prove an affliction after all.

It would easily be possible to go through the play and point out dozens of more or less equally effective examples of unconscious verbal irony, but it hardly seems necessary, once a reader is alive to such meanings. There are many ironical prophecies — Samson's that God will conquer Dagon without further help from him (460-71), which is accepted by Manoa (472-78), or Manoa's suggestion that God may let Samson off and permit him to return home (516-20). There is the constant assumption, discussed in the previous chapter, that Samson is no longer capable of accomplishing anything. There is Manoa's hope, several times expressed, that God may restore Samson's eyesight. No one understands Samson, nor does Samson, until the end, fully understand himself. No one knows what course Samson must take, though it is increasingly evident to Samson what courses he may not take. One major result of all this irony is to underscore the difficulty of Samson's choice. Another is to emphasize the mysteriousness of divine providence. In the end, the meanings of what has happened are revealed to everyone, but until that moment they must remain in varying degrees of ignorance. The audience is allowed to seem wiser, but it can take no pride in that fact, since its wisdom is the product of an unearned knowledge that the characters happen not to possess. So a third effect of the irony should be to induce an emphatic sense of humility in the reader. If he knew as little as Samson — or as Manoa and the Chorus — he certainly could do no better. (It must be noted that not all the critics of *Samson* have agreed with this.) But it would appear that irony does more than produce such logical results; it is almost an end in itself as well as a means, or at least it contributes very basically to the play's spirit.

4

Conscious verbal ironies in *Samson* play an important part in developing the atmosphere; they are sufficiently prominent to impress themselves forcibly on most readers. Yet, unlike the unconscious ironies, there are relatively few instances of the device—partly, perhaps, as Parker suggests, because it is only toward the end of the play that any of the characters know what to expect or to be ironic about,[10] but mostly because throughout the play, until Samson confronts the Public Officer and the Philistine crowd, everyone is interested in communicating as directly as possible, in order to get at the truth or to put some point across. Thus, although the opportunities for conscious irony are more frequent than Parker allows— particularly in the interviews with Dalila and Harapha—the characters seldom indulge in it. The Chorus permits itself a single thrust at Samson:

> In seeking just occasion to provoke
> The *Philistine,* thy Countries Enemy,
> Thou never wast remiss, I bear thee witness:
> Yet *Israel* still serves with all his Sons.
>   (237-40)

This might be considered a human slip, since it is hardly a soothing or comforting statement. But it has the unintended effect of goading Samson into responding and thus achieving a better understanding of the extent of his guilt. Manoa allows himself one similar remark, in the speech that begins, "I cannot praise thy Marriage choises, Son" (420); its effect is similar.

When Samson confronts Dalila, he has much to be ironic about in analyzing her behavior, but he limits himself to two uses. First is his ironic remark, "such pardon therefore as I give my folly, / Take to thy wicked deed" (825-26). He immediately drops the irony, however, to explain that he has no intention of pardoning his own guilt. It should also be noted that the irony is directed as much at himself as at Dalila. If all his words to her are closely considered, it will be seen that, although Samson bitterly attacks her behavior, he is not interested in mocking her but rather in communicating with her, in somehow getting through to her. The other instance of irony in their interview occurs in Samson's last words to Dalila:

> At distance I forgive thee, go with that;
> Bewail thy falshood, and the pious works

[10] Parker, p. 157.

> It hath brought forth to make thee memorable
> Among illustrious women, faithful wives:
> Cherish thy hast'n'd widowhood with the gold
> Of Matrimonial treason: so farewel. (954-59).

At first, these bitter words seem unnecessarily cruel and heartless. They seem also to contradict what I have said about Samson's desire to reach Dalila with his arguments; but as I will show in Chapter 7, Samson has good reasons to speak this way at this point, and his intention still is to communicate.

Harapha would seem, even more than Dalila, to be a natural butt of satire or verbal irony. Certainly Samson succeeds in making a fool of him. But irony appears only once in his speeches to Harapha, nor is it directed at the Philistine champion. Harapha has been contrasting Samson's ignominious state with the honorable condition of the Philistines, and has just made his remark about Samson's need of a wash. Samson replies:

> Such usage as your honourable Lords
> Afford me assassinated and betray'd,
> Who durst not with thir whole united powers
> In fight withstand me single and unarm'd. . . .
>   (1108-11)

Samson begins with the one ironic epithet, "honourable Lords," which he has picked up from Harapha's protestations about honor (a parallel with Mark Antony's speech about Brutus naturally suggests itself), but he then drops irony to argue directly and conclusively that the behavior of the Philistine lords toward him has been extremely dishonorable.

The most important instances of conscious irony in the play are Samson's last speeches, following the turning point at which the "rouzing motions" (1382) persuade him to go with the Public Officer. Parker calls the irony in these passages "very evident."[11] In fact, its use is still limited to only two speeches, but there is no doubt that its effect is far more prominent and powerful than that would suggest. Both speeches will be analyzed further in Chapter 9, since their full meaning can only be understood in relation to

---

[11] Parker, p. 158.

Milton's theories of vengeance; but a preliminary examination can be made here. Samson makes the first speech to the Public Officer, as an explanation of why he has changed his mind:

> Because they shall not trail me through thir streets
> Like a wild Beast, I am content to go.
> Masters commands come with a power resistless
> To such as owe them absolute subjection;
> And for a life who will not change his purpose?
> (So mutable are all the ways of men). (1402-07)

These, of course, are only professed reasons, not real ones. Samson speaks with "superb" irony that reveals "the degree of self-mastery" he has won.[12] He is now completely in control of the situation, and the Public Officer, the instrument of force, has instead become his dupe. There are two further things to notice about this speech. First, it reveals Samson's new unconcern for appearances. "His is a special kind of irony, an irony of humility which operates at his own expense."[13] Throughout most of the play, as we saw in the last chapter, Samson is extremely sensitive to what his enemies think of him. The worst thing about his blindness and slavery is the mockery it draws on him. Now, however, he allows the Public Officer and the Philistines completely to misinterpret his actions and intentions, to believe that he is submitting shamefully and slavishly to their yoke. He is still concerned about the opinion of his friends, and tells them:

> I with this Messenger will go along,
> Nothing to do, be sure, that may dishonour
> Our Law, or stain my vow of *Nazarite*. (1384-86)

This concern is less for his own sake, however, than for the sake of their peace of mind. Samson has learned that shameful appearances can be turned into a positive good, that the world's opinion, and especially the opinion of enemies, is unimportant. This recognition, a necessary part of his spiritual development, also serves him in a practical sense, since it is by submitting himself to the ridicule of the

---

[12] Parker, p. 158.

[13] Stanley Fish, "Question and Answer in *Samson Agonistes," Critical Quarterly*, 9 (1969), 262.

Philistines that he is able to destroy them and thus save his own people.

The second thing to notice about this speech is that it is an equivocation. Perhaps it is not literally a lie, since everything Samson says has an underlying truth; but it is deliberately calculated to give the Public Officer a false impression. This is the first moment in the play that Samson speaks not to communicate or enlighten, but instead to mislead. The reasons are obvious: it is plainly impossible at this point to convert the Philistines to his point of view; he is being confronted with the whole force of the Philistine state; and so he must resort to whatever weapons are at his disposal. In effect, he uses against the Philistines their own moral weakness, their willingness to believe that such "prudence" as he pretends to is only natural. Here, as later, they draw their own destruction on themselves.

Falsehood in the service of truth is plainly a ticklish matter. Samson avoids a direct lie; but equivocation — truth which misleads — was also in bad repute among seventeenth-century Protestants. It was generally considered merely a hypocritical method of lying — and it was associated, moreover, with the Jesuits. Milton does defend this kind of apparent falsehood, however, in a rather lengthy and tortuous analysis in the *Christian Doctrine*. He might almost be speaking directly about the behavior of Samson:

> Veracity consists in speaking the truth to all who are entitled to hear it, and in matters which concern the good of our neighbor.
> . . . Hence falsehood is not justifiable, even in the service of God. . . . No rational person will deny that there are certain individuals whom we are fully justified in deceiving. Who would scruple to dissemble with a child, with a madman, with a sick person, with one in a state of intoxication, with an enemy, with one who has himself a design of deceiving us, with a robber?
> . . . Yet, according to the above definition, it is not allowable to deceive either by word or deed in any of the cases stated . . . . If every answer given to every interrogator with the intent of deceiving is to be accounted a falsehood, it must be allowed that nothing was more common even among the prophets and holiest of men.

Hence, falsehood may perhaps be defined as follows: Falsehood is incurred when any one, from a dishonest motive, either perverts the truth, or utters what is false to one to whom it is his duty to speak the truth. . . . It follows from this definition, first, that parables, hyperboles, apologues, and ironical modes of speech are not falsehoods, inasmuch as their object is not deception but instruction. . . . Thirdly, it is universally admitted that feints and stratagems in war, when unaccompanied by perjury or breach of faith, do not fall under the description of falsehood. . . . We are undoubtedly commanded to speak the truth; but to whom? not to an enemy, not to a madman, not to an oppressor, not to an assassin, but to "our neighbor," to one with whom we are connected by the bonds of peace and social fellowship.[14]

Thus Manoa and the Chorus deserve, and receive, the truth from Samson, because they are his neighbors; against the Public Officer, however, Samson is entitled to use deceit, because he is (to use words that Samson has spoken to Harapha) an enemy, an oppressor, an assassin; metaphorically, the Philistines are even described as mad and intoxicated. But Samson still does not lie directly: he uses the Philistines' evil assumptions against them. What has been said about Samson's words to the Public Officer holds true for his last ironic speech, which also reveals his control over the situation, his unconcern with the appearance he makes, and his special use of equivocation:

> Hitherto, Lords, what your commands impos'd
> I have perform'd, as reason was, obeying,
> Not without wonder or delight beheld.
> Now of my own accord such other tryal
> I mean to shew you of my strength, yet greater;
> As with amaze shall strike all who behold.
>   (1640-45)

The density, complexity, and boldness of the irony in these two last speeches explains why they have made so great an impression on most readers.

[14]*Works*, XVII, 297–305; small capitals removed.

5

Thus far, I have discussed only those instances of irony in *Samson* that involve reversal of one kind or another. To these familiar types of irony, which Milton has developed with great mastery, may be added another which is more unusual, possibly unique to *Samson* in its extensiveness and explicitness. This irony is characterized by a hypothetical choice, posited by one of the characters: either this is true or that, or more usually, either this will happen or that; but in the working out, both choices eventuate, even though they were thought to be mutually exclusive. Milton, in his *Art of Logic,* calls this form of proposition a contingent disjunct axiom (*axioma disjunctum contingens*), and cites two examples: "when Caesar said to his mother: 'Today you will see me pontifex or an exile'"; and when Ovid wrote "in the *Epistle of Leander:* 'Either good hap shall now unto me fall, / Or else fierce death, the end of loving thrall.'" [15] Neither of these propositions is worked out ironically, however; so it may be said that in *Samson Agonistes* Milton has developed a form of irony whose only precedent, to my knowledge, is a minor instance in Sophocles' *Trachiniae.* The precedent to lines 1387-89 is noted by J. C. Maxwell, who compares the lines to the *Trachiniae,* lines 79-81: "The alternative possibilities remind us of the 'tablet' which Heracles left with Deianeira, containing oracles to the effect 'that either he shall meet his death, or, having achieved this task, shall have rest thenceforth, for all his days to come.'" [16] But as Maxwell also points out, the first half of the oracle is dropped from consideration when Heracles returns to it at the end of the play (1169-73); and it is rather "ambiguous" than "unsearchable." Moreover, the oracle, unlike that in *Oedipus,* has at most a potential relation to the action that remains effectively undeveloped. Nevertheless, the device is so unusual that it leads Maxwell, a scholar particularly careful of such parallels, to propose a debt to the *Trachiniae* in this passage of *Samson.*

[15] *Works,* XI, 365.

[16] Maxwell, "Milton's Samson and Sophocles' Heracles," *Philological Quarterly,* 33 (1954), 90-91.

According to the *Art of Logic,* only one of the parts of a disjunct axiom can logically be true; but a reconciliation of opposites in *Samson* is possible because the irony is only apparent, or holds on only one level. The irony results, usually, from the ignorance of the speaker. It differs, however, from the unconscious dramatic irony discussed earlier since the unexpected issue is not the working out of the prediction in an opposite sense, but the reconciliation of the two apparent contradictions, so that both events occur, contrary to preliminary understanding or expectation. Some minor examples may be given first. When Manoa enters for the first time, the Chorus, directing his attention to Samson as he lies sprawling before the prison, tells him: "As signal now in low dejected state, / As earst in highest, behold him where he lies" (338-39). But Samson is already beginning his inward growth, though his appearance belies it, and at the end of the play he will be both lowest *and* highest, at the same time dying and performing his most glorious deed. The implied opposition between terms thus reveals the ignorance of the Chorus concerning Samson's kind of heroism or of what is truly high and low in human existence. When Harapha enters, the Chorus tells Samson that "His habit carries peace, his brow defiance" (1073). Again the sharp distinction is dissolved, however, for the issue of the visit is both peace and defiance — in a different way than the Chorus expected, because they thought that Harapha, not Samson, would dominate the confrontation and have the choice of peace or war. In a third minor example, the Messenger says that either he has been guided to the Danites by "providence or instinct of nature," or he has found them by "reason" (1545-46); but the reader learns that the hidden workings of providence and the promptings of right reason are the same. This fact is hidden until the end from most of the characters, who have their own ideas about reasoning. A fourth instance of this kind consists of the disjunctive prophecies of Manoa and Samson. Manoa argues: "His might continues in thee not for naught, / Nor shall his wondrous gifts be frustrate thus," to which Samson replies: "All otherwise to me my thoughts portend, / That these dark orbs no more shall treat with light" (588-92). A fifth and final example occurs near the end of the play, when Samson is described by the Messenger "as one who pray'd, / Or some great matter in his mind revolv'd" (1637-38). In fact, insofar as Samson both chooses freely and is led by divine providence, both alternatives are true.[17]

This kind of irony, based on the reconciliation of apparent contradictions, or, in the technical language of Milton's *Art of Logic*, on the ironic resolution of contingent disjunct propositions, I shall call the irony of alternatives. In the balance of this chapter it will be seen that the more important examples of the device, not yet mentioned, play an important role in the play as a whole, that they answer in a fruitful way a question that has often bothered critics — whether Samson is an active or a passive hero — and that they contribute further to the double plot and the double nature of the play as a tragedy and as a religious drama. Like the action, or the play itself, they are at once double and single: and thus they help to fuse and synthesize the disparate elements.

Milton's use of dichotomies in his poetry is well known. The most obvious example consists of the twin poems, "L'Allegro" and "Il Penseroso." Tillyard traces Milton's habit of taking opposing sides to his academic training in debate.[18] Certainly there are many actual debates in his poems, between characters or between opposing points of view: joy and melancholy in "L'Allegro" and "Il Penseroso," The Lady and Comus or the Elder and the Younger Brother in *Comus,* Eve and Satan or Adam and Eve when they part in *Paradise Lost,* Christ and Satan in *Paradise Regained,* Samson and Dalila or Samson and Harapha in *Samson Agonistes.* The further productive reconciliation of opposites has often been noticed as well, especially in

---

[17] I owe the last two examples to Joseph H. Summers, "The Movements of the Drama," *The Lyric and Dramatic Milton,* ed. Summers (New York: Columbia Univ. Press, 1965), pp. 158–59. When I published a version of this part of Chapter 4 in 1969 I had not noticed that Summers briefly noted several instances of this kind of irony. He mentions these two I had not noticed, and one I had, *S. A.* lines 1388–89. I take this opportunity to apologize for my earlier neglect of Summers' insight.

[18] E. M. W. Tillyard, *The Miltonic Setting* (London: Chatto & Windus, 1938), pp. 1–28.

Lycidas.[19] Milton's use of dialectic, conscious or unconscious, may also owe something to his interest in Ramistic logic, which characteristically splits and divides what it examines. He constantly uses literary examples to illustrate his points in the *Art of Logic,* thus revealing that he connected the study of different kinds of logical propositions with the writing of poetry. Still another possible influence — though much of what has been said on this subject is rather questionable — was the intellectual and artistic milieu, specifically the Mannerist and Baroque esthetics.[20] Paradox characterizes much of the poetry of the period, "strain" and conflict are seen in the painting and architecture. Whatever the influences, however, Milton was his own man and made his own artistic choices. Probably one of his deepest habits of mind was to divide, to oppose, and to reconcile contraries, and reading and training only sharpened this natural tendency. The irony of alternatives, which must have been used quite deliberately, is one more instance of his predilection for paradoxical structures and devices. I hope to show, in the rest of the chapter, that it is distinctive and important enough to deserve separate notice and a separate name.

When Samson has passed the final testing and strengthening of his spirit by his resistance to the Public Officer, God returns to him clearly for the first time since his fall. He feels "Some rouzing motions in me which dispose / To something extraordinary my thoughts" (1382-83). He knows immediately that this is a divine calling, and that therefore he will do nothing "that may dishonour / Our Law, or stain my vow of *Nazarite*" (1385-86). But the exact nature of what he is to do remains unknown to him, for he can particularize it only by the phrase "something extraordinary." He

[19]See Jon S. Lawry, "'Eager Thought': Dialectic in 'Lycidas,'" *PMLA,* 77 (1962), 27–32; and B. Rajan, *"Lycidas:* The Shattering of the Leaves," *Studies in Philology,* 44 (1967), 51–64.

[20]See Roy Daniells, *Milton, Mannerism and Baroque* (Toronto: Univ. of Toronto Press, 1963); and Rosemond Tuve, "Baroque and Mannerist Milton?" *JEGP,* 60 (1961), 817–33. Although Miss Tuve questions the application of the terms to literature, she provides extensive references. For another approach to Milton's dialectic, see Thomas Kranidas, *The Fierce Equation* (The Hague: Mouton, 1965).

concludes with this prophecy, which hesitates between two alternatives:

> If there be aught of presage in the mind,
> This day will be remarkable in my life
> By some great act, or of my days the last.
> (1387-89)

The irony in this prediction, as in the examples previously quoted, is that it is more true than Samson realizes: this will be both the last and the greatest day in his life. He means only to say that one alternative or the other will result, that he will either succeed or fail. That in one and the same action he can do both occurs neither to him nor to the Danites whom he is addressing. The reader, however, familiar with the biblical story of Samson's death in the temple of Dagon, perceives an additional meaning in his words.

After Samson goes out, Manoa returns, ironically and pitifully happy that he has nearly succeeded in ransoming his son. He grows more and more sanguine. Not only will he bring Samson home with him and tend his eyes, but God, who may have a "purpose / To use him further yet in some great service," "since his strength with eyesight was not lost," will "restore him eye-sight to his strength" (1498-99, 1502-03). These hopes, the Chorus agrees, "are not ill founded nor seem vain" (1504). Their speculations are interrupted by the second shout, which signals the catastrophe. "They have slain my Son," Manoa cries, to which the Chorus answers, "Thy Son is rather slaying them" (1516-17). The ironies in the preceding speeches culminate in the statement of these two alternatives, both of which prove to be true. Manoa spoke truly when he said that his son would be ransomed, but not as he expected. Like the Messiah, Samson pays the ransom with his death. Manoa was also right in thinking that God has a purpose to use Samson again "in some great service"; but that service will not involve the restoration of Samson's sight. All these ironies converge on the paradox that Samson, finding victory in death, wins by losing, slays by being slain.

Wavering between hope and fear, Manoa and the Danites decide to wait where they are for news to be brought. This news, the Chorus points out, must be either "good or bad" (1537). But when the

Messenger comes, he brings news both good and bad. He delivers first the good, that the Philistines have been slain by Samson; then he offers "the worst in brief, *Samson* is dead" (1570). His explanation has only begun at this point, however, for he must also explain how the two events are involved with one another. It is only by this final defeat and death, the destruction of all Manoa's hopes, that Samson's victory is made possible. "Inevitable cause" has led him to the point where contradictions are brought together and made inseparable, "At once both to destroy and be destroy'd" (1587). Samson is "tangl'd in the fold, / Of dire necessity" (1665-66), and so must die with his victims. But although this ending is terrible, it is also happy, for God is with him at the end, "favouring and assisting" (1720). Moreover, it should be pointed out that the Messenger's words express only a partial insight into the mystery of divine providence. Unlike many of the Greek tragic heroes, Samson has gone freely to his destiny, gladly choosing to obey the divine prompting, aware of the possible consequences though ignorant of the exact outcome. And the Messenger's description of him as either praying or revolving some great matter in his mind, before pulling down the temple, suggests that he has an opportunity for free choice even at the last moment; that he makes his decision with his own intellect but at the same time unites his will with the will of God.

These events reveal how individual instances of the irony of alternatives in *Samson* are related to one another, and how they build to a cumulative effect. The distinctions of the Chorus between "low" and "highest" in Samson's life and between war and peace in the confrontation with Harapha indicate their misapprehension of the nature of Samson's heroism. The forecasts of Manoa and Samson, Samson's prophecy of his end that hesitates between the possibilities, the speculations of Manoa and the Chorus about what is happening in the temple, and the explanations of the Messenger — all turn on the dual nature of the catastrophe. The specific statements of ironic alternatives are, in fact, concentrated in that part of the play immediately preceding and surrounding the catastrophe. These individual instances are closely connected with the structural pattern of the play's complication and resolution. Though less important than the persistent reversal of intention, the irony of alternatives is nevertheless basic to the play's method and meaning. Milton presents a whole series of difficulties and conflicting alternatives before the catastrophe, then solves them with a stroke of action calculated to reveal the simplifying and resolving power of God's providence. The pattern of resolved alternatives can be further related to the action, which simultaneously and inevitably leads Samson both to triumph and to catastrophe; and also to Samson's character as a hero whose every step toward God separates him from men, but whose final action reconciles him with both. The explicitly stated individual examples of the disjunct axiom ironically resolved are important, because they are demonstrably present: they point up the meaning of the larger patterns, which by themselves would shade into conventional paradox.

6

One major instance of the irony of alternatives has not yet been mentioned. A central question posed in the play itself, and later taken up by many of the critics, is the problem of what kind of hero Samson is or should be. He has, evidently, the choice of action or suffering. Manoa, in his hopeful mood, speculates that God may restore his eyesight so that he can resume his heroic career; at other times Samson and his friends fear that God has abandoned his champion forever. After Samson has shown some of his old fire and sent Harapha off in disgrace, the Chorus is led to speculate on the nature of heroism. It divides the matter into the two traditional categories, acting and suffering—related to the long-standing controversy over the merits of active and contemplative lives. Drawing upon Samson's former exploits, the Chorus first portrays the active hero:

> Oh how comely it is and how reviving
> To the Spirits of just men long opprest!
> When God into the hands of thir deliverer
> Puts invincible might
> To quell the mighty of the Earth, th' oppressour,

> The brute and boist'rous force of violent men
> Hardy and industrious to support
> Tyrannic power, but raging to pursue
> The righteous and all such as honour Truth;
> He all thir Ammunition
> And feats of War defeats
> With plain Heroic magnitude of mind
> And celestial vigour arm'd,
> Thir Armories and Magazins contemns,
> Renders them useless, while
> With winged expedition
> Swift as the lightning glance he executes
> His errand on the wicked, who surpris'd
> Lose thir defence distracted and amaz'd.
>
> (1268-86)

Samson, despising the weapons and armor of the chivalric hero, as he did at Ramath-lechi (see also lines 340-48, 1119-29), relies instead on his own "plain Heroic magnitude of mind" and the "celestial vigour" given him by God's grace. But although his heroism is not like that of the Philistines — glorious on the surface but ignoble when examined closely — it nevertheless answers force with force. Milton makes it clear that this force is used in behalf of freedom, against tyrants and the supporters of tyranny, and is therefore not incompatible with Christian doctrine. As Samson answers Harapha, in a retort that echoes Milton's justification of the deposition of kings in the prose tracts, "force with force / Is well ejected when the Conquer'd can" (1206-07).

There is another kind of heroism, however, more common to saints or heroes in religion. This is the way of the passive hero or the martyr, the sufferer for truth's sake:

> But patience is more oft the exercise
> Of Saints, the trial of thir fortitude,
> Making them each his own Deliverer,
> And Victor over all
> That tyrannie or fortune can inflict,
> Either of these is in thy lot,

> *Samson,* with might endu'd
> Above the Sons of men; but sight bereav'd
> May chance to number thee with those
> Whom Patience finally must crown.
> (1287-96)

Although the decorum of his Hebrew story prevents Milton from saying so explicitly, this statement is clearly Christian rather than Stoic. (Milton disagreed in a number of places with the Stoic doctrine of suffering without complaint, and it is evident that Samson is never an uncomplaining Stoic hero.) Reading the Chorus' words, one cannot doubt that "Patience" will finally crown these saints with the crowns of Revelation.

Neither kind of heroism, active or passive, can actually be ruled out as unchristian. Critics have, therefore, differed as to which sort the Chorus, or Milton, prefers. Active heroism, enthusiastically described and supported, is divinely sanctioned and is given a longer passage. But passive suffering is "the exercise / Of Saints"; the language describing it is more nearly openly Christian; and it is given the rhetorically advantageous second place. Not only is it unclear which kind of heroism is best, critics even disagree as to which category Samson finally falls into. Tillyard and Stein think the tragedy ultimately supports the necessity of action.[21] Ralph Nash finds Milton preferring the passive course but tied to an active ending by his source: "That Samson chooses the path of action, rather than saintly suffering, seems clear. The Biblical story could hardly be made into a legend of passive martyrdom, the trial of Samson's fortitude; he chooses of his own accord to make other trial of his strength."[22] William O. Harris, to the contrary, feels that Samson's final victory does consist in patience, the virtue of the saints. "Victory through patience was to Milton the nobler triumph, though we and the Danites may feel otherwise"; and Samson's final victory is "the

[21]Tillyard, *Milton,* p. 301, and *The Miltonic Setting,* pp. 85–88; Stein, *Heroic Knowledge,* pp. 178–91, 197.

[22]Nash, "Chivalric Themes in *Samson Agonistes," Studies in Honor of John Wilcox,* ed. A. D. Wallace and W. O. Ross (Detroit: Wayne State Univ. Press, 1958), pp. 33–34.

one within—a victory over despair, whose antidote is patience, the higher attribute of fortitude."[23]

For the most part, critics have seen the choice between active and passive heroism in *Samson* as a matter of exclusive possibilities. Their basis for this is, of course, the Chorus' assumption. "These are real alternatives: 'Either of these is in thy lot.'"[24] More recently, several critics have suggested that Samson is both an active and a passive hero, that his passive heroism is a necessary prelude to his final action, but that the two states are mutually exclusive, experienced one at a time. Samson first suffers, then acts.[25] Thus the distinction drawn by the Chorus is still tacitly accepted. But before the catastrophe the Chorus is only groping in puzzled fashion for the truth.[26] Part of its "new acquist" (1755) after the event is the realization that God has cut the knot of its earlier intellectual difficulties. For Milton's solution is once more to combine the alternatives, as he does in all the instances discussed above, in one action that unexpectedly reconciles the seeming opposites. Samson's final act is both active and passive: he conquers in defeat, suffers and inflicts, slays and is slain, is reborn and dies. Thus he combines Christian

---

[23] Harris, "Despair and 'Patience as the Truest Fortitude' in *Samson Agonistes,*" *ELH,* 30 (1963), 119–20. See also Ann Gossman, "Samson, Job and 'the Exercise of Saints,'" *English Studies,* 45 (1964), 212–24; Kenneth Fell, "From Myth to Martyrdom: Towards a View of Milton's *Samson Agonistes,*" *English Studies,* 34 (1953), 145–55; and M. A. N. Radzinowicz, "*Samson Agonistes* and Milton the Politician in Defeat," *Philological Quarterly,* 44 (1965), 454–71. Radzinowicz seems at one point (p. 470) about to anticipate my thesis here, but draws back from it because she believes that Milton's purpose in the play is to advocate patience and self-mastery as alternatives to political action.

[24] Nash, "Chivalric Themes in *Samson Agonistes,*" p. 33.

[25] See, e.g., Joseph Summers, "The Movements of the Drama," p. 169; John M. Steadman, *Milton and the Renaissance Hero* (Oxford: Clarendon Press, 1967), p. 34.

[26] The question of the Chorus' wisdom or ignorance is discussed below in Chapter 6, and by a number of critics there cited.

and nonchristian, or two kinds of Christian, heroism.[27] In this act he is both the doer of great deeds, like Hercules, Achilles, or Judas Maccabeus; and the lowly sufferer, prevailing through degradation, pain, and death, like Job, the Christian martyrs, or Christ himself. The pulling down of the temple is a return to action that explicitly surpasses the active deeds of his youth, made possible only by the return of his strength and inward resolution; and it is also the culmination (not merely the product) of his inner development and regeneration, made possible by his new self-knowledge and humility, his victory over despair, and his confirmation in Christian patience. By the reconciliation of alternatives that to other characters in the play have seemed irreconcilable, divine providence vindicates itself and fulfills with Samson's cooperation predictions that seemed impossible of fulfillment. Before the event, human reason is inadequate to prophesy truly, revealing its weakness in statements of conflicting possibilities; after the event, everything is made clear, and God sends his servants away "with new acquist."

Two precedents may be suggested for Milton's combination of the active and the passive in his hero. The first lies in the field of devotional theory. Although most Protestants in the period disapproved of the passive, contemplative life, or valued it only as it issued in action,[28] one Catholic solution to the debate between the active and the contemplative lives was to praise a mixture of the two. St. Paul, St. Francis, and, preeminently, Christ were often said to be men who combined at once the best of both kinds of spirituality. Although it is more characteristically Catholic than Protestant, there

[27] Chapter 9 will suggest more clearly how Samson's action as well as suffering is Christian. It may be noted here that the word "Saints" in the description of the passive hero seems to refer back also to the active hero, as a close examination of the syntax will show: "But patience is more oft the exercise / Of Saints. . . ." In other words, some saints are given an active task to perform, but most must suffer.

[28] See Howard Schultz, *Milton and Forbidden Knowledge* (New York: Modern Language Association, 1955), pp. 71–82; Helen White, "Some Continuing Traditions in English Devotional Literature," *PMLA*, 57 (1942), 966–80; and my *Augustine Baker* (New York: Twayne, 1970).

is nothing in this idea that Milton would have rejected. Indeed, such a life can be thought of as action continually issuing from contemplation, a balance preferable to mere alternation between the two. The second precedent lies in the field of Renaissance commentary on the epic hero. Spenser remarks, in his well-known letter to Raleigh prefacing *The Faerie Queene,* that in the figure of Aeneas Virgil successfully combined the "good governour" Agamemnon with the "vertuous man" Ulysses — that is, that he combined public and private virtue, which previously had been embodied in separate heroes. Tasso wrote that Virgil combined the active *Iliad* with the contemplative *Odyssey* to produce an epic concerned with both kinds of life.[29] These commonplace interpretations of the *Aeneid* were certainly known to Milton. Although the combination of elements mentioned by Spenser is different, and the mixture of active and contemplative that Tasso saw in the *Aeneid* consisted rather in alternation and variety than in fusion, the principle is similar. There is no need, however, to suggest that either precedent was a source. The form the solution takes in *Samson Agonistes* and even more the preparation for it are Milton's own. Critics have pointed out that Milton was not responsible for the exact nature of the catastrophe, and indeed could not have changed it. But he was able to lead up to and prepare for Samson's final deed in his own way. What he chose was an action that prepares Samson internally, giving him the patience necessary to a suffering martyr, but which also goads him out of his despair and lethargy to a resumption of his former valor and activity.

Unlike the voice out of the whirlwind that answers Job, or the unexpected arrival of a *deus ex machina* in *Philoctetes,* God's solution in *Samson Agonistes* is logical and comprehensible, if terrible. What is unforeseen is its simplicity. By its perfect fitness, disparate ends are accomplished. The Philistines are appropriately punished for their idolatry and their tyranny over the Jews; the Jews are rebuked for their lack of faith yet set back mercifully in the right way. In one action Samson makes final payment for his sin and is given the chance

---

[29] *Le prose diverse di Torquato Tasso,* ed. Cesare Guasti (Firenze, 1875), I, 116–20; cited by Steadman, *Milton and the Renaissance Hero,* p. 13.

to achieve his purpose in life: thus he is both rewarded and punished. God finds a way, as in *Paradise Lost,* to combine justice with mercy to the detriment of neither. In a catastrophe prepared for by the irony of alternatives, itself the resolution of conflicting possibilities, Samson is given the opportunity to combine active with passive heroism, both bravely doing and patiently suffering. In the conclusion, Milton achieves a fusion of the disparate elements of genuine tragedy and religious drama. As an active hero, Samson achieves his purpose but dies tragically; as a martyr he gains tragic dignity and wins a spiritual victory and the crown of patience. Neither alternative is ruled out; all the possibilities are reconciled.

5

IMAGE AND BLINDNESS

Samson Agonistes is full of paradoxes at nearly every level, and among
the most difficult of them is a question of its spirit: Is the play essentially rational or irrational? Both views have been confidently
argued. In some ways, *Samson* is obsessively rational. It begins with
questionings and intellectual probings; its middle consists mostly
of argument, discourse, and debate; and it ends with explanations
and reassurances. Logic, argument—above all, talk—are its very
substance. It was long a commonplace that Milton stripped from the
play the kind of sensuous richness that characterizes *Paradise Lost,*
and until recently everyone agreed that it contained hardly any
images or metaphors—the means by which poetry usually speaks
through the senses and feelings instead of directly to the intellect.
It is obvious to a sensitive reader of the play, however, that what
has been said thus far is partly wrong, and partly too simple and
narrow. All the arguments in *Samson* are permeated with human
feelings, and we are constantly aware of each speaker as well as of
what he says. The questionings in the play are as much emotional as

intellectual; the final reassurances are meant to calm our hearts as well as satisfy our minds.

No other work of Milton matches this one in the intensity of its passions. Even the exposition, the least exciting part of most plays, is designed so that every piece of background information we are given — Samson's birth, his vocation, his betrayal, the loss of his eyes, his defeat and imprisonment — is seemingly introduced only for its psychological power. What other play could move, while still making its exposition, and by what seems a completely natural and gradual process of mental development, in a space of eighty lines, to words like these:

> O dark, dark, dark, amid the blaze of noon,
> Irrecoverably dark, total Eclipse
> Without all hope of day! (80-82)

How many playwrights, for that matter, would dare to begin a play at this level of emotional intensity? How many could carry on from a beginning like this without sinking into anticlimax?

The question of whether passion or rationality in Samson predominates can be answered in several ways. The first and most general answer is that, as we have learned to expect, Milton succeeds in reconciling them. The exposition both gives the facts and conveys the emotions: so does the rest of the play. It was suggested in the last chapter that the play raises doubts, hesitations, alternatives, and mysteries of various kinds, and that it then solves them by one simplifying stroke of divine providence working through Samson. This implies that the God of the play is ultimately rational. Although he is infinite, omnipotent, uncircumscribable by human intellect, not to be tied to his own prescripts — capable, in the powerful image from *Paradise Lost* (VI. 139-42), of reaching out "beyond all limit" to whelm Satan's legions under darkness — nevertheless, as in all Milton's works, the God of *Samson Agonistes* chooses to reveal his ways to men in order to enlighten them. Milton writes in the *Second Defense:* "It is impious to believe that God is grudging of truth or does not wish it to be shared with men as freely as possible."[1]

---

[1] Cited by Sherman H. Hawkins, "Samson's Catharsis," *Milton Studies,* 2 (1970), 211. Cf. *Works,* VIII, 64.

"As freely as possible": the Chorus and Manoa, or Milton's reader, do not understand all the secrets of the universe after the catastrophe has taken place. God still remains mysterious, and much in the fate of Samson remains mysterious too. Yet much is revealed, including the comforting assurance (rather than any particular knowledge) that there is a plan behind the providential inscrutability; that although God will remain a mystery, he is a mystery one can trust in: a God whose beneficence will ultimately be confirmed. *Samson* does not close with a voice from the whirlwind that says nothing to the intellect, if much to the spirit; neither does it close with a complete revelation of all mysteries — especially of the residual human mysteries of sin, suffering, and death in a fallen world.

One major way that Milton succeeds in balancing the senses against the intellect in *Samson* is to employ the chief means of poetry or fiction, which he himself characterized as *simple, sensuous,* and *passionate:* that is, to speak to the reader through what may broadly be called *images,* rather than by discourse alone. The term "image" has been much abused in recent criticism, the fate of all important or convenient words, but (fortunately) it is not our task to rescue it. Rather than attempt to define it rigorously here, I shall suggest a few of its possible meanings: both in order to let its significance emerge for itself, and because too much rigor is undesirable in this matter. "Image" means, first of all, something which appeals to vision and the other senses. Second, it means, in terms of Renaissance psychology, one of the units manipulated by the faculty of imagination or fantasy in the human mind — a mental unit derived from the outer world through the senses and used in all natural thought processes. Third, the most important images or clusters of images in heroic poetry — to which broad class *Samson* belongs — are *exempla,* great images for imitation or avoidance, whether persons, actions, descriptions of places, or embodiments of ideas. Imagery in *Samson* can be understood in all these senses. They are not contradictory; in fact, the whole matter is ultimately quite simple, as all good art is simple — but this is an area somewhat difficult to explore discursively without falsification. One approach, an indirect one, is through Samson's blindness.

2

The central fact of *Samson Agonistes* is the blindness of the hero. It is both a symbol of his punishment, degradation, and suffering, and an instrument for his spiritual convalescence. Indeed, it can be argued that everything in the play, in a sense, is perceived as if through the eyes of a blind man — that is one reason why the action is so narrow, stifling, and intense, and why there is so little consciousness of the outside, physical world and so much concentration on an inner psychological and spiritual world.[2] At first, blindness is the torment of which Samson complains most bitterly:

> but chief of all,
> O loss of sight, of thee I most complain!
> Blind among enemies, O worse then chains
> Dungeon, or beggery, or decrepit age! (66-69)

He has lost the comfort of light, "the prime work of God" (70). As he rises gradually from this hopeless state, however, to a spiritual readiness for his final act of heroism, the emphasis changes and he realizes that

> The base degree to which I now am fall'n,
> These rags, this grinding, is not yet so base
> As was my former servitude, ignoble,
> Unmanly, ignominious, infamous,
> True slavery, and that blindness worse then this,
> That saw not how degeneratly I serv'd. (414-19)

He who has lived uxoriously in "perfet thraldom" is now free, his jail a "house of Liberty" (946-49). Like Oedipus, or Gloucester in *King Lear,* Samson was blind while he saw, and sees when he is blind. The true light of God is not the light of the sun but the light of con-

---

[2]Since I first drafted this chapter two suggestive studies of the sensory imagery in *Samson* have appeared, independently citing many of the same passages, though for purposes different from mine. They are Anne Ferry, *Milton and the Miltonic Dryden* (Cambridge: Harvard Univ. Press, 1968), pp. 127–77; and Marcia Landy, "Language and the Seal of Silence in *Samson Agonistes,*" *Milton Studies,* 2 (1970), 175–94.

science, the inner guidance that Samson finally regains when his regeneration is complete. Such was Milton's view even before his own blindness:

> Vertue could see to do what vertue would
> By her own radiant light, though Sun and Moon
> Were in the flat Sea sunk.
>
> .   .   .   .
>
> But he that hides a dark soul, and foul thoughts
> Benighted walks under the mid-day Sun;
> Himself is his own dungeon. (*Comus,* 372-74, 382-84)

Samson's blindness, and especially the paradox of physical and spiritual blindness, often remarked on by critics, is obvious to any perceptive reader. It is somewhat less obvious that Milton extends this paradox to the other characters and, indeed, to the whole ambience of the poem. For the symbolism of blindness and seeing is much more extensively worked out than first appearances suggest. Samson's gradual regeneration, his movement from physical blindness to spiritual vision, takes place against a background of spiritual blindness that gives an added brilliance to his last victory. The difficulty and rarity of spiritual seeing is emphasized, so that at his death Samson stands out like one of those single just men of *Paradise Lost,* among

> the common rout,
> That wandring loose about
> Grow up and perish, as the summer flie,
> Heads without name no more rememberd . . . .
>   (674-77)

He is like an "ev'ning Dragon" among chickens, an eagle among common birds,[3] a unique and self-begotten Phoenix (1692-1707). Even Manoa and the Danites, though they do not suffer from the extreme blindness and *hybris* of the Philistines, lack insight. Samson alone truly sees, and by his action in the temple brings to them and the rest of the Jews perception of the truth.

An examination of *Samson* reveals, apart from the obvious ref-

---

[3] The same image is associated with Samson in *Areopagitica* (*Works,* IV, 344).

erences to Samson's blindness, an extraordinary number of references to vision and seeing, or to their lack. The angel ascends in flames to to Heaven "in sight / Of both my Parents" (24-25); men "enjoying sight" complain of imprisonment but Samson's is worse (157); fools who think there is no God "walk obscure" (296); Samson, once God's nursling, grew up "Under his special eie" (636); God's "ear is ever open; and his eye / Gracious to re-admit the suppliant" (1172-73); Samson pretends to worry that it will upset the Philistines to "see me girt with Friends," for "the sight" may exasperate them (1415); the Chorus tells Samson that God has never given man greater strength "As in thy wond'rous actions hath been seen" (1440); Manoa will not go to the temple of Dagon "Lest I should see him forc't to things unseemly" (1451); he describes how he will bring the ransomed Samson home and "tend his eyes," "And view him sitting in the house" (1490-91).

All these references to vision remind the reader that Samson is a blind man among people who see, and keep his attention on kinds and degrees of seeing. English is full of fossilized metaphors of seeing, of which Milton takes full advantage, in accordance with his habitual awareness of the root meanings of words and his constant play on their original senses. There are many further instances, which taken together in their cumulative effect result in a powerful pattern of physical and spiritual seeing which is of considerable thematic importance. The theme is not, of course, original with Milton: *Oedipus* and *Lear* have been mentioned, and even more relevant are the biblical passages, often referred to in the *Christian Doctrine,* which use seeing as a spiritual metaphor. "Having eyes, see ye not? and having ears, hear ye not? and do ye not remember?" (Mk. 8.18); "And Jesus said, For judgment I am come into this world, that they which see not might see; and that they which see might be made blind" (Jn. 9.39).

Throughout the play, Samson is a visual object for all to look on, held up to the "scorn and gaze" of his enemies (34), the "mirror of our fickle state" (164), "to visitants a gaze" (567), God's champion and the "Image" of his strength (706), finally a public "spectacle" to all the Philistines, the center of their attention (1604). But not all those who have eyes to see can see, and Samson, who should be the

cynosure of the Jews and a warning to the Philistines, is foolishly
ignored or misunderstood. Like the Messiah, there are those who
cannot understand him even when his mission is most openly mani-
fested to their eyes:

> . . . *Israel*'s Governours, and Heads of Tribes,
> Who seeing those great acts which God had done
> Singly by me against their Conquerours,
> Acknowledg'd not, or not at all consider'd . . .
> But they persisted deaf, and would not seem
> To count them things worth notice. (242-45, 249-50)

Though they see the great acts God performs through Samson, "signs
and wonders," nevertheless the Jewish leaders are blind and deaf to
the testimony of their senses. There is a similar insensibility in the
Philistines — who, however, prove incurable.

Each of Samson's visitors comes to *see* him, literally as well as
figuratively. The Chorus, entering quietly, is immediately struck by
his appearance. "See how he lies at random, carelessly diffus'd . . ./
In slavish habit, ill-fitted weeds / O're worn and soild; / Or do my
eyes misrepresent?" (118, 122-24). At this moment their vision is
accurate, however, for the external appearance of Samson is a true
indication of his inner state. As Samson himself says, "Yee see, O
friends, / How many evils have enclos'd me round" (193-94). But
already he is undergoing the beginnings of an interior change, for
his blindness which shortly before was "worst" now "least afflicts"
him (195). As he grows within, the physical sight of his visitors will
reveal to them less and less accurately what kind of man he really is.

Manoa enters next. The Chorus ironically or forgetfully tells
Samson, "see here comes thy reverend Sire" (326), and then directs
Manoa's attention to his son's appearance: "As signal now in low
dejected state, / As earst in highest, behold him where he lies" (338-
39). Like the Chorus, Manoa too goes by outward appearances; he
therefore sees nothing but a "miserable change" from what Samson
once was (340). But this appearance is no longer an entirely reliable
indication of Samson's inner strength, since interaction with the
Chorus has begun to change him. "What not in man / Deceivable and
vain!" (349-50) Manoa exclaims, thinking of Samson's downfall

from his promising start, but the words apply in an opposite sense to Samson as he lies before him. Manoa himself is instrumental in his son's further growth. He reminds him that his worst crime and his worst sorrow are not present suffering but betrayal of God and magnification of Dagon, "Which to have come to pass by means of thee, / *Samson,* of all thy sufferings think the heaviest" (444-45). Samson, who in spite of his soul-searchings has previously managed not to think of this, suffers a heavy blow;[4] but one he is able to bear without giving in to absolute despair.

Dalila comes in, "With all her bravery on, and tackle trim" (717), a visual contrast to Samson's wretched state. "Some rich *Philistian* Matron she may seem" (722). Like the Chorus and Manoa, she has come to *see* her husband. She sweeps up to him, and the Chorus tells Samson that she "now stands and eies thee fixt" (726). "Conjugal affection," she tells him, has "led me on desirous to behold / Once more thy face" (739, 741-42). But her vision, like that of the Jews, is incapable of seeing him aright; she sees but does not see. Her tendency to distort objectivity by twisting perception in her mind is revealed by the passage in which she describes her marriage before the betrayal:

> I saw thee mutable
> Of fancy, feard lest one day thou wouldst leave me
> As her at *Timna,* sought by all means therefore
> How to endear, and hold thee to me firmest:
> No better way I saw then by importuning
> To learn thy secrets. . . . (793-98)

She incorrectly "saw" Samson to be mutable, revealing an inability to interpret sense data; she foolishly "saw" that the solution to her imaginary problem was to get Samson's secret and hold it over him, showing that she is incapable of right reasoning. From endearing him to her, to holding him "firmest," to the thought of blackmail — then to betrayal — her sophistical logic moves by an ambiguous middle term. Thus, even if her words are believed, Dalila reveals her blindness. Samson rejects her plea and says that he will give her as much

[4] A point made by Arnold Stein, *Heroic Knowledge* (Minneapolis: Univ. of Minnesota Press, 1957).

pardon as he gives himself: "which when thou seest / Impartial, self-severe, inexorable, / Thou wilt renounce thy seeking, and much rather / Confess it feign'd" (826-29). But she is unable to see; what she sees is not justice, merited punishment, or even the means of expiation, but implacable severity, "more deaf / To prayers, then winds and seas" (960-61), and she leaves not convicted of error — the first step in genuine repentance and regeneration — but furious with Samson and rejoicing in her fame among the Philistines. Samson had the vision to understand and accept his guilt when Manoa reminded him of its true nature; Dalila does not. She sees nothing and repents nothing. While Samson is growing in spiritual stature underneath his rags, she reveals bareness under her finery: "In vain thou striv'st to cover shame with shame" (841), Samson tells her. "These false pretexts and varnish'd colours failing, / Bare in thy guilt how foul must thou appear?" (901-02).[5]

The Chorus now announces the appearance of Harapha: "But had we best retire, I see a storm?" (1061). Harapha has come to "see" and to "survey" limb by limb the man of whom he has "heard" so much, but Samson counters that "The way to know were not to see but taste" (1082-91). Harapha has come not to learn or to know, however, but only to gratify his expectations. He knows beforehand what he wants to see, and he is not prepared to experience anything different. Samson tells him to leave imaginings for present reality: "Boast not of what thou wouldst have done, but do / What then thou would'st, thou seest it in thy hand" (1104-05). Harapha, however, is another of those who seeing does not see, hearing does not hear, because he chooses not to. Once again, Samson offers to make him "see, or rather . . . feel, whose God is strongest, thine or mine" (1154-55), but Harapha will not. Appropriately, he is called a "Tongue-doubtie Giant" (1181), for although he has come to "survey" Samson (1227) he lacks the organs of receptivity; he is only a foolish tongue. Like Dalila, he departs in a "sultrie chafe," with "lower looks" (1246).

Samson might have been the instrument to reveal justice and genuine love to Dalila. His stern behavior at their interview was necessary for her sake as well as his, for she must be convicted of

[5]Dalila's response is discussed further below in Chapter 7.

sin before she can be converted to loyalty and righteousness. He might also have shown Harapha, who as the Philistines' champion is no mere buffoon, what true courage and strength, or honor and glory, consist of. But each visitor comes with his own purpose, and so is not open to what he might see, to the truths that might be revealed through Samson. Both are seemingly reprobate, up to this point at least and within the context of the play, and their visit to Samson proves to be an "evil temptation" for them, which encourages them to sink further into error, at the same time that they serve as "good temptations" to strengthen him.[6] Samson's interpretation of Dalila's visit applies to her rather than to him: "God sent her to debase me, / And aggravate my folly" (999-1000). On the contrary: Dalila and Harapha have been sent to strengthen him, but they are allowed to debase themselves. While Samson's inner sight grows, his visitors confirm themselves in blindness.

Samson's last visitor is the Public Officer, who alone has come not to look at him but to bring him a message. It is the Philistine Lords who now wish to see Samson; they require a "public proof" (314) of his strength at the feast of Dagon, where he will "appear as fits before th' illustrious Lords" (1318). Samson asks whether the Philistines expect him to make a spectacle of himself, like a juggler or mummer, "To make them sport with blind activity" (1328)—a phrase that vividly suggests the blind Samson at the center of the Philistine gaze. He refuses, showing that he has gained back all of his old courage and strength of will; then, enlightened by God's inspiration, he submits. The course of his spiritual growth is almost completed. As at Ramath-lechi, once more he will be a spectacle for many to look upon, not as the Philistines propose, however, but as God disposes.

While Manoa and the Chorus talk, the first shout tears the sky. As the Chorus correctly guesses, it is the Philistines catching their first sight of the blind Samson. But they, "Insensate left, or to sense repro-

---

[6]In the *Christian Doctrine* (*Works,* xv, 86), Milton speaks of "mala" and "bona tentatio," those temptations which God sends to 1) confirm the wicked in their wickedness, and 2) strengthen and purify the good. The passage is discussed and analyzed by Ann Gossman, "Milton's Samson as the Tragic Hero Purified by Trial," *JEGP,* 61 (1962), 535-36.

bate" (1685) — the one phrase in the play which best sums up the state
of all the reprobate characters, not merely blind but deaf and sense-
less — they are the ones who are blind while Samson, now under
providential guidance, is the only one in the whole theater who sees.
They call for their own destruction, "shouting to behold / Thir once
great dread, captive, and blind before them" (1473-74). Then the
second shout goes up: the truth has finally been brought home to
the Philistines, in the only way they can understand. The Messenger,
who has escaped the wreckage, is terrified by the very sight:

> O whither shall I run, or which way flie
> The sight of this so horrid spectacle
> Which earst my eyes beheld and yet behold;
> For dire imagination still persues me.
>   (1541-44)

The after-image lingers on his eyes as Samson, the Image of God's
strength (706), reveals himself to all. Like a bringer of the gospel,
the Messenger has been an "Eye-witness" (1594) to the manifestation
of Samson's power, and through him of God's. His terror is partly
the terror which numinous events inspire.

The Messenger brings with him yet another picture of the blind
Samson, watched by the spiritually blind Philistines, consulting his
interior vision and the guidance of God before acting:

> with head a while enclin'd,
> And eyes fast fixt he stood, as one who pray'd,
> Or some great matter in his mind revolv'd.
> At last with head erect thus cryed aloud,
> Hitherto, Lords, what your commands impos'd
> I have perform'd, as reason was, obeying,
> Not without wonder or delight beheld.
> Now of my own accord such other tryal
> I mean to shew you of my strength, yet greater;
> As with amaze shall strike all who behold.
>   (1636-45)

With his "eyes fast fixt," Samson is like one who sees, while the
Philistines look on with a superficial and besotted gaze, "thir hearts
. . . jocund and sublime, / Drunk with Idolatry, drunk with Wine"

(1669-70). If idolatry is the worship of a false image instead of the true, then this describes their state in more than one sense. As Harapha can be taught only by touching and tasting, so the audience in the temple must be struck with amazement, as Samson puts it: for them, mere seeing is not enough.

The semichoruses which celebrate Samson's transfiguration conclude with an explicit contrast between the Philistines and Samson. They are "Insensate," so far gone in their *hybris* and inebriation that their spiritual senses no longer can bring them any messages. Out of their dark ruin Samson rises like the Phoenix from its ashes:

> They only set on sport and play
> Unweetingly importun'd
> Thir own destruction to come speedy upon them.
> So fond are mortal men
> Fall'n into wrath divine,
> As thir own ruin on themselves to invite,
> Insensate left, or to sense reprobate,
> And with blindness internal struck.
>   *Semichor.* But he though blind of sight,
> Despis'd and thought extinguish't quite,
> With inward eyes illuminated
> His fierie vertue rouz'd
> From under ashes into sudden flame,
> And as an ev'ning Dragon came. . . .
>   (1679-92)

The two semichoruses are like a dyptich or a pair of wings: on one side is pictured the fall of the Philistines into darkness and final blindness; on the other Samson rises out of ashes into sudden flames of illumination. Blindness is the point on which these two motions turn, first down into it, then upward and out, like some huge wheel of the tragic and Christian pattern, or like apocalypse itself. More particularly, the movement echoes the twofold fate of Samson, who goes down into final tragic death but rises in triumphant vindication.

Manoa and the Danites, although earlier they were unable to see Samson's spirit regaining its heroic strength under their eyes, are not lost to understanding like the Philistines, and so they can profit from the manifestation in the temple. God has shown to his faithful

people his "uncontroulable intent"; Manoa and the Chorus acknowledge the message:

> His servants he with new acquist
> Of true experience from this great event
> With peace and consolation hath dismist,
> And calm of mind all passion spent. (1755-58)

Through the agency of Samson a separation has been made between
Jews and Philistines, not unlike that in *Paradise Lost* between the
fallen angels and fallen man: "Man therefore shall find grace, / The
other none" (III.131-32).

The Chorus has spoken of Samson as the "Image" of God's strength
and his mighty minister (706). As God's champion, he has been an
instrument revealing God's "great acts" (243). During his youth,
while acting as God's image, he has grown up under his "special
eie" (636). When he falls to Dalila's temptation, both his function
as image and his "visual" relationship with God are ended: he is
totally blind both physically and spiritually; his appearance is totally
changed from hero to slave—the first thing Manoa and the Chorus
remark on; and instead of an image to direct the Jews toward God,
he becomes an example to turn them away. By the end of the play,
however, when Samson's regeneration is complete, both aspects of
seeing and *being seen* are restored to him one last time, in a single,
swift action of God. Once more the Chorus expresses itself in visual
terms:

> All is best, though we oft doubt,
> What th' unsearchable dispose
> Of highest wisdom brings about,
> And ever best found in the close.
> Oft he seems to hide his face,
> But unexpectedly returns
> And to his faithful Champion hath in place
> Bore witness gloriously. . . . (1745-52)

God's wisdom is unsearchable, meaning that man cannot see into it.
But God can reveal himself through his instruments. God hides his
face, a phrase from the Psalms that is especially appropriate, for

throughout the play he has hidden from Samson while secretly preparing him for this revelation. Finally, God bears witness, a phrase usually used of bringers of the gospel or revealers of truth by martyrdom. The witness is borne both *to* Samson, who now sees God's face as he had in his youth, and *through* him as image or agent to the Philistines and Jews.

Samson had spoken earlier of a contest between the God of Abraham and the Philistine Dagon. As Manoa puts it, "God, / Besides whom is no God" is compared with idols "By th' Idolatrous rout amidst thir wine" (440-43). But an idol, or *eidolon,* is a false image, as Steadman has pointed out[7]—a witness to falsehood rather than truth. God can have no stone image like Dagon's, but he can make Samson his living image and witness. In his early heroic actions as well as his person, Samson is an Image of God's strength, intended to focus the attention of the Jews; but the changeable Jews refuse to see. When he falls, he permits a false *eidolon* of Dagon to stand in his place as the focus of all eyes, to the detriment of God and truth. But in his final act, he expiates this worst of his sins by a sacrifice neither Philistine nor Jew can fail to see. Even after his death, Samson will continue to play the role of Image, as Manoa foresees; for to his "Monument"

> shall all the valiant youth resort,
> And from his memory inflame thir breasts
> To matchless valour, and adventures high. . . .
>   (1738-40)

Samson will now be an image and exemplar for all times, a model for emulation, especially by the young, who are still in the process of learning and so can open their eyes and *see.* From Samson's memory they will "inflame their breasts," as if the fire of the Phoenix and of Samson's sacrifice were to spread to their resinous hearts and there take flame. The building of the tomb has been deprecated by recent critics as an attempt to institutionalize Samson's deeds, and

[7]John M. Steadman, "Image and Idol: Satan and the Element of Illusion in *Paradise Lost," JEGP,* 59 (1960), 650–53; see also Steadman, *Milton's Epic Characters* (Chapel Hill: Univ. of North Carolina Press, 1968).

therefore as a basic misunderstanding of his spirit on the part of Manoa and the Chorus. On the contrary: the tomb serves only as a reminder, but heart will speak to heart and soul to soul, the only way Milton thought that goodness could be spread — not by force or by institutions, but by persuasion and example, resulting in the free choice of the "paradise within."

During the course of the play, none of Samson's visitors, nor the audience in the temple, have really been able to see him as he lies or stands before them in the flesh, hidden under an appearance of rags and slavery that less and less accurately reveals his true state or potential for action. The Philistines, their spiritual senses dead, no longer capable of listening to the messages their physical senses bring to them, lost in drunkenness and the worship of *eidola* or false images, are incapable of this vision; they are lost to the truth. Closing their eyes and ears, they choose death, the ultimate darkness and insensibility. But for the Jews, who though recurrently unfaithful are still the chosen people, God makes Samson in his death and after it a saving image, a revelation of his face.

3

The imagery of sight and seeing in *Samson,* balanced against the various kinds of blindness, forms a symmetrical and pervasive pattern. Linked to it are the images of fire and ashes summed up in the resurrection of the Phoenix; and also the recurrent images of light and darkness. Light-dark imagery appears, in various forms, in all of Milton's important poetry. It will not be necessary to examine it broadly here, beyond what has already been suggested in the discussion above. However, the play's time scheme should be noted. Beginning quietly in the early morning, by a bank with "choice of Sun or shade" (3), the action ends at high noon in the temple of Dagon. Much has been made in this connection of the "noonday devil" (the time is the same as that of Eve's fall) and of the mystical equivalence in Milton of noon and midnight;[8] but the major significance of the temporal pattern is a journey from darkness into light, from beginnings to maturity, and from the depths to the heights.

Noon is dominantly the moment of the day's greatest light, and these
other meanings can be no more than undercurrents to the theme of
radiance. Thus when Samson dies he goes, in a sense, not only into
darkness but into light, and like Andrew Marvell's description of
the soul returning to Heaven like a drop of dew, "does, dissolving,
run / Into the Glories of th' Almighty Sun."[9]

Also linked to the pattern of sight imagery are related patterns
made up of other sensory imagery, especially hearing. Sometimes
sight and hearing are brought very close together, fused or confused,
as when the leaders of Israel are both blind and deaf to Samson's
deeds, or when, in Samson's first speech, he moves by a kind of
synesthesia from one sense to another and back again:

> The Sun to me is dark
> And silent as the Moon,
> When she deserts the night
> Hid in her vacant interlunar cave. (86-89)

Similarly, just as the pulling down of the temple is visually overwhelming, and persists on the frightened Messenger's interior
retinas, the eyes of his imagination, so the sound which it makes is
also terrifyingly overwhelming, as Manoa and the Chorus testify,
even at a distance:

> *Man.* I know your friendly minds and — O what noise!
> Mercy of Heav'n what hideous noise was that!
> Horribly loud unlike the former shout.
> *Chor.* Noise call you it or universal groan
> As if the whole inhabitation perish'd,

---

[8]See Albert L. Cirillo, "Noon-Midnight and the Temporal Structure of
Paradise Lost," *ELH*, 29 (1962), 372–95; and deriving from this article Lynn
Veach Sadler, "Typological Imagery in *Samson Agonistes:* Noon and the
Dragon," *ELH*, 37 (1970), 195–210. In his latest article, Cirillo drops these
paradoxes in favor of an interpretation with which I essentially agree: see
his "Time, Light, and the Phoenix: The Design of *Samson Agonistes*," *Calm
of Mind*, ed. Joseph Anthony Wittreich, Jr. (Cleveland: Press of Case Western
Reserve Univ., 1971), pp. 209–33.

[9]"On a Drop of Dew," *The Poems and Letters of Andrew Marvell*, ed. H. M.
Margoliouth (Oxford: Clarendon Press, 1952).

Blood, death, and deathful deeds are in that noise,
Ruin, destruction at the utmost point. (1508-14)

So too when the Messenger describes the catastrophe from the viewpoint of an eyewitness:

As with the force of winds and waters pent,
When Mountains tremble, those two massie Pillars
With horrible convulsion to and fro,
He tugg'd, he shook, till down they came and drew
The whole roof after them, with burst of thunder
Upon the heads of all who sate beneath. . . .
                    (1647-52)

Both sight and sound are so intense that they seem to overload the senses; and the Philistines must also *feel*.

Similarly, Harapha is invited to touch and taste Samson as well as look at him, while the Philistines are not merely blind but totally insensate. There is frequent biblical precedent for coupling hearing and seeing in the context of spiritual enlightenment or hardening of the heart; and, as Milton notes in the *Christian Doctrine,* enlightenment is occasionally pictured in terms of the other senses as well: "it is sometimes spoken of under the metaphor of hearing or hearkening . . . sometimes under that of tasting."[10] In the gospel account, the apostle Thomas was invited to confirm his faith by touching. Thus when Samson invites Harapha not to look at but to taste and touch him, though his primary meaning is a mocking, ironic invitation to battle, his words mean more.

The result of the interconnection of sensory imagery is to extend the implications of seeing to all the other evocations of sense in the play. While each instance keeps its local meaning, it also contributes to the portrayal of a spectrum of sensory perception: from Samson's irritable hypersensitivity to words or to stares — or to Dalila's offered touch — to his complete withdrawal into self, as suggested by his portrait of his earlier self as a "fort of silence" (236), battered by Dalila's peals of words — or to the description of the Philistines' final retreat from the possibility of perception into the inebriation and darkness of absolute, self-imposed isolation from the real world.

[10]*Works,* XV, 355.

Anne Ferry expresses a useful perception when she suggests that *Samson Agonistes* is a world governed by Samson's blindness, and that many of the outward happenings in the play are subtly mediated to the reader as if he perceived them through the blind Samson's senses.[11] That effect accounts in good part for the play's claustrophobic closeness and frequent hypersensitivity—qualities which are not limited to Samson's speeches alone. Milton gives us not the broad world of his visual imagination, as in *Paradise Lost,* but the narrow, tortured world of the blind Samson, a world where the other senses are magnified, where footsteps echo, where seeing is constantly spoken of, and sensed, and used metaphorically, yet little can be directly seen. Both Ferry and Landy move from this perception of the play's atmosphere to a similar conclusion: a theory that in *Samson* Milton portrays the inadequacy of language, by means of a hero who moves into the darkness and silence within, gradually isolating himself from the sounds of the world and retreating into a "fort of silence": achieving at last, through "increasing reticence," a state of "heroic silence."[12]

This interpretation can be accepted only in part. That Samson is increasingly isolated from his friends I have already argued. That the wells of his strength are within (though ultimately from above) can also be agreed on. But that he becomes suspicious of language to the point that he grows reticent or silent simply is not true. Samson tries earnestly to communicate with all his visitors, friends and enemies, for that is his duty. The very essence of his mission in life is to manifest God's truth. Only at the end of the play is he forced, in two speeches, to prevaricate with the Public Officer and with the Philistines in the temple. This is not the result of a growing reticence, however, nor does it accompany his slowly increasing isolation. His special use of irony in the last speeches, which is like nothing else in the play, results simply from the tactical necessity of concealing his plans from his enemies, following upon his decision to act. The

---

[11]Ferry, *Milton and the Miltonic Dryden,* pp. 127–77.

[12]The quotations are from Ferry, p. 165; Landy, "Language and the Seal of Silence in *Samson Agonistes.*" A brilliant evocation of the meaning of blindness in the play is also given by Balachandra Rajan, *The Lofty Rhyme* (London: Routledge & Kegan Paul, 1970), pp. 128–45.

irony in these speeches, it might be added, does have the additional effect of giving the reader a sense that providence itself acts unexpectedly and ironically — but only toward the reprobate or the overly confident, not toward those of good will. While Samson hides his intentions from the Public Officer, he reveals himself as fully as he can — for he himself does not know the details of what is about to happen — in his last words to his friends.

Samson must learn to escape his sensitivity to appearances, his constant concern for the opinions of others, especially of his enemies. His sense of shame at his blindness and slavery, his sense of being constantly watched and mocked, while human enough, influence him too much at the beginning of the action. He must learn to see his predicament not through the eyes of enemies, or even of father and friends, but in terms of his divinely-appointed mission and, as it were, through the eyes of God. In this sense, he must escape from the world. He must not simply retreat inward, however, away from communication with others. He was a "fort of silence" *before* his fall, but that kind of withdrawal failed to prevent his betrayal and defeat at the hands of Dalila. If he goes inward and receives a strength and purpose out of the depths of his own being which his father and friends cannot offer him from without, this spiritual motion is not a withdrawal from and condemnation of society or of public commitment; it is a regroupment, a preparation for more effective action and communication.

The pattern here — also discussed in the last chapter — is both an archetypal pattern of tragic and of Christian heroism and a recognizable and universal psychological process. In her study of "the rebirth archetype" in literature, part of her excellent book *Archetypal Patterns in Poetry,* Maud Bodkin notes many similar instances of such a pattern, from the classical epics to *The Ancient Mariner.* Moments of intense creativity, Jung noted, are usually preceded by periods of frustration and blockage. "Before 'a renewal of life' can come about, Jung urges, there must be an acceptance of the possibilities that lie in the unconscious contents 'activated through regression . . . and disfigured by the slime of the deep.'"[13] This regression is often reflected in the myth of a "night journey," either literal or, as in the case of Samson, figurative. Miss Bodkin's further gen-

eralizations about these motifs could have been written specifically
about the psychological processes in *Samson Agonistes:*

> Within the image-sequences examined the pattern appears of
> a movement, downward, or inward toward the earth's centre,
> or a cessation of movement—a physical change which, as we
> urge metaphor closer to the impalpable forces of life and soul,
> appears also as a transition toward severed relation with the
> outer world, and, it may be, toward disintegration and death.
> This element in the pattern is balanced by a movement upward
> and outward—an expansion or outburst of activity, a transition
> toward redintegration and life-renewal.
>
> To the pattern thus indicated in extreme generality we may
> give the name of the Rebirth archetype.[14]

To speak only of a journey by Samson into darkness and silence is
to recognize only a part of the pattern and of the play's impact on
the reader.

Neither in fact nor in spirit is Samson a man who abandons language as a means of communication or persuasion. He argues from
time to time that deeds speak louder than words alone, or than empty
protestations; he adds gesture and action to words (with a vengeance)
when he brings down the temple; he even doubts in the end that
anything short of having the temple pulled down around their ears
can get through to the Philistines. But he grudges no one the right
to rational argument and the opportunity to be convinced first
through words. If he fails to communicate his message, the fault is
not in words, but in eyes and ears; if his last action opens some eyes
and ears among the survivors, it will be in part an opening that will
enable them to hear and to understand words that he has earlier
spoken and deeds that he has earlier done. On another level, insofar
as God is the cause of the catastrophe, he brings it about as a sign to
the Jews, significant in itself—"the use of miracles is to manifest

---

[13]Maud Bodkin, *Archetypal Patterns in Poetry* (London: Oxford Univ. Press,
1934, 1963), p. 52. Miss Bodkin is citing Jung, *Contributions to Analytical
Psychology* (London: Kegan Paul, 1928), p. 38.

[14]Bodkin, p. 54. Her entire book is relevant to an understanding of the play
from this perspective, and is highly recommended to anyone who is interested in poetry.

the divine power, and confirm our faith"[15]—but also as a means of
recalling to the chosen people the words and commandments he
has spoken to them through Moses. The Philistines, hard of heart,
must suffer by hard experience; the Jews can still open their eyes and
ears and learn by precept and example. Samson does not abandon
his people except for a time: he withdraws from the world into the
depths of soul-searching, suffering, and degradation in order to return
to them with a hard-won and more persuasive truth. This is also
true of the poet as creator, as Miss Bodkin suggests. His journey into
the depths of his creativity is not unlike what he portrays in his hero,
and it may involve a similarly difficult effort. His purpose too is to
communicate, to return from the depths of his being with some truth
for mankind.

The Renaissance believed firmly that it was better to learn by
listening to words, advice, or example of another than by painful
experience, and they confidently believed that such vicarious learning was possible. Milton, in his prose tracts and his many efforts in
poetry to justify the ways of God to men, demonstrates that he too
believes in the possible efficacy of words, even if their fit audience
prove but few. The many arguments and debates, the sheer weight
of discussion and persuasion in *Samson,* show that he had not changed
his mind when he wrote the play. Often both the disputants in a
given debate may seem near-sighted and may reach no conclusion
for the moment; but by the end of the play what they had argued
about, uncertain at the time, grows clear. From the beginning to the
end of his career, Milton grew more pessimistic about the difficulties
of persuading others of the truth, and of the numbers who could be
so persuaded. In *Areopagitica* truth prevails in a fair field over falsehood; in *Paradise Lost,* it retires from battle beslandered and stuck
with darts. In *The Reason of Church Government* Milton hopes to
educate a whole nation through poetry and drama; in *Paradise Lost*
he addresses only a saving remnant. *Samson* itself, instead of becoming part of a public, national drama like the plays of Athens, cannot
even be given on stage. Nevertheless, Milton continued to believe
in the existence of truth, and the utility of words and poetry in

[15]*Christian Doctrine; Works,* XV, 95.

furthering it. He would never have argued against the attempt to
persuade by the arts of language, whether in tract or debate, or
through the subtler, sense-related methods of poetry.

4

The conveyance of truths, whether intellectual, emotional, or spiritual, by means of images was central to Renaissance critical theory
and literature, and to Milton's practice in his poetry. Samson is the
image of God's strength, a rare "example" (166) in his person, his
words, and especially his actions. Although *Samson Agonistes* is a
tragedy, not an epic, it clearly falls into the Renaissance class of
heroic poetry — or, if one prefers, it is in the heroic mode. The function of such poetry is to teach and to inspire to active virtue by means
of examples for imitation or avoidance. Thus, for example, Samson
is a true exemplar of courage whom the Jews, or the reader, may
emulate; while Harapha is an exemplar of false or falsely-based
courage, which collapses under pressure and is to be avoided.[16]

Renaissance educational theory was heavily based on the theory
of emulation and imitation of examples — this was the major justification for making schoolboys read literature. Milton writes, in *Of
Education,* that the main duty of the schoolmaster toward his pupils is

> To temper them such Lectures and Explanations upon every
> opportunity, as may lead and draw them in willing obedience,
> enflam'd with the study of Learning, and the admiration of
> Vertue; stirr'd up with high hopes of living to be brave men,
> and worthy Patriots, dear to God, and famous to all ages. That
> they may despise and scorn all their childish, and ill-taught

[16]Milton's use of contrasting examples for imitation or avoidance is best
discussed by John M. Steadman, in *Milton and the Renaissance Hero* (Oxford:
Clarendon Press, 1967) and *Milton's Epic Characters.* There are many useful
discussions of heroic poetry and exemplary literature among studies of
Sidney and Spenser: for example, Maurice Evans, *Spenser's Anatomy of
Heroism* (Cambridge: Cambridge Univ. Press, 1970) or two articles on
Sidney's *Arcadia* by Alan D. Isler in *Studies in Philology,* 65 (1968), 171–91;
and *PMLA,* 83 (1968), 368–79.

qualities, to delight in manly, and liberal Exercises: which he
who hath the Art, and proper Eloquence to catch them with,
what with mild and effectual perswasions, and what with the
intimation of some fear, if need be, but chiefly by his own example, might in a short space gain them to an incredible dili-
gence and courage: infusing into their young brests such an
ingenuous and noble ardor, as would not fail to make many
of them renowned and matchless men.[17]

Children are to be persuaded to learn, rather than forced, and the
chief means of doing this is by example. In speaking to an adult
audience, with whom the threat of physical punishment must be
abandoned, effectual persuasion must use the same methods. Examples for imitation, presented by means of art and proper eloquence,
the chief tools of a good schoolmaster, would still be appropriate
methods for a committed poet.

In *Areopagitica,* Milton calls Spenser "a better teacher than *Scotus*
or *Aquinas*" because he describes "true temperance under the person
of *Guion*"[18] — that is, probably, because Spenser teaches his reader
by example rather than precept. In the *Apology for Smectymnuus,* Milton mentions the primary importance in his own education of "the
divine volumes of *Plato,* and his equall *Xenophon.*"[19] Xenophon is
put beside Plato as a moral teacher because while Plato taught
mainly by precept, Xenophon, in his *Cyropaedia,* was thought to
be among the most notable of those who taught by example.[20] His
Cyrus was the figure of a perfect ruler, whom all men in positions of
authority would do well to emulate. In *The Reason of Church Government,* Milton takes time from his main concern in the treatise to
discuss his plans for one day carrying out a program of teaching
Englishmen by means of his poetry. He is uncertain what kind of

[17]*Works,* IV, 282.

[18]*Works,* IV, 311.

[19]*Works,* III, 305.

[20]See my "'Plato, and his Equall Xenophon': A Note on Milton's *Apology
for Smectymnuus," Milton Quarterly,* 4 (1970), 20–22. The same conclusion
was simultaneously reached by Lawrence A. Sasek, "Plato and his Equal
Xenophon," *English Language Notes,* 7 (1970), 260–62.

poetry will best suit this purpose, but he is in no doubt of the purpose itself. The only question is whether epic or "those Dramatick constitutions, wherein *Sophocles* and *Euripides* raigne shall be found more doctrinal and exemplary to a Nation."[21] Doctrinal and exemplary: for a serious poet in the Renaissance tradition, the two concepts could scarcely be separated, since poetry by definition taught by examples.

One well-known statement of this principle was Spenser's letter to Raleigh which was printed as a preface to *The Faerie Queene*. The general end of his poem, Spenser writes, is "to fashion a gentleman or noble person in vertuous and gentle discipline." This he means to accomplish by means of twelve principal heroes, who will embody the moral virtues; and, summing them all up, by means of Prince Arthur, "the image of a brave knight." Thus he will follow the example of Xenophon, who is to be preferred to Plato because he taught virtue "in the person of Cyrus"; for "so much more profitable and gratious is doctrine by ensample, then by rule."[22] The chief English authority for this principle, however, is Sir Philip Sidney. The central thesis of *An Apology for Poetry* is that the function of poetry is to please and instruct the reader and thus move him to virtuous action, and that poetry accomplishes this end by its *images*, in the broad sense we have been using.

The philosopher, Sidney writes, teaches by dry and difficult precepts, which can reach only those who are already philosophers; the historian presents specific men in action but can impose no meaningful form on his work; the poet uses the best of both philosophy and history, and so is the best and most pleasing teacher. "It is that fayning notable images of vertues, vices, or what els, with that delightfull teaching, which must be the right describing note to know a Poet by." What Sidney means by "images," which is a key term here, is best explained by the examples he gives. His exemplars or images of virtue are such men as Achilles, Cyrus, Aeneas, Turnus, Tideus, and Rinaldo; the image is not merely the man, however, but

<hr/>

[21]*Works*, III, 237.

[22]*Spenser's Faerie Queene*, ed. J. C. Smith (Oxford: Clarendon Press, 1909), II, 485–86.

also his various actions, or the action of the poem itself, as the following passage shows:

> For as the image of each action styrreth and instructeth the mind, so the loftie image of such Worthies most inflameth the mind with desire to be worthy, and informes with counsel how to be worthy. Only let *Aeneas* be worne in the tablet of your memory; how he governeth himselfe in the ruine of his Country; in the preserving his old Father, and carrying away his religious ceremonies; in obeying the Gods commandement to leave *Dido,* though not onely all passionate kindenes, but even the humane consideration of vertuous gratefulnes, would have craved other of him; how in storms, howe in sports, howe in warre, howe in peace, how a fugitive, how victorious, how besiedged, how besiedging, howe to strangers, howe to allyes, how to enemies, howe to his owne; lastly, how in his inward selfe, and how in his outward government. . . .[23]

This is the key to how the English Renaissance read the ancient heroic poems, and what they intended to accomplish in their own heroic poems, such as *The Faerie Queene* or the *Arcadia.*

Milton was a subtler teacher in poetry than Sidney, but his aim and his methods were essentially similar. In the same passage in which he speculates whether epic or drama is more "doctrinal and exemplary" to a nation, he discusses the potentialities of poetry, rightly used. The passage is one of the best glosses on Milton's major poems, among them *Samson Agonistes.* The ability to write poetry, Milton says, is "the inspired guift of God rarely bestow'd"; it is

> of power beside the office of a pulpit, to inbreed and cherish in a great people the seeds of vertu, and publick civility, to allay the perturbations of the mind, and set the affections in right tune, to celebrate in glorious and lofty Hymns the throne and equipage of Gods Almightinesse, and what he works, and what he suffers to be wrought with high providence in his Church, to sing the victorious agonies of Martyrs and Saints, the deeds and triumphs of just and pious Nations doing valiantly through faith against the enemies of Christ, to deplore the general relapses of Kingdoms and States from justice and Gods true worship. Lastly,

[23]G. Gregory Smith, ed., *Elizabethan Critical Essays,* I, 160, 179–80. I have regularized *u* and *v* in the Sidney and Spenser quotations.

whatsoever in religion is holy and sublime, in vertu amiable, or grave, whatsoever hath passion or admiration in all the changes of that which is call'd fortune from without, or the wily suttleties and refluxes of mans thoughts from within, all these things with a solid and treatable smoothnesse to paint out and describe. Teaching over the whole book of sanctity and vertu through all the instances of example with such delight to those especially of soft and delicious temper who will not so much as look upon Truth herselfe, unlesse they see her elegantly drest, that whereas the paths of honesty and good life appear now rugged and diffi-cult, though they be indeed easy and pleasant, they would then appeare to all men both easy and pleasant though they were rugged and difficult indeed. And what a benefit this would be to our youth and gentry. . . .[24]

The heroism and the particular virtues which interest Milton are somewhat different from those which interest Sidney; his examples are to work through what we call the unconscious as well as the conscious mind of the reader, to allay his perturbations and set his affections in right tune, moving him through senses and feelings as well as the intellect; but otherwise the two poets are in close agree-ment about both aims and methods.

Against the exemplars of virtue are set exemplars of vice. In Spenser, Duessa, Archimago, or Acrasia show us persons, states of mind, or actions to avoid, just as Una, Guyon, Britomart, or Arthur show us persons and actions to imitate. So Comus is an example of intemperance to be avoided just as the Lady is an example of virtue to be emulated. In *Paradise Lost* (to simplify), while Adam and Eve are the protagonists and therefore the heroes in one sense, the image for emulation *par excellence* is Messiah, and the *eidolon* to be seen through and repudiated is Satan. Adam and Eve are in a middle state, and like the reader, participate in some of the qualities of both ex-tremes. While less good or evil than Christ or Satan, they are easier for us to identify with. Although, reading the critical works of the Renaissance, a modern reader might judge the theory of example and emulation to be somewhat simple-minded, artistic practice was more subtle and effective than the theory of imitation, barely stated, might

[24]*The Reason of Church Government; Works,* III, 238–39.

suggest. Examples of good to imitate, and of evil to avoid: ultimately the matter is simple, as art must be; but the heroes for emulation are never mere cardboard figures, at least in the works of major writers. Spenser's heroes, or Sidney's, are never unqualifiedly good. Not even Prince Arthur is perfect, while Guyon must be helped by an angel's intervention, and the Red Cross Knight fails miserably in his task until he is himself rescued. Sidney's Musidorus and Pyrochles are likewise only too human.

It is a matter of opinion what should be called a major poem; but one would not be too far wrong to say that only two English poets have given us major poems with heroes who are examples of perfection: Milton in *Paradise Regained* and Shelley in *Prometheus Unbound.* Neither of these poems is an inconsiderable achievement, in fact both must be called highly successful: they are among the greatest accomplishments in the language. But this success, real as it is, is somewhat qualified by the inaccessability of both works: the level of emotion begins and persists so high that to many readers there seems to be no emotion that they can share, and they have great difficulty in identifying with the heroes and their actions. Therefore, Shelley's poem may seem simply effusive because it is not properly felt, while Milton's appears cold, schematic, and too purely theological. It will be evident that I think these judgments wrong, but given the nature of the two poems, they are understandable.

Milton and Shelley fall into this problem because they are both poets who are ultimately idealists and absolutists, with visions of perfect love, beauty, and truth. It is easier for a poet less concerned with final ends to present mixed and ambiguous heroes and actions — for Ariosto, for example, or Malory. Milton got around the problem in *Paradise Lost* by using the device of what might be called the triple protagonist: Satan, Adam-Eve, and Messiah. In *Paradise Regained* he confronted his ideal vision almost directly (there is some mediation because Jesus is hidden under his humanity). In *Samson Agonistes,* if the traditional dating is assumed, he returned to a method of greater indirection and humanity. Speaking only of the heroes, *Samson Agonistes* may well be judged Milton's most successful work, though the play as a whole is outweighed by the much larger accomplishment of *Paradise Lost.* It is not necessary or desirable, however, to weigh

Milton's major works or their heroes against each other, since, in fact, each hero helps to illuminate the others.

In Samson, Milton gives us an image of debasement and greatness, both human and more-than-human. He is an image whom we perceive: we see him in his rags and careless, defeated posture or as he gradually grows more upright and active; we hear him, as a voice in darkness, a speaker of magnificent words; we even come close to smelling, tasting, and touching him. Unlike the other characters in the play, we are able to approach him internally, sensing and feeling what he feels; then, toward the close, we are moved to a distance, our final understanding, vision, emotional catharsis mediated through the Messenger, Manoa, and the Danites. Finally, we are dismissed, with "true experience from this great event," with "peace and consolation," and with "calm of mind all passion spent." In these phrases, Milton unifies the head, the heart, and the senses. The culmination of our intellectual and emotional education, according to the Chorus, is brought about by the "great event": the terrible *exemplum* of Samson in the temple, acting out his role as God's champion, the image of his strength and of his uncontrollable purpose. As Sidney came away from the *Aeneid* with a series of images — Aeneas in action, carrying his father out of flaming Troy, Aeneas in war or in peace — so the reader leaves *Samson* with a series of images. There are many of these images: Samson in chains, lying on the ground; Samson disputing with his father and friends; Samson sinking into near despair, but as a result taking new hope and growing beyond his visitors' grasp or gaze; Samson confronting the gorgeous Dalila and revealing her for what she is, while he learns better what he is himself; Samson and Harapha, circling around one another in debate and in near-physical contact, the champions of two different ideals; finally, Samson and the Philistines, who come together to confront one another in the temple, the blind champion and his blind conquerors. These are, in Sidney's words, images both of "inward self" and of "outward government." All of them lead up to and are presided over by one great image: Samson as Phoenix in the temple of Dagon, rising to new heights but pulling down in destruction, dying and triumphing, an image whose very violence to the eyes and ears terrifies the beholders: the image and example of the champion of God.

6

JEWS AND PHILISTINES, MANOA AND THE CHORUS

It might seem to an unsophisticated reader that the characters in *Samson Agonistes* fall naturally into two rough groups, the good ones and the bad ones, and that these two groups are defined by the forces lying behind them, in contention with one another: God and Dagon, or, on the human level, Israel and Philistia. Ultimately, "good" and "evil" are indeed the terms that are appropriate, for in Milton's view the God of *Samson* is absolute goodness itself, while Dagon, a false god or *eidolon*, who sets himself up against God (and is revealed in *Paradise Lost,* though not in *Samson,* to be a fallen angel in disguise), is the very opposite of goodness, and for that reason evil. Israel, as the nation and people of God, also appears to have a special claim to be considered good, while Philistia, the opponent of Israel and the oppressor of God's people, must apparently be considered bad. Then it would follow that Samson, Manoa, the Chorus, and the Jewish

people are good, and Dalila, Harapha, the Public Officer, and the
Philistine leaders and people are evil.

Put this way, the statements become increasingly untrue, or rather
true only in part. One can agree, in principle, that Milton's God is
good. Even this, however, requires further discussion. As I have tried
to show elsewhere in connection with the God of *Paradise Lost*,[1] the
God of *Samson* should not be thought "good" simply as a kind of
arbitrary axiom, or as a recognition of his sheer power and assigned
position in the Miltonic universe. It is not merely by virtue of his
power, but also by his very nature, his merit, and his love that Milton's God rules: that is made evident in *Paradise Lost*. It cannot appear
quite so evidently in *Samson,* because in the play the action remains
in the human world, with the author, the characters, and the reader
"Standing on Earth, not rapt above the Pole." Its God, who is unseen
and never directly heard, must, therefore, remain more mysterious
than the God of the epic. But, on the human level of *Samson,* Milton
does insist on enforcing the same point he makes against the wider
background of the cosmos in *Paradise Lost:* that just and unjust rule,
true authority and force, the golden scepter and the iron rod, are not
one and the same. Those critics are mistaken, then, who view the God
of *Samson* as a particularly arbitrary or Calvinistic deity. Milton was
never an admirer of sheer force and authority. On the contrary: in
human affairs, he was a rebel and a disrespecter of authorities, while
in divine matters he admired not God's power in itself, but rather
the coupling in God of light, goodness, and love with omnipotent
power, thereby ensuring the ultimate rule of these qualities over the
universe. Moreover, it is by virtue of this absolute power and love
that Milton's God is able to extend the gift of freedom to angels and
men, to use or abuse as they decide.

One of Milton's first principles was the belief that God withholds
from no one the opportunity to choose the right path and thus to be
saved, that no one is damned by fiat or by eternal predestination.[2]
Even in their fallen state, all men are extended the opportunity for

---

[1]"Milton's God: Authority in *Paradise Lost,*" *Milton Studies,* 4 (1972), 19–38.
[2]*Christian Doctrine; Works,* XIV, 91–175.

life. This belief appears to conflict with the possibility that the Jews can somehow be called "good" and the Philistines "evil." Milton also believed, however, that beyond ordinary election some individuals or nations are specially elected by God, chosen for special purposes above the rest of men. The special mission of the Israelites was to live under the law, and to follow the precepts given them by Moses:

> with a promise of life to such as should keep them, and a curse on such as should be disobedient; to the end that they, being led thereby to an acknowledgment of the depravity of mankind, and consequently of their own, might have recourse to the righteousness of the promised Savior; and that they, and in process of time all other nations, might be led under the Gospel from the weak and servile rudiments of this elementary institution to the full strength of the new creature, and a manly liberty worthy the sons of God.[3]

The Jews thus have a special mission in preparing the way for the new dispensation. Although the Law is in itself inadequate, it is God-given, and those who follow it are promised the gift of life. On the other hand, the Israelites will lead the way to the new covenant almost as much by the example of their individual failures as by obedience. They are a specially elected nation, but among them individuals can either choose or not choose to live up to the covenanted terms.

Israel as a nation, or as an ideal, is good; Philistia, and what it stands for, is depraved. Among the Philistines, however, as among the Jews, individuals may be either good or bad. In the temple catastrophe, for example, Milton distinguishes between those Philistines who are killed and those who escape: a distinction which he did not find in the Bible. "Lords, Ladies, Captains, Councellors, or Priests, / Thir choice nobility and flower" (1653-54), are all caught and destroyed, while the "vulgar" crowd standing outside the roofed-in area of the temple escape. This is not a sign of modern democracy on Milton's part, in the strict sense of the word, for he was a classical

---

[3]*Works,* XVI, 103-05. This and the following quotation are reduced from small capitals.

republican, who believed in rule by merit and excellence and had little respect for the virtues of the mob. The common people of Philistia escape because less is expected of them, because they have few responsibilities to abuse. Philistia's rulers are destroyed because they have arrogated power to themselves, literally because they put themselves forward into the best seats, the better to watch Samson's humiliation. They merit destruction because they are closely associated with and responsible for the policies of Philistia and Dagon, in particular the policy of tyrannizing over the Jewish nation, holding its people in captivity, and attempting to force or seduce them from their duties to the God of Israel. Individually, each Philistine has a choice which would allow him to save himself, but this choice, at least in some cases, must involve conflict with what Philistia and Dagon have come to stand for. Dalila especially has this alternative, to follow her husband's God or Philistia's. As an adopted Israelite, her choice is clear.

What is expected of the rest of the Philistines is less clear. Each must find salvation in his own way. None, except for Dalila, is bound to follow the Law of Israel, or even to leave the worship of Dagon, as long as they follow the natural law and behave as well as they know how. Milton notes in the *Christian Doctrine* that "The Mosaic law was . . . intended for the Israelites alone."[4] It is up to the Philistines, therefore, only to live as "virtuous pagans" in the traditional phrase.

The chief sin of the Philistine leaders is essentially that of Pharoah in Exodus: the failure to let God's people go in the face of unmistakable miracles and warning signs. God has appointed Samson to perform in front of the Philistines, as well as the Jews, several miracles, whose significance they are at liberty either to recognize and act on, or ignore. Clearly Samson's escape from his bonds and his slaughter of a thousand Philistines at Ramath-lechi, with only his bare hands and an ass's jawbone, must be classed as a miracle, and moreover an unmistakable miracle performed in full sight of both the Philistines and Jews, or reported back to those who were absent. In the last chapter, Milton was briefly quoted on the purpose of miracles

---

[4]*Works,* XVI, 103.

in converting witnesses or confirming them in their faith. Here his comments may be cited more fully:

> The extraordinary providence of God is that whereby God produces some effect out of the usual order of nature, or gives the power of producing the same effect to whomsoever he may appoint. This is what we call a miracle. Hence God alone is the primary author of miracles, as he only is able to invert that order of things which he has himself appointed [a point that the Chorus and Manoa make concerning Samson's marriages, without fully realizing how it applies to his heroic deeds] .... The use of miracles is to manifest the divine power, and confirm our faith .... Miracles are also designed to increase the condemnation of unbelievers, by taking away all excuse for unbelief .... John XV.24. "if I had not done among them the works which none other man did, they had not had sin: but now they have no cloak for their sin."[5]

The role of Samson's deeds in confirming the faith of the Jews has already been mentioned. The obverse effect also applies. Because the Philistines continue to oppress Samson and the Jews, because they ignore events which have been plainly "done among them," which they could hardly fail to see or hear about, "they have no cloak for their sin." Nothing in the play is plainer than the extensive fame of Samson's miraculous deeds at Ramath-lechi. His reputation extends as far among the Philistines as among the Danites. Harapha, for example, comes to view Samson because of his fame:

>   Much have I heard
>   Of thy prodigious might and feats perform'd
>   Incredible to me. . . .   (1082-84)

He has come to learn more about these rumors; he has in his grasp everything he needs for a realization of the true state of affairs; but he will not see what is right in front of him. As Milton elaborately explains in the *Christian Doctrine,* such a reaction, the confirmation in wickedness by a miracle or a "bad temptation," is only in one sense caused by God. A miracle becomes a means of condemnation only

[5]*Works,* XV, 95–97.

when the individual exercises his free choice of hardening his heart or closing his eyes and ears.

What is true for the Philistines in *Samson* is also true for the Jews. As members of the people of Israel, they are all, in a sense, specially elected. Theirs, however, is the plainer task of being loyal to their nation, their law, and their God, while for the Philistines (though less is expected of them) the course of action is less clear. Nevertheless, each Israelite has it in his power to stand or fall, to choose rightly or wrongly. Beyond that, some who choose rightly are more preeminent in virtue than others. Samson is specially elected, beyond his birthright as a Jew; Manoa and the Chorus are loyal to Samson and to their God, but often weak or ignorant; the rest of the Jews fall away almost entirely, and are on the verge of reprobation. In the rest of this chapter, we will consider further the cases of Manoa and the Chorus, who are actors near the center of the special providential history of Israel, which leads toward the new dispensation. They play a special role, but they are also fallible and human like us.

2

In the past few years, a growing number of Miltonists have belittled the characters of Manoa and the Chorus far beyond what they deserve, and thus have distorted the whole meaning of the play. As yet there has been no critical response. This criticism grows out of certain long-standing attitudes toward *Samson,* perhaps especially the often-repeated view that Manoa and the Chorus are very like the comforters of Job. (About this, more will be said later.) But while Manoa and the Chorus have their faults, they are by no means predominantly evil or malicious, nor any more foolish and blind than might be expected of good men in a fallen world. Naturally, in comparison with Samson, the other characters look small and ordinary. This is partly the result of Milton's Aeschylean handling of the characters and their relationships to one another. More important, Samson's force, eloquence, and spiritual magnitude—his guilt and suffering as well as his final triumph—dwarf everyone around him. Nevertheless, the Danites and Manoa are not merely fools or "of men the common rout" (674). They are just and upright, the flower of Israel, the "saving remnant" at this moment in Israel's difficult history. Although in comparison with Samson, a great hero of faith and also a great tragic hero, they appear deficient, they are never foolish or immoral, nor can the critic safely patronize them. They represent human nature neither at its most heroic nor at its mediocre average, let alone its worst: they are what might properly be called its ordinary best.

The recent revaluation of the Chorus and Manoa was touched off by John Huntley, in an article published in 1966.[6] Huntley's discussion is generally judicious. His main point is that the Chorus in *Samson* is not the voice of Milton commenting omnipotently on the action, as many earlier critics assumed, especially in objecting to the misogynistic remarks after Dalila's exit. Rather, the Chorus is a group of fallible men, who often speak ignorantly, and who attain spiritual insight only at the end of the play. This thesis is entirely reasonable, nor would such a Chorus of fallible and ordinary men be foreign from the practice of the Greek tragedians whom Milton imitated. At several points, however, Huntley is unnecessarily harsh with the Chorus and Manoa. He accuses them of representing not "common morality" but "common immorality." They "are neither vicious nor saintly, but represent the vast ambivalent mass of mankind which neither knows what it feels nor feels what it knows." They are among those who "love bondage more than liberty."[7] None of these accusations is defensible. While it is true that the Chorus is neither vicious nor saintly, it is not true that they represent the masses, are commonly immoral, or desire slavery. On the contrary, they are among the few faithful members of Israel, they remain Samson's friends in spite of adversity and possible penalty, and they deeply desire their nation's freedom, as their praise of Samson's victories and their paean to national liberators clearly reveal. The nature of Samson's mission and the character of his heroism are beyond their initial understanding — but that is hardly surprising. Not even Samson himself knows what to expect.[8]

[6]Huntley, "A Revaluation of the Chorus' Role in Milton's *Samson Agonistes*," *Modern Philology*, 64 (1966), 132–45.

[7]Huntley, p. 139.

[8]I should repeat that these remarks are from an otherwise excellent essay; had they not influenced other critics, they would need no attention.

Huntley's passing strictures on the Chorus and Manoa have been taken up by an increasing number of other critics.[9] Louis Martz, the most prominent of them, argues that not only is the Chorus spiritually ignorant, but that Milton undercut many of its speeches with deliberately bad poetry. This interpretation, if it is allowed, makes the play less a tragedy than a comic satire. Martz characterizes the Chorus as generally stupid, while its various speeches are called trite, commonplace, trivial, feeble, undignified, heavy, flat, and unintentionally comic. A detailed discussion of these opinions would be out of place, but one example may be given. The Chorus' lament for the fall of great men, at the end of the *parodos,* is called a "trite view of Samson's disaster."[10] Readers may judge for themselves whether they agree:

> O mirror of our fickle state,
> Since man on earth unparallel'd!
> The rarer thy example stands,
> By how much from the top of wondrous glory,
> Strongest of mortal men,
> To lowest pitch of abject fortune thou art fall'n.
> For him I reckon not in high estate
> Whom long descent of birth
> Or the sphear of fortune raises;
> But thee whose strength, while vertue was her mate,
> Might have subdu'd the Earth,
> Universally crown'd with highest praises.   (164-75)

It is true that this commentary on Samson's predicament must be revised in the light of later events. Nevertheless, it is accurate for the time, and also it is a universal and moving expression of sorrow at a significant human problem. Characteristically Miltonic are the vertig-

[9]Louis Martz, "Chorus and Character in *Samson Agonistes,*" *Milton Studies,* 1 (1969), 115–34; Franklin R. Baruch, "Time, Body, and Spirit at the Close of *Samson Agonistes,*" *ELH,* 36 (1969), 319–39; Roberts W. French, "Rhyme and the Chorus of *Samson Agonistes,*" *Laurel Review,* 10 (1970), 60–67; Irene Samuel, "*Samson Agonistes* as Tragedy," *Calm of Mind,* ed. Joseph A. Wittreich, Jr. (Cleveland: Press of Case Western Reserve Univ., 1971), p. 250. Unlike the others, French argues that the Chorus has been educated by the play's end.

[10]Martz, p. 121.

inous, interrupted fall in lines 166-69 (from "stands" to "fall'n"), the false rising motion in lines 170-72, and the hypothetical, exultant rising motion in lines 173-75: now ruled out, alternative to actual events, but foreshadowing the conclusion. Critics commonly compare this speech to the "medieval" view of tragedy as the fall of great men on Fortune's Wheel, which is somehow thought naive, but only by a partial misreading. The Chorus, in fact, specifically qualifies or rejects most earlier, "trite" conceptions of heroism and tragedy. It rejects the medieval wheel of fortune, the conventional stress of tragedy on great lineage, which is found even in Shakespeare, and the strength without virtue which typifies the heroic drama of the Restoration.

The critics have been equally hard on Manoa. At his first entrance, for example, Martz describes him thus: "Manoa is utterly broken and pathetic. He moans pitifully to his son, clearly so wound up in his own grief that he cannot think about the effect that his groans may have upon Samson."[11] This is only a part of the truth. Manoa is sorry for his son as well as himself. Indeed, he is so involved with his son's fate that the two motives are difficult to separate. His sorrow is not merely maudlin, for he has perfectly good reasons to mourn. Manoa is a complex character. He hopes and despairs, chides and comforts, sympathizes but misunderstands, irritates but loves. He is vengeful toward his enemies but willing to swallow his pride to get what he wants from them; he is stern toward his son's faults, but willing to forgive them. His concerns are not narrow, considering the exigencies of the situation, but touch on himself, his son, his people, his God, all in varying mixture. If he seems simple or simple-minded, compare him with Job's comforters.

Perhaps the most crucial thing Manoa does in the play is to remind Samson of the true nature of his crime. How we interpret that reminder is equally crucial to our understanding of *Samson Agonistes* as a whole. Martz suggests that we should hear in the speech "self-centered moaning" and "the quavering voice of aged self-pity":

> So *Dagon* shall be magnif'd, and God,
> Besides whom is no God, compar'd with Idols,

[11]Martz, p. 122. Manoa is defended by Nancy Y. Hoffman, "Samson's Other Father: The Character of Manoa in *Samson Agonistes*," *Milton Studies,* 2 (1970), 195–210, but her defense salvages little.

> Disglorifi'd, blasphem'd, and had in scorn
> By th' Idolatrous rout amidst thir wine;
> Which to have come to pass by means of thee,
> *Samson,* of all thy sufferings think the heaviest,
> Of all reproach the most with shame that ever
> Could have befall'n thee and thy Fathers house.
>   (440-47)[12]

Is there really a "quavering voice of aged self-pity" in these lines? As Arnold Stein points out, this stern indictment of Samson's action is a crucial turning-point in the play.[13] It brings home to Samson for the first time what the real nature of his sin has been. Before this, he has been able to say: "but chief of all, / O loss of sight, of thee I most complain!" (66-67). Now he is immediately forced to admit that bringing honor to Dagon and dishonor to God, and thus being the cause of misleading many, is his "chief affliction, shame and sorrow, / The anguish of my Soul" (457-58).

Instead of querulous self-pity, one might rather hear in Manoa's words the tone of fierce rebuke, mingled with anxiety for his son's guilt, characteristic of Old-Testament prophecy. His words are hard, but true, and he is unable to hold them back. Their tone is very like the narrator's voice in describing the profanation of the Temple by the alienated daughters of Judah in *Paradise Lost* (1.452-57), for Samson too has profaned the sacred, and though he should have been a bulwark of strength, has betrayed his trust. In speaking of shame to "thy Fathers house," Manoa is expressing the orthodox Jewish view that righteous behavior honors one's ancestors and nation, while sin results in dishonor before man and God. There are similar phrases throughout the Old Testament. As in line 1733, there may also be a covert reference to God the Father. Manoa is not concerned with dishonor done to himself personally, which might be called selfish; he is concerned with dishonor to his family, his tribe, his nation, and above all to the God of Israel. Nor is he concerned with honor as mere external reputation, but rather with blasphemy to God and harm done

---

[12]Martz, pp. 123–24.

[13]Stein, *Heroic Knowledge* (Minneapolis: Univ. of Minnesota Press, 1957), pp. 152–53. Stein too calls Manoa's tone "thin and weak" and "distressingly overpersonal." It is certainly distressing, but rightly and curatively so.

to men as a result of an ill example. His indictment of Samson is accurate, it immediately results in a critical moment of self-realization and repentance on Samson's part, and thus it contributes essentially to Samson's spiritual regeneration. At this one point, at least, Manoa sees further into the situation than his greater son.

What has perhaps most troubled critics recently, however, is Manoa's attitude and his speeches toward the end of the play. He and the Chorus are criticized for being unable to understand Samson's death. They are thought to be too preoccupied with externals: washing the blood off Samson's body, having a funeral, building a monument.[14] One might equally well criticize Fortinbras for ordering Hamlet's body borne off the stage, or Lear with being concerned with a tight button. It this last scene we see Manoa acting as a man naturally and properly does in the face of tragedy and death: restoring order, organizing the necessary ritual observances, undertaking the traditional duties of a survivor (there is, of course, an irony in that he must do these things for Samson, and not Samson for him). He must also see to it that Samson's example and his sacrifice will not be forgotten, but will continue to benefit the nation.

> The weight of this sad time we must obey;
> Speak what we feel, not what we ought to say.
> (*Lear* V.iii.323-24)

Manoa, however, speaks and does both what is natural and what is proper: the two are not incompatible.

Manoa's proposal, in his last speech, to build a monument for the dead Samson has particularly troubled the critics, who think the idea too nationalistic, materialistic, or selfish. The proposal is even compared with Dalila's desire to perpetuate her fame. Surely, however, any such parallel, like that between the Satanic and divine trinities in *Paradise Lost,* is meant to contrast true fame with false, true heroism with false heroism. Dalila's dream is flawed in its very foundations, since it is built on wedlock treachery and the illusory strength of Philistia and Dagon. Manoa's dream is built on the solid foundation of Samson's true heroism, on Israel's place in providential history,

---

[14]Huntley, p. 143; Martz, pp. 131–33; Baruch, passim.

and on the God of Israel himself. Besides, there is the elementary distinction that Dalila wants fame for herself, Manoa for his son, not as a private person, but as a national hero and especially as an exemplar of God's purposes.

Since the matter of Samson's tomb has so often been misunderstood, it deserves close consideration. Wishing to bring Samson home to his tomb cannot be attributed to the initial ignorance of Manoa and the Chorus. It is one of the last decisions taken in the play, only fourteen lines from the conclusion, and on our interpretation of it rests our view of what effect the "great events" of Samson's tragedy have had on Manoa, the Chorus, the Jews, and even the reader. If a desire to build a commemorative tomb for Samson is a mistaken one, if as several critics have suggested it is a foolish attempt to institutionalize what should remain purely spiritual, then it indicates a basic inability to understand the meaning of Samson's sacrifice, and the whole ending of the play is neither tragic nor triumphant, but merely ironic and bitter. Samson's acts and his final great deed, in this case, have not shown us that "all is best"; they do not lead us through catharsis to a state of earned emotional peace and wisdom; instead, we are left at the end of the play with a group of characters who have missed the whole point, who in the words of a recent critic are nothing but "a contented, peaceful lot, well out of the active process that Milton always envisioned at the unalterable center of true Christian being."[15]

Before proceeding further, we should have the passage before us and examine it in more detail:

> Let us go find the body where it lies
> Sok't in his enemies blood, and from the stream
> With lavers pure and cleansing herbs wash off
> The clotted gore. I with what speed the while
> (*Gaza* is not in plight to say us nay)
> Will send for all my kindred, all my friends
> To fetch him hence and solemnly attend
> With silent obsequie and funeral train
> Home to his Fathers house: there will I build him
> A Monument, and plant it round with shade
> Of Laurel ever green, and branching Palm,

[15]Baruch, p. 338.

With all his Trophies hung, and Acts enroll'd
In copious Legend, or sweet Lyric Song.
Thither shall all the valiant youth resort,
And from his memory inflame thir breasts
To matchless valour, and adventures high.
(1725-40)

When Manoa proposes to bring his son "Home to his Fathers house," he is not putting in a selfish claim: he is following Jewish law and custom, doing all things in decent order. (He is unaware, of course, of any typological meaning.) So too with the washing off of the blood and the effects of violence. This is not simply concern with bodily matters at the expense of spirit. How else would Samson be prepared for burial? In the *Christian Doctrine*, Milton stresses the importance of "decent burial." Although any decent place may be chosen, Milton praises the decision of Jacob and Joseph "to be gathered unto the sepulchre of their fathers in the land of promise."[16] Milton might have added the promise which God made to Abraham in Genesis: "Thou shalt go to thy fathers in peace; thou shalt be buried in a good old age" (xv.15). In fact, a common synonym for dying in the Old Testament is that a man has been "gathered to his fathers."

Samson's last journey to his father's—or fathers'—house will be an ironic one, for Manoa had hoped to ransom him and bring him home in quite a different manner. That is a tragic irony; not cheap satiric irony at Manoa's expense. Manoa does not simply visualize the monument as an institutionalized means for spreading Samson's reputation. The example of his deeds will be perpetuated by means of monument, song, and poetry, but it will travel essentially from spirit to spirit and from heart to heart, as youths "inflame thir breasts" from Samson's memory. *Samson Agonistes* itself may be thought of as part of this living process, although, while Manoa cannot foresee it, the principal means of memorializing Samson's story will be the Bible itself.

Every year, while the youths of Israel come to emulate Samson, the maidens will bring flowers and mourn at his tomb. Milton writes in the *Christian Doctrine* that, while mourning must not be "immod-

[16]*Works*, XVII, 263.

erate," it is "the appropriate mark of respect paid to the memory of all who are not utterly worthless."[17] Manoa's speech concludes with a description of the mourning, lines which are among the most troubling in the play:

> The Virgins also shall on feastful days
> Visit his Tomb with flowers, only bewailing
> His lot unfortunate in nuptial choice,
> From whence captivity and loss of eyes.
>
> (1741-44)

Most critics have seen this as anticlimactic and puzzling—as, in my experience, do most readers coming to the play for the first time. Why mention loss of eyes and marriage troubles at this point? Greater events have pushed them into the background. Even before his complete spiritual recovery, Samson was able to dismiss his blindness as the least of his problems. These lines do have a function, however: with the reference to "clotted gore," they are among the few reminders toward the play's conclusion that Samson was human, and that he suffered. The *exodos* is almost entirely triumphant, and perhaps such a reminder of the events which preceded the triumph is necessary. More, the specific meaning of the lines, turning on the word "only," is that the only aspects of Samson's life and death that can really be mourned are these earlier difficulties. His death itself is not a cause for mourning; his worst crime of betraying God and exalting Dagon has been wiped out; therefore, the maidens can "only" bewail sufferings and sins that now appear relatively unimportant.

This is not to say that Samson's many sufferings were not real, or that his death itself is not tragic, but that—as in so many of the greatest tragedies as well as the Christian paradigm—in his death and in the total pattern of his life, in Manoa's words:

> Nothing is here for tears, nothing to wail
> Or knock the breast, no weakness, no contempt,
> Dispraise, or blame, nothing but well and fair,
> And what may quiet us in a death so noble.
>
> (1721-24)

---

[17] *Works*, XVII, 261–63.

We can dismiss, I think, the thought that Manoa is pleased with the manner of Samson's death because it reflects no dishonor on himself. Nor does his assertion mean that he feels no sorrow or loss at his son's death, or that he has forgotten Samson's tragic suffering. Far from it. What it means is that suffering, sorrow, and loss have been subsumed in an even greater triumph, not his own triumph but Samson's. The peace which Manoa speaks of is an earned peace, the calm after a storm, much like the peace and reconciliation which accompany the long-suffering Oedipus to his end, or which Shakespeare found at the close of his great tragedies, or portrayed at greater length in such plays as *The Winter's Tale*. It is also similar to the mood which closes *Lycidas* and *Paradise Lost*. Manoa's last words are no half-truths; they show no lack of sensibility; he is speaking of a greater peace, of a spiritual calm, which has recognized, lived with, come to terms with, and finally risen above suffering, sorrow, and death.

3

"On the introduction of the gospel, or new covenant through faith in Christ, the whole of the preceding covenant, in other words the entire Mosaic law, was abolished."[18] With Christ, Milton believed, began the covenant of the spirit, written "in the hearts of believers," and bringing eternal life to all who have faith. It was toward this new freedom and sonship that the Mosaic law was to lead mankind. Under the law, men were in bondage, and could merit only eventual death; but the benefits of Christ's sacrifice were extended back in time to such as Adam, Abraham, or Samson—all those who under the old dispensations had lived well according to their lights. In itself, however, the law could promise only life and prosperity in this world, not immortality.

Knowing how much Milton stressed the spirit—the paradise within the individual soul rather than the secular rule of the Church, faith and not works in themselves, not ceremonies but a devout heart—

[18]*Works,* XVI, 125. For the rest of the discussion, see the *Christian Doctrine* I.xxvi–xxviii and xxxiii (*Works,* XVI, 98–163, 336–81).

even those critics who do not consider *Samson* to be a Christian play have blamed Manoa and the Chorus for being insufficiently spiritual: for clinging to the works and ceremonies of the law in the face of the divine revelation through Samson. Several times in *Samson* it is made evident that God is not bound to his own law. He can permit Samson to marry a Philistine wife, in spite of the law forbidding marriages outside the nation of Israel. He can allow Samson to attend and take part in a pagan religious festival, though normally that would be a serious sin. Those who would tie God to his own laws, the Chorus realizes quite early in the play, are mistaken:

> As if they would confine th' interminable,
> And tie him to his own prescript,
> Who made our Laws to bind us, not himself,
> And hath full right to exempt
> Whom so it pleases him by choice
> From National obstriction, without taint
> Of sin, or legal debt;
> For with his own Laws he can best dispence.
>   (307-14)

It is one thing to say that God can dispense with his own laws, however, and quite another to say that men can ignore them. The Jews were freed from the laws with the coming of Christ. Until that time, they were obliged to obey them unless specifically exempted by God himself.

Thus, Milton makes it clear that Samson married the woman of Timna under divine guidance. When he married Dalila, however, no divine impulse is mentioned: Samson says only that "I thought it lawful from my former act" (231).[19] If Samson married Dalila without specific divine sanction, but only through his own effort to improve on God, then clearly he broke the law and behaved wrongly, and this action was responsible for beginning the train of events which led to his downfall. The terms of the Mosaic law are simple, as Milton analyzes them in the *Christian Doctrine:* they are intended for the Jews alone, and all the Jews are bound to them until the coming of

---

[19]See Arnold Stein, pp. 145–46. This is a likely interpretation, although it rests only on the turn of one phrase.

Christ; obedience to them will be awarded by a prosperous life; disobedience by death. If God determines to award eternal life to those living under the law, this is not part of the terms, but an unmerited and unexpected addition. No one but God himself can release the Jews from these conditions. Even Samson, though he is enabled to die triumphantly, and as Milton's readers would expect, to gain eternal life, must pay the penalty. He has broken the law, and so he must die — however much this justice is mitigated, in the manner and circumstances of his death, by mercy. The penalty for betraying his trust, under the Mosaic covenant, is immediate adversity and early death.

Although Manoa and the Chorus learn a lesson from the life and death of Samson, that lesson is not that they should abandon the law for the spirit. Such implications are only possible for Milton's presumedly Christian reader. What Manoa and the Chorus do learn — as far as it can be defined at all — is that God is all-powerful and just; that he cannot be successfully resisted by false gods or by human might; that his prophecies, however dark things seem, will be fulfilled; that he is above human understanding and above his own law; that although he is just, he is also merciful. From Samson they learn that faith and trust can conquer worldly probabilities, and that it can be better to die in the service of God than to leave it and live. They also learn something about vicarious sacrifice, although they cannot know what will be its fulfillment. The death of Samson must have a double meaning: to the reader, it imperfectly but clearly imitates Christ's sacrifice and suggests the insufficiency of the earlier covenant; to the survivors in the play, it is only a dim preparation for that event, which still lies in the future. The Chorus and Manoa are left, at the play's end, with a realization that the law is not absolute or final, or even entirely adequate: yet it must be obeyed, not for its own sake, but as a means of showing faith to its author.

The "new acquist" which the Chorus speaks of, the lesson they have learnt, is as much emotional as intellectual, an experience rather than dead knowledge. Religious wisdom, though it originate in precept or example, must be felt, tasted, and lived through, not merely known. Similarly, the lesson of tragedy is a lesson of doing and of power, of catharsis, as much as it is one of self-recognition or enlightenment.

In one sense, Manoa and the Chorus have learned nothing which they did not already know; in another, they are made new men by the power of Samson's example. They still follow the law, but they do so with a new faith and conviction in the author of that law, and not merely because they have been told that there are so many rules, precepts, and ceremonies to be followed. From the beginning they had thought, in theory, that the God of Israel was the one true God and that Dagon was a false idol, but they had much reason to doubt. In the end, they know by experience and renewed faith. When contrasted with the light and freedom of full revelation, the last condition of Manoa and the Chorus can still be called darkness and slavery. But they are no figures for contempt. Readers of the Bible knew that Samson's death failed within a few years to bring freedom to the Jews; that their history was to consist of one bondage after another, one apostasy after another. Nevertheless, his deed and others led finally upward to Christ's victory, and so the Old-Testament heroes proved triumphant in the long run after all, even in terms of human history.

It depends where one puts the stress; the implied outcome of *Samson Agonistes* is no more — and no less — pessimistic in historical terms than the conclusion of *Paradise Lost*. And in the light of eternity, Samson's sacrifice and the new faith of Manoa and the Chorus are primarily important in themselves, not in terms of their immediate success or failure. Not their failure, but the blindness of others, will set Israel back again for a time. But for themselves, Manoa and the Chorus have earned, and have been given by God and his Champion Samson, the right to return home in peace — dismissed from the tension of great events to face the day-to-day trials of life which still await them with a new wisdom and conviction, whatever the eventualities may bring.[20]

[20]In its close *Samson* follows the pattern of *Lycidas,* which descends from the beatific vision with its new acquist and sets narrator and reader back in nature, prepared to face other woods and fields "tomorrow." Similarly, the protagonists of *Paradise Lost* and *Paradise Regained* descend from the heights of spiritual crisis with new knowledge and experience with which to "enter" life.

4

The negative view of Manoa and the Chorus recently expressed by Milton's critics is not entirely new. Manoa especially has seldom been accorded much dignity. When the Chorus announces his approach, before he has actually entered, Samson exclaims:

> Ay me, another inward grief awak't,
> With mention of that name renews th' assault.
>   (330-31)

This has too often been interpreted to mean simply that Samson finds his father an irritation, and would rather not see him. Proceeding from this point, the rest of Manoa's behavior can be made to appear ludicrous and somewhat contemptible — if finally worth our patronizing pity. In part, this attitude arises because Manoa seems to play the rather thankless role of a Job's comforter — ultimately helpful to Job, perhaps, but foolish in his own right. Knowledge of Milton's respect for his own father might prepare us to doubt the likelihood of such an interpretation, however, and a close reading of the play must cause us to dismiss it. Samson's first words at his father's coming are not a contemptuous reference to Manoa's character, but rather the words of someone who feels guilty, and who hesitates to face a loved one whom he has, in effect, betrayed. Dalila is a thorn intestine to Samson, but her coming awakens no grief of this sort, only pain, anger, and resolve. Now, however, Samson is grieved, because he loves Manoa.

After Manoa has brought into the open for the first time in the play the nature of Samson's real sin and sorrow — betrayal of God and people — Samson reacts by immediately agreeing, and by according to Manoa the dignity of a father-confessor. Although Milton was not a believer in the sacrament of penance, or in any human rite of confession and absolution, he has Samson confess his deepest guilt to Manoa in an almost ritual manner, as one might to a priest. Thomas B. Stroup points out that this speech, in which Samson reveals how important he feels Manoa's opinion to be, begins like a *confiteor*: "Father, I do acknowledge and confess" (448).[21] In his confession Samson errone-

---

[21]Stroup, *Religious Rite and Ceremony in Milton's Poetry* (Lexington: Univ. of Kentucky Press, 1968), p. 58.

ously assumes that he can no longer be a part of the struggle, that "all the contest is now / 'Twixt God and *Dagon*" (461-62), a proposition which Manoa understandably but wrongly receives as a prophecy. Before Samson can be forgiven he must make his confession not just to Manoa, but, in spirit, to God. But it is through his relations with Manoa that Samson is enabled to discover within himself how to repent his real sins. This is revealed by the rest of his dialogue with Manoa. There is constant reference to confession, expiation, punishment, and absolution. Manoa begins by accepting the confession itself, realizing Samson's need for absolution and relief from emotional stress. "With cause this hope relieves thee, and these words / I as a Prophecy receive" (472-73). It is a prophecy ironically only half true, yet Manoa's response is not unwise. It especially reveals his empathic understanding. When Samson continues to speak of his crime and his passionate desire for expiation, Manoa's advice is unexceptionable:

> Be penitent and for thy fault contrite,
> But act not in thy own affliction, Son,
> Repent the sin, but if the punishment
> Thou canst avoid, self-preservation bids.
> (502-05)

The principles Manoa puts forward cannot be faulted. If he goes wrong, it is in applying the principle to the specific case. This was known as the art of casuistry, an art sufficiently difficult that even the name has fallen into disrepute.

Manoa cannot comfort his son or give him the absolution he so badly wants: not because he fails either in love or wisdom, but because only God can give Samson what he needs. Nevertheless, just as the mutual confessions and forgiveness between Adam and Eve in *Paradise Lost* are a vital step both religiously and psychologically toward their confession to God, so Samson's confession to Manoa, who can forgive him insofar as he has sinned against him personally, lays his guilt bare and thus proves a vital step toward his spiritual cure. His father cannot forgive Samson's crimes against God, for no man has this power, but he can help him realize clearly what his crime has been, what his present state is, and what may be his future hopes or limitations.

If Manoa helps Samson, it is not in the way he expects or intends. Can it be said that he helps him in spite of himself, like one of Job's comforters? The comparison has often occurred to Milton's critics. Certainly many useful parallels can be drawn between *Samson Agonistes* and the Book of Job: the suffering of the two central figures, their comparative immobility, the presence of comforters, their mis-understanding of the situation, the painful effect of their words on the heroes, and the final working out of the problem in a way quite contrary to what the comforters expected. Nevertheless, there are also major differences. The pain that Job's comforters cause him re-sults from groundless accusations, while many of the uncomfortable points raised by Manoa and the Chorus are perfectly true, and often spiritually helpful. Although the effect of the "comforting" is simi-larly painful, and in both works there is a reversal of intention, the basic character of the two groups of comforters is quite different. Job's companions are self-righteous and basically unsympathetic, while Samson's err only through being too human and even too hu-manly sympathetic.

Another biblical parallel may be suggested instead of the Book of Job, which throws a more revealing light on the character of Samson's friends. It involves a central heroic figure, who must like Samson suffer and go willingly to his death, but whose friends wrongly try to dissuade him from his duty because of their well-intentioned human love for him. I refer, of course, to Christ and his disciples.

Half-way through the Gospel of Matthew, Peter proclaims for the first time that Jesus is the Messiah: "Thou art the Christ, the Son of the living God" (xvi.16). Jesus honors him with the well-known words, "Thou art Peter, and upon this rock I will build my church." Jesus then proceeds to introduce his disciples to a new conception of the Messiah and his role, as one who will not enjoy worldly king-ship, but will suffer and die for his people:

> From that time forth began Jesus to show unto his disciples, how that he must go unto Jerusalem, and suffer many things of the elders and chief priests and scribes, and be killed, and be raised again the third day. Then Peter took him, and began to rebuke him, saying, Be it far from thee, Lord: this shall not be unto thee. But he turned, and said unto Peter, Get thee behind me, Satan:

thou art an offense unto me: for thou savorest not the things that
be of God, but those that be of men. Then said Jesus unto his
disciples, If any man will come after me, let him deny himself,
and take up his cross, and follow me. For whosoever will save
his life shall lose it: and whosoever will lose his life for my
sake shall find it.   (xvi.21-25)

The point is not that Peter is a bad or a weak man — indeed, he has
just been called the rock on which the Church is to be built — but that
even the best of men is insufficient *as a man*: "Thou savorest not the
things that be of God, but those that be of men."

In each of the gospels, Christ prophesies his own death before going up to Jerusalem; nevertheless, he must go. Toward the end of
Acts, St. Paul undergoes a similar experience, pointing up once
more the opposition between the divine and the human. Again the
other disciples act toward Paul as Peter acts toward Christ, and as
Manoa and the Danites in a similar situation act toward Samson:

As we tarried there [in Caesarea] many days, there came down
from Judaea a certain prophet, named Agabus. . . . He took Paul's
girdle, and bound his own hands and feet, and said, Thus saith
the Holy Ghost, So shall the Jews at Jerusalem bind the man that
owneth this girdle, and shall deliver him into the hands of the
Gentiles. And when we heard these things, . . . [we] besought
him not to go up to Jerusalem. Then Paul answered, What mean
ye to weep and to break mine heart? for I am ready not to be
bound only, but also to die at Jerusalem for the name of the Lord
Jesus. And when he would not be persuaded, we ceased, saying,
The will of the Lord be done.   (xxi.10-14)

When St. Peter attempts to dissuade Jesus from sacrificing himself,
he is motivated chiefly by human love, not by selfishness. His motives,
though limited, are good, and his advice must be refused only because it conflicts with a higher good which he does not yet understand. Similarly, the motives of Paul's friends are good, and have a
powerful effect on him, but they too must give way before the higher
principle that supersedes all lesser ones: the "will of the Lord."

When Manoa seeks to ransom Samson and to bring him home, he
is quite unconscious that his actions are an inadequate paradigm of
the ransom that will be brought about by Christ in the future, or that

Samson must, like Jesus and Paul, suffer and die. His intentions and his actions are good in themselves, proper to a loving and concerned father. They are negated only because God has another, irresistible purpose for his champion that neither Manoa nor anyone else in the play can anticipate. Manoa and the Chorus are not the secret enemies of Samson (as Job's comforters often appear to be), but his bewildered friends and followers. When Samson must leave them in the end, to go out and die alone, he has outdistanced them spiritually. Thus his death is something like Christ's, who for a while left his disciples behind and was deserted by them. Yet Manoa and the Chorus are no more weak and evil for their inability to follow Samson on his interior journey than are the apostles: they are good men, better than the average, faithful to their friend, but with human limitations that can be tempered or raised up only by God's intervention.

Samson is not Jesus, or even Paul, because he can do no more than foreshadow and typify the new dispensation. He can only partly understand the implications of his own self-sacrifice, although he makes it willingly and perhaps with a high degree of intuitive understanding. Manoa and the Danites are even less likely to comprehend at first the nature of his providential destiny. Even after Samson's death their understanding cannot be full: he has given them no more than a dark image. Nevertheless, as just and good men they are enabled to move a long way beyond the initial human insights with which they began the play—a starting-point only relatively limited, for they are never ignorant men. Manoa and the Danites are given an example of heroic self-sacrifice which, like Isaiah's Suffering Servant, anticipates the new Christian heroism. Even though the implications of Christ's death will go far beyond Samson's, nevertheless dying for one's friends, country, and God is an act that hardly requires a special Christian insight to admire it. Moreover, it is evident in the *exodos* that Manoa and the Chorus are given a sense of some intimate connection between this kind of death and God's providential plans for men. Their dim grasp of these realities, by emotion and reconfirmed faith, raises them at least for a time above themselves.

In nearly all of Milton's poems, human values are celebrated. Although in the later poems the purely human is put in its place, it is put high. Even in *Paradise Regained* the hopes and fears of the apostles and the love of Mary are given their due. In *Paradise Lost,* Milton insists that the human love of Adam and Eve must come after the love of God, but this should not be allowed to obscure the high value he puts on true human love and companionship in the poem. They are placed above everything else. The moving portrayal of love between Adam and Eve has affected many diverse critics, even though not all of them admit that Milton meant it to do so. In *Samson Agonistes* we are given not marital love, since Dalila has destroyed it, but filial-paternal love, and also friendship. Here too, however, divine love must come first. The fatherly love of Manoa and the faithful friendship of the Chorus must give way before God's purpose, to be augmented and transformed. Nevertheless, they are clearly good in themselves. Because they are genuine, they increase the poignancy of the drama when human values come into conflict with, and are finally raised and disciplined by, the divine. Adam and Eve, thinking to choose between love of God and love of each other, choose human love, and as a result lose both for a time. After failing once, Samson chooses divine love, and instead of losing his human ties, leaves them knit even more closely by death.

Manoa's fatherly offices, and the proffered friendship of the Chorus (180-86), gratefully accepted by Samson (187-93, 202), are never condemned anywhere in the play, though they must find higher expression. Samson's friends are not, like Job's comforters, condemned for their sentiments or sent away in disgrace; they are not, like Dalila, exposed as false friends or lovers; but they do resemble the disciples of Christ and the friends of Paul, in that their human affections, temporarily checked, find an ultimate, higher meaning in their friendship and love. In short, their last, illuminated condition is built on the foundations of an earlier misguided but human love, which is tried in the fire, refined, and purified.

When ultimate and human values conflict, Christianity has always insisted that the ultimate come first, but it has never denied the legitimacy of human feelings. Thus Paul is torn by his friends' good wishes, thus Jesus weeps over the forthcoming destruction of Jerusalem. A passage in St. John's Gospel was traditionally cited against the Stoic insistence that men must totally suppress their human feelings in the face of the eternal: that is, Jesus' reaction to the death of

Lazarus. Jesus comes to Lazarus' house in Bethany and is met by his sister Mary:

> When Jesus therefore saw her weeping, and the Jews also weeping which came with her, he groaned in the spirit, and was troubled, And said, Where have ye laid him? They said unto him, Lord, come and see. Jesus wept. Then said the Jews, behold how he loved him! (xi.33-36)

Although in the Judaeo-Christian view death must be accepted as the will of God, and indeed it is the "Gate of Life" (*Paradise Lost* XII.571), the example of Jesus permits and encourages human pity and grief—as also did custom among the Israelites in Samson's time.

Milton condemned the Stoic approach to suffering in *Paradise Regained* (IV.300-08) and in the *Christian Doctrine*.[22] Samson himself, like Job, is never stoical. Indeed, his lengthy complaints led one critic to suggest that he embodies not patience but impatience.[23] Samson goes to the festival of Dagon not merely resigned to death, but willing to suffer death for the sake of his God and his people. Earlier he had wished to die, but he gives up his life only when it is once more of value to him, because he has regained his purpose and his special relationship with God. Samson retains his human feelings to the last, and although he is caught up in "the fold, / Of dire necessity" (1665-66), he acts freely. His death is "necessary" only insofar as he chooses to do his duty, and because, choosing duty, he must die with the Philistines. Manoa too must be allowed his human emotions. Though they may in part be selfish at the beginning of the play, they are mainly good and admirable. At the end of the play they are more complex: a mixture of sorrow and gladness not unlike the close of *Paradise Lost*. But they are still human: human sorrow at his son's death, human gladness at his heroism and his vindication, and complex human acceptance of God's guidance of the day's events—exalted and resigned, joyful and sorrowful, weary but consoled. His passions have been refined by catharsis and religious experience, but they are

[22]*Works*, XVII, 253; see also Paul R. Baumgartner, "Milton and Patience," *Studies in Philology*, 40 (1963), 203–13.

[23]Mason Tung, "*Samson Impatiens:* A Reinterpretation of Milton's *Samson Agonistes*," *Texas Studies in Literature and Language*, 9 (1968), 475–92.

no simple ones because of that. Since they are the acquist of experience, they can best be understood by a reader who feels some of the same emotions, by sympathetically experiencing the action of the play which has produced them.

7

DALILA AND HARAPHA

In some respects, Samson's encounter with Dalila is the most accessible and humanly understandable in the play. Everyone knows the story of Samson and Delilah, and of the love and treachery between them. Goethe, on hearing Dalila's speeches read aloud to him by Crabb Robinson, is reported to have said: "See the great poet! he *putt* her in right!"[1] On the other hand, too much prior familiarity with the story might actually distort our understanding of Milton's version. One is unsure, as one is unsure with Milton's God or his Satan, how much can legitimately be brought in from outside the play. In practice, then, although the encounter with Dalila would seem to be straightforward enough, it has proven to be one of the play's most puzzling episodes. Critics have been unable to agree about her character, her motivations, or, as a result, the impact of the confrontation on the play as a whole. With characteristic and amusing

[1]Cited by J. B. Leishman, *Milton's Minor Poems* (London: Hutchinson, 1969), p. 228, from W. P. Ker, *The Art of Poetry* (1923).

perversity, William Empson has suggested that Dalila is actually the heroine of *Samson Agonistes,* like Satan in *Paradise Lost.* "A modern jury," he writes, "would at once regard Delilah as a deeply wronged wife."[2] Few other critics would go quite so far, nor is one sure just how serious Empson really is. But certainly many readers have been sympathetic to Dalila's plight, unable to understand or entirely to forgive Samson for finally rejecting her. Rejection is the right course for Samson and for his mission, it turns out, but is it fair to Dalila, the "wronged wife"? The arguments of the many critics and readers who question Samson's conduct toward Dalila are usefully summed up by Virginia Mollenkott:

> Samson's conduct is at least as reprehensible as Dalila's. . . . If Samson can justify the breaking of law by an appeal to private inspiration, so can Dalila. . . . Rationalization is treacherously easy. . . . Samson's name will be a stench no less than the stench of Dalila's name in Israel. Samson and the Chorus regard Dalila as "a manifest Serpent" and a "viper"; yet surely her final words are the face-saving device of a woman whose every advance has been scorned. She had eaten the bread of humiliation as surely as Eve ate it after the fall; but unlike Eve, she has met with total repudiation. On the natural level of the drama, she has much truth on her side; but on the supernatural level, inasmuch as by her allegiance to Dagon she has been one of those who "band them to resist" God's "uncontrollable intent," she is clearly wrong.[3]

That Samson does not break the law merely by "private inspiration"

[2] Empson, *Milton's God,* rev. ed. (London: Chatto & Windus, 1965), p. 211.

[3] Mollenkott, "Relativism in *Samson Agonistes," Studies in Philology,* 67 (1970), pp. 98, 99–100. On the Dalila episode, see also Empson; Arnold Stein, *Heroic Knowledge* (Minneapolis: Univ. of Minnesota Press, 1957); Charles Mitchell, "Dalila's Return: The Importance of Pardon," *College English,* 26 (1965), 614–20; Thomas Kranidas, "Dalila's Role in *Samson Agonistes," Studies in English Literature,* 6 (1966), 125–37; Allan H. Gilbert, "Milton on the Position of Women," *Modern Language Review,* 15 (1920), 240–64; Ralph Nash, "Chivalric Themes in *Samson Agonistes," Studies in Honor of John Wilcox,* ed. A. D. Wallace and W. D. Ross (Detroit: Wayne State Univ. Press, 1958).

will be argued in Chapter 9 below. Samson's inspiration is quite different from Dalila's (who indeed claims no inspiration, but invokes only the pressures put on her by the priests of Dagon), because it has an objective reality in the play. More important, however, is the separation of the action in *Samson Agonistes* into two levels, human and divine. Although two such levels are operative in the play, they cannot be thus easily separated from one another. One cannot, in Milton's eyes, be right in human terms and wrong in divine terms, for his God, though often inscrutable, is never irrational. There can be strong human pressures and temptations—as indeed there are in almost all of Milton's works—but there is always a right course, not only in absolute terms, but also in terms of present human happiness. When, for example, Adam chooses love for Eve over love of God in *Paradise Lost,* he not only reverses the priorities and betrays his creator, but he temporarily destroys the love between himself and Eve as well. When the divine love is rejected, their human love is also lost, changing first into lust, then into recrimination and hatred. Only by the renewal of divine love is their human love renewed. There is actually no choice in Milton's poems between right conduct and human happiness: the temptations are real enough, but their fruits prove illusory. So Adam and Eve learn to their sorrow; so Satan emblematically discovers, when in the moment of his triumph, he and his followers are forced to eat the bitter fruit for which they have traded obedience to God:

> greedily they pluck'd
> The Frutage fair to sight, like that which grew
> Neer that bituminous Lake where *Sodom* flam'd;
> This more delusive, not the touch, but taste
> Deceav'd; they fondly thinking to allay
> Thir appetite with gust, instead of Fruit
> Chewd bitter Ashes. . . .   (x.560-66)

The parallel between Milton's Dalila and his Eve is a natural one, which most readers immediately draw. Adam's first reaction to Eve's plea for forgiveness is very much like Samson's. But Adam receives Eve back, while Samson remains adamant to the end. There is, however, an obvious explanation for this difference: Eve is genuinely

penitent, while Dalila is not. It is not the seriousness of their crimes
that matters — for the consequences of Eve's act are far worse than
Dalila's, nor can she plead the excuse of natural concupiscence — but
the sincerity of their repentance afterward. Dalila points out, quite
rightly, that Samson has been as guilty in the past as she has been:

> E're I to thee, thou to thy self wast cruel.
> Let weakness then with weakness come to parl
> So near related, or the same of kind,
> Thine forgive mine. . . .   (784-87)

There is, in fact, little doubt that Milton would have considered
Samson's sin much more serious than Dalila's: because he is a man
whose intellect should be stronger, because like Adam he falls knowing that he is wrong, and because he has, but abuses, the special
guidance of God. Samson admits his guilt, but he will condone
neither his own crime nor Dalila's:

> I led the way; bitter reproach, but true,
> I to my self was false e're thou to me,
> Such pardon therefore as I give my folly,
> Take to thy wicked deed. . . .   (823-26)

It must be particularly noted that Dalila seeks "forgiveness" in a
special sense — she wants Samson to admit that her deed — like his —
was *understandable,* "well meaning" (813), not to be repented but
simply glossed over and forgotten. But that is not what Milton
understood forgiveness to mean. True forgiveness must first be
preceded by repentance. In the *Christian Doctrine,* Milton takes as
the thesis of one of his chapters the following statement: "Repentance
. . . is the gift of God, whereby the regenerate man perceiving with
sorrow that he has offended God by sin, detests and avoids it, humbly
turning to God through a sense of the divine mercy, and heartily
striving to follow righteousness." In particularizing on this statement, Milton makes several observations that are pertinent to Dalila:

> We may distinguish certain progressive steps in repentance;
> namely, conviction of sin, contrition, confession, departure from
> evil, conversion to good. . . . Confession of sin is made some-
> times to God . . . Sometimes to men. . . . Repentance is either

general, which is also called conversion, when a man is converted from a state of sin to a state of grace; or particular, when one who is already converted repents of some individual sin.[4]

From these last observations, it will be evident that Dalila has both general sinfulness and a particular sin to repent, and that she should, going through the various stages, repent of them both to God and to Samson.

Dalila's recognition of the absolute importance of repentance in gaining forgiveness is evidenced by her first words to Samson:

> With doubtful feet and wavering resolution
> I came, still dreading thy displeasure, *Samson,*
> Which to have merited, without excuse,
> I cannot but acknowledge; yet if tears
> May expiate (though the fact more evil drew
> In the perverse event then I foresaw)
> My penance hath not slack'n'd, though my pardon
> No way assur'd. (732-39)

At first Dalila seems to show all the signs of true repentance, but as it turns out, this is not the case. She is sorry (perhaps), if we take her tears to be genuine: but sorry to lose Samson, not sorry for her sins against him or against God. Her entire argument is an attempt to palliate her sins: "it was a weakness / In me, but incident to all our sex" (773-74); it was well-meaning love that motivated her (813); it was duty, religion, and "public good" that prevailed over her (850-69). These are like the shifts that Adam and Eve resort to shortly after their fall, each attempting to lay the blame on the other, or on God, or on their natures—on anything but themselves. Dalila puts the blame on Samson, on her weakness as a woman, on the Philistine magistrates and priests, but never for a moment on herself. Instead, in the last parts of her argument, she simply drops the question of guilt altogether. Samson too has earlier tried to shift his guilt onto others—onto God or the Jews. It is only too natural a reaction. But even from the beginning Samson undergoes spiritual growth and change, a process of gradually accepting and repenting his own culpability. From the first he dimly realizes, "Whom have I

[4]*Works,* XV, 379, 385. The first quotation is reduced from small capitals.

to complain of but my self?" (46). Thus Samson, like Adam and Eve
in *Paradise Lost,* undergoes the process of conversion, regeneration,
and repentance. Dalila, however, takes quite a contrary course.

The first necessity for repentance, "perceiving with sorrow that he
has offended God by sin," or "conviction of sin," is absent. Although
Dalila admits that the consequences of her act have been unfortunate
(and, she claims, unforeseen), she is not interested in the question
of guilt. Nor is she conscious that she has "offended God." By marrying Samson, as he points out, Dalila has made his nation hers. Unlike
the other Philistines, she falls under the jurisdiction of the Mosaic
law. Her God is the God of Israel. But Dalila is conscious of no
offense to God. She argues that her deed was pleasing to Dagon:

> the Priest
> Was not behind, but ever at my ear,
> Preaching how meritorious with the gods
> It would be to ensnare an irreligious
> Dishonourer of *Dagon.* . . .   (857-61)

She speaks as if she had been fooled and seduced by Dagon's priests,
but when this argument has been refuted and her pleas rejected, she
actually concludes by glorying in her deed and her service to Dagon,
boasting of the "piety" (993) for which she will be famous in Philistia.
Nowhere does she offer to join Samson's nation or to turn to the God
of Israel and ask forgiveness. Instead, she wants to bring him back
with her into spiritual captivity. Thus there is no evidence whatever
that she is "heartily striving to follow righteousness," the final re-
quirement for repentance. She need no longer repeat her old crime,
for Samson is now blinded for good, and apparently vanquished for
good. But she wants to prolong the results of her crime, to enjoy
the fruits of it, to bring Samson home to her, a prisoner of love, in
tacit submission to the Philistine lords, whose permission is needed
(920) — where he will become, if not a Philistine himself, no longer a
true Israelite or a follower of the true God. Repentance and resigna-
tion, when they are genuine, require a total reorientation and a
change of heart. But Dalila, unlike Samson, or unlike Eve, is just the
same as she was before her betrayal and his fall: nor does she show
the slightest desire to repent or reform.

2

Dalila has done nothing, and said nothing, to merit Samson's forgiveness. Is she then to be understood as totally evil, acting out of conscious malice like Satan in *Paradise Lost?* Thomas Kranidas has shown that, like Satan, Dalila uses on Samson all the devices of rhetoric and persuasion.[5] He clearly demonstrates that she is more than the innocent, wronged wife that Empson makes her out to be. Most critics have commented on the great cleverness and persuasiveness of her arguments, the care with which she mounts first one kind of attack, then, when that fails, another. Like Milton's other great tempters, Comus and Satan, Dalila is as convincing as she well can be, and employs every possible device to make her pleas attractive. But as critics have recently shown, especially in connection with *Paradise Lost,* persuasive rhetoric is for Milton a suspect tool.[6] Direct plainness, the word for the thing, the "pure milk of the word"—these are the qualities he associates with goodness and innocence. God the Father and his Son, the innocent Adam and Eve, use some of the parts of rhetoric: schemes, rhythm, verbal patterning and formal elaboration. But they avoid the devices of emotional persuasion, or of letting a word's meaning slide from one significance to another. None of the characters speak plainly at all times in *Samson Agonistes,* for they are in a fallen and imperfect world. Samson's language, especially toward the end of the play, is the most complex and ironic of them all; but it is Dalila who makes special use of rhetoric for persuasive purposes, unremittingly except in her final outburst, thus revealing herself for what she is. Dalila's role, of course, is a traditional one. She may be compared with Homer's Circe, Tasso's Armida, or Spenser's Acrasia, or perhaps with Virgil's Dido—not to speak of a long tradition of earlier Delilahs. Or one can also compare her with the fallen Eve; and that parallel, already instructive in the matter of repentance, reveals still more about her.

Some Milton critics have been sympathetic to Eve, mainly by

[5] Kranidas, "Dalila's Role in *Samson Agonistes."*

[6] See Stanley Fish, *Surprised by Sin* (London: Macmillan, 1967), and Anne Ferry, *Milton and the Miltonic Dryden* (Cambridge: Harvard Univ. Press, 1968).

glossing over her actions between her fall and Adam's. Others have pointed out that she acts very badly. While protesting that she is willing to die for Adam because she loves him so much, what she actually wants is for him to die with her. This, technically, is murder. When she tells him she has missed him during her absence and thought of him constantly, the reader knows that her words simply are not true. During most of the time after the serpent's appearance she has forgotten Adam entirely. But, as I have suggested in Chapter 2, it seems unlikely that Eve is deliberately lying. Instead, she is a victim of self-delusion, in particular of the self-delusion which often accompanies fallen human love. Although Eve plays the serpent's part with Adam, she is not, like Satan, a deliberate destroyer. Her rhetoric is less the product of evil intention than of her own captivity to sin, her strong feelings, mixed intentions, and confused illusions. Satan is the father of evil, but "Man falls deceiv'd" (III.130).

Just so, one can argue that Dalila may have acted partly out of malice, partly because she is pressured by the Philistine leaders and priests, partly for gold, partly out of desire for fame, but that she is also a victim of her own sinful confusion and what she calls "love." This is not to excuse her, since unlike Eve she does not repent, and Milton deeply believed that all men receive sufficient grace from God to repent if they choose to. But it does explain not only the sympathy we feel for Dalila, but also her own somewhat obscure motives. As Virginia Mollenkott points out, Dalila's motives in coming to visit Samson have puzzled a succession of critics, and none of their suggestions persuasively explain more than in part just what it is that she is after:

> What good is in it for Dalila? If her object were to break her husband, he is already broken; if her object were to jeer, why didn't she jeer? She is beautiful and is free to remarry; why should she seek to spend the rest of her life playing nursemaid to a blind giant? If she merely wants to demonstrate her power over her husband, as Samson says, why doesn't she move on to new conquests instead of bearing repeated rebuffs from a man who is already ruined?[7]

[7] Mollenkott, "Relativism in *Samson Agonistes,*" p. 94.

One must point out that if Samson is ruined, Dalila played a major part; but that bears only on Samson's motivations in the confrontation, not Dalila's. The argument, as far as Dalila's motivations are concerned, is persuasive. One may, therefore, agree in part with Mollenkott's conclusion: "Unless we are willing to accept Dalila's reason for coming to Samson, we are forced to assume with certain critics that the whole episode is doubtfully motivated and dramatically weak."[8]

Dalila's basic reason for coming may be quite simple: she thinks she has acted, and is acting, out of love. There is no need entirely to disbelieve her. This may be precisely what she thinks, this has been and is her intention. At the same time, however, the "love" of which she speaks is poles apart from the mutual married love and companionship that Milton describes in the divorce tracts and movingly portrays in *Paradise Lost,* and — one presumes — quite different from what most readers would want in their spouses, whether husband or wife. Milton's ideal of love is portrayed in Adam and Eve, both before Eve's fall and later when they go out into Eden hand in hand, promising to be faithful to each other and to help each other through future tribulations. This is the love of Milton's paean: "Haile wedded Love, mysterious Law . . . Founded in Reason, Loyal, Just, and Pure" (IV.750, 755). It is not Dalila's love, either in the past or in the present. Her kind of love is often indistinguishable from jealousy or hatred, nor is it incompatible with treachery or malice.

Dalila's first speech reveals her primary reason for visiting Samson:

> conjugal affection
> Prevailing over fear, and timerous doubt
> Hath led me on desirous to behold
> Once more thy face, and know of thy estate.
> (739-42)

Samson reacts violently: "Out, out *Hyæna;* these are thy wonted arts, / And arts of every woman false like thee" (748-49). He does not accuse all women of falsehood, only Dalila and those who are like

8Mollenkott, p. 95.

her. He then describes Dalila's technique: transgression, repentance; transgression, repentance; until the husband is "drawn to wear out miserable days" (762). He realizes now, however, that Dalila's repentence is false. It is nothing but "feign'd remorse" (752); she is "not truly penitent" (754); she is merely probing and trying her husband, in order to find his weaknesses.

In her second speech, Dalila appeals once more to love. Her elaborate and involuted argument now reveals just what it is that love means to her. It is necessary to quote her words in full; they should be read closely:

> And what if Love, which thou interpret'st hate,
> The jealousie of Love, powerful of sway
> In human hearts, nor less in mine towards thee,
> Caus'd what I did? I saw thee mutable
> Of fancy, feard lest one day thou wouldst leave me
> As her at *Timna,* sought by all means therefore
> How to endear, and hold thee to me firmest:
> No better way I saw then by importuning
> To learn thy secrets, get into my power
> Thy key of strength and safety: thou wilt say,
> Why then reveal'd? I was assur'd by those
> Who tempted me, that nothing was design'd
> Against thee but safe custody, and hold:
> That made for me, I knew that liberty
> Would draw thee forth to perilous enterprises,
> While I at home sate full of cares and fears
> Wailing thy absence in my widow'd bed;
> Here I should still enjoy thee day and night
> Mine and Loves prisoner, not the *Philistines,*
> Whole to my self, unhazarded abroad,
> Fearless at home of partners in my love.
> These reasons in Loves law have past for good,
> Though fond and reasonless to some perhaps;
> And Love hath oft, well meaning, wrought much wo,
> Yet always pity or pardon hath obtain'd.   (790-814)

What Samson calls hate, Dalila begins, is actually love, or rather the "jealousy of Love" (the terms are interchangeable). Dalila "saw" —

that is, imagined — that Samson was "mutable / Of fancy" because he once married the woman of Timna and then left her. In fact, Samson was faithful to the woman of Timna until she betrayed him. From this false beginning, Dalila's jealousy or love leads her to fear that Samson will leave her. She desires somehow to endear herself to him, which becomes transmuted to "hold thee to me firmest"; and from holding in love she imperceptibly moves into holding by force, imprisoning: "To learn thy secrets, get into my power / Thy key of strength and safety." At first she thinks of using the secret to blackmail him into remaining captive to her love, then she reveals it to the Philistines so they can keep Samson in "safe custody, and hold." Thus she will be assured that her lover will not escape. Thus he will no longer enjoy liberty, to go out on dangerous adventures, while she wails his absence in her "widow'd bed." Finally, all that she has done has been done in order to make Samson "Loves prisoner." Even if one believes everything that Dalila says here, this is still a devastating revelation of character.

The closest parallel to this kind of "love" in Milton's verse — jealous, selfish, possessive, destructive — is displayed by Satan when he peers out from behind the bushes in Paradise and sees Adam and Eve embracing:

> O Hell! what doe mine eyes with grief behold,
> Into our room of bliss thus high advanc't [?]
>
> .   .   .   .
>
> League with you I seek,
> And mutual amitie so streight, so close,
> That I with you must dwell, or you with me
> Henceforth. . . .   (IV.358-59, 375-78)

Satan's proffered embrace, "so streight, so close," is menacing and claustrophobic: his is a jealous and possessive love-hate just like Dalila's. He too wishes to bring man home with him, to clasp him close, never to let him go. And the home to which he hopes to bring mankind is hell, which as he ironically notes, is not as pleasant a dwelling place as Paradise.

This kind of imprisoning love has a long tradition behind it. It is the love of Circe, Dido, Alcina, Armida, and Acrasia, a love that prevents the hero from going on his journey or crusade, turns him aside from duty, and binds him in fetters of soft arms or flowers.[9] Samson has already recognized that his relationship with Dalila was a worse imprisonment than the Philistines' mill (414-19), and the meeting with Dalila ends by his even more explicit statement of the same theme:

> How wouldst thou use me now, blind, and thereby
> Deceiveable, in most things as a child
> Helpless, thence easily contemn'd, and scorn'd,
> And last neglected? How wouldst thou insult
> When I must live uxorious to thy will
> In perfet thraldom, how again betray me,
> Bearing my words and doings to the Lords
> To gloss upon, and censuring, frown or smile?
> This Gaol I count the house of Liberty
> To thine whose doors my feet shall never enter.
>
> (941-50)

Such is the love of Dalila: jealous, possessive, destructive, nor does she yet repent of it. She sees nothing basically wrong with her previous behavior; in fact, her revelation of character is wholly unintended, since her appeal to love, and her description of her own love, are meant to be persuasive. Her love, she concludes, whatever may have come of it in the past, is "well meaning," and so it deserves "pity or pardon" from the hardest heart. Dalila's motto might well be "Amor vincit omnia."

Samson, for these reasons, is thoroughly justified when he replies to Dalila's specious and misguided plea of love:

> But Love constrain'd thee; call it furious rage
> To satisfie thy lust: Love seeks to have Love;
> My love how couldst thou hope, who tookst the way
> To raise in me inexpiable hate,
> Knowing, as needs I must, by thee betray'd?
> In vain thou striv'st to cover shame with shame,
> Or by evasions thy crime uncoverst more.
>
> (836-42)

---

[9] See Ralph Nash, "Chivalric Themes in *Samson Agonistes*."

Dalila is not repenting but evading, yet her evasions do nothing but reveal her for what she is. If Samson does Dalila any injustice, it is in not realizing how much she has become the prisoner of her own love and lust, and how much evil makes a victim of itself as well as of others. But Samson is hardly to be blamed for not making such subtle distinctions. As most critics have argued, he feels strongly drawn toward Dalila at the same time that he resists and rebukes her; old habits die hard and still must be overcome. His arguments, and his new understanding, result in part from her own present self-revelations. Her attractiveness is the temptation by which he previously fell; it is only just within his strength to resist her now. Probably the critics are right when they suggest that his savage reaction to her last effort at persuasion, the plea to touch his hand, is at least partly motivated by his fear of giving in after all.

Samson's last words to Dalila are bitter and satirical, showing, as Dalila says, that he is "implacable, more deaf / To prayers, then winds and seas" (960-61):

> At distance I forgive thee, go with that;
> Bewail thy falshood, and the pious works
> It hath brought forth to make thee memorable
> Among illustrious women, faithful wives:
> Cherish thy hast'n'd widowhood with the gold
> Of Matrimonial treason: so farewel.   (954-59)

Although the words are bitter, they are the only response Samson can make to a Dalila who refuses to repent or change. Her only hope, in fact, is to bewail her falsehood, finally to realize what she has done and what she is, and then to repent. If Samson's words seem cruel, they are also salutary, since only such biting words are likely to pierce her defenses. Satire and "grim laughter," "indignation and scorne," Milton writes in the *Animadversions,* "hath oft-times a strong and sinewy force in teaching and confuting." And in the *Apology for Smectymnuus* he writes: "And I would ask, to what end *Eliah* mockt the false Prophets? was it to shew his wit, or to fulfill his humour? doubtlesse we cannot imagine that great servant of God had any other end in all which he there did, but to teach and instruct the

poore misledde people."[10] Thus it can well be argued that just as
Dalila proves a "good temptation" to Samson, strengthening him by
his resistance to her, so Samson's rejection is a necessary trial for
Dalila. To accept her back would only be to re-establish their old
relationship and to confirm her in her ways. There is no hint in the
play whether or not Dalila will ever repent, but Samson's final words
refer to the future, when if ever her heart may change. His words
carry a sting along with their admonition to think over what she has
done—and that, if anything can help, is what is needed to pierce
through the armor of her self-enclosing spiritual blindness. "Chastisement is often the instrumental cause of repentance."[11]

Lust, the word which Samson uses in summing up Dalila's behavior, is not entirely adequate to describe her passion. There are
flashes of lust here and there in her speeches, no doubt, but what
she feels is better described as romantic love mixed with lust. Lust
by itself ranges "among the bestial herds" (*Paradise Lost* IV.754), and
is indifferent how it is satisfied or by whom; love, pure or sinful, is
fastened to a single object. It becomes not indiscriminate, but
obsessive. Dalila's passion, then, does not consist merely of physical
attraction, although that is plainly strong: it is also a deep spiritual
perversion. It is a love that is not life-giving but death-dealing, that
wishes not the good of its object, but its own satisfaction. So it easily
becomes jealousy or, to all appearances, hatred. It binds close not in
mutual amity and support, but in guilty imprisonment. It is, in short,
the familiar state so commonly described in western literature.
Yet there is still another complexity to Milton's portrayal of Dalila:
one is never quite sure just how much she is telling the truth, or
where she is lying; how much she is the conscious temptress and how
much the victim of her own passions. Perhaps she is inventing her
love, as she invents other excuses. If so, then the kind of love she
chooses to invent and describe still is a revelation of character. One
may assume that her triumphant exit is also a revelation of character, that the desire for fame and dominance which it reveals, and

---

[10] *Works,* III, 107, 317. Italics removed.

[11] *Christian Doctrine; Works,* XV, 387.

her sense of triumph over Samson and his God and people, are
genuine too, perhaps the last word on her character — revealing, as
the Chorus says, the sting in the scorpion's tail. Yet these last
revelations still need not be incompatible with the kind of love she
has earlier spoken about. Indeed, her last words can be read as a
twisted and frustrated cry of love, turned inevitably into hatred and
destructiveness. Dalila quite properly remains inscrutable. It is
precisely this ambiguity that gives her so much force as a character
in the play. There should be no doubt that her actions, past and
present, and all that she stands for, must be rejected: by Samson, by
the reader, and if she is ever to be saved, by Dalila herself. Nevertheless, she remains a woman, with a human subtlety that still
draws our sympathy and baffles certainty — not about her crime, but
about the nature of her character and motivations.

3

Harapha is Milton's own creation. His name, in Hebrew, means
simply "the giant," and that is his nature and lineage. He belongs to
a famous Old-Testament family of giants:

> I am of *Gath*
> Men call me *Harapha,* of stock renown'd
> As *Og* or *Anak* and the *Emims* old
> That *Kiriathaim* held, thou knowst me now
> If thou at all art known.   (1078-82)

Harapha's son is the better-known giant and Philistine champion
Goliath, who fell at the hand of the shepherd David.[12] Harapha is a
boaster, who takes particular pride in his family and position, in his
chivalric honor, his weapons, his martial prowess, and the fame
and glory he has won on the battlefield. Because of his frequent
boasts, one can say that his portrait owes something to the traditional *miles gloriosus* or boasting soldier of Roman comedy. In

---

[12] See John M. Steadman, *Milton's Epic Characters* (Chapel Hill: Univ. of
North Carolina Press, 1968), pp. 185–93.

some respects, he also resembles the cowardly, mock-chivalric braggart, a stock character in a number of Renaissance comedies, who constantly boasts of his great deeds and his delicate honor, but if he is challenged to a battle or duel can always find some "honorable" excuse for avoiding it.[13] More particularly, Harapha's argument that he cannot fight with Samson because they are not social equals — he being a noble soldier and Samson a blind slave and traitor — resembles the excuse for avoiding combat of many a Renaissance comic braggart.

Harapha is undeniably a partly comic figure, whose bragging and high consciousness of his own worth are comically humbled, both by Samson's arguments and by his refusal of single combat. Harapha leaves the stage shamed and dishonored, reduced to little more than a figure for ridicule and scorn, all the more laughable because of his size and pretentions. On the other hand, although Harapha acts a comic part, he is nevertheless the Philistine champion. His objections to fighting with Samson were commonly accepted and no mere excuses, since a slave could hardly expect to fight with a free man on an equal basis. Boasting has characterized a number of genuine heroes as well as cowards, from the Greeks to the Anglo-Saxons. Milton had small use for the conventional hero, of course, which is a key point. Although Samson makes Harapha into a figure of fun, he is not normally either a coward or a clown. He leaves a coward, but he does not enter as one. He is genuinely the Philistine champion, and in the past he has been a man of deeds as well as words.

In the preface to *Samson,* Milton makes it very plain that he dislikes the Elizabethan playwrights' practice of mingling comic scenes with serious in their tragedies. According to Milton, many people hold tragedy itself in contempt on account of this practice, and so he feels the necessity to

> vindicate Tragedy from the small esteem, or rather infamy, which in the account of many it undergoes at this day with other common Interludes; hap'ning through the Poets error of intermixing Comic stuff with Tragic sadness and gravity; or

[13] Daniel C. Boughner, "Milton's Harapha and Renaissance Comedy," *ELH,* 11 (1944), 297–306.

introducing trivial and vulgar persons, which by all judicious
hath bin counted absurd; and brought in without discretion,
corruptly to gratifie the people.

It is unlikely that Milton would have changed his mind, between
writing the play and writing the preface, on so substantial a point.
He could not have intended Harapha merely to be a "trivial and
vulgar" person, nor can he have meant Harapha's interview with
Samson to a predominantly comic interlude, in a play whose prevailing tone is grave and serious, and which he himself calls tragic.
That does not mean, however, that there is no room for comedy of
any kind in a Miltonic tragedy. One must distinguish between one
kind of comedy and another.

Milton's idea of decorum, or of what can properly be admitted
into a poem and what must be kept out, was extremely broad.[14] Not
for him the narrow restrictiveness of such contemporary critics as
Thomas Rymer. It has already been seen that heroic seriousness in
Samson is wide enough to include a number of elements normally
thought trivial or disreputable.[15] If the actual practice of Milton's
poetry is allowed to speak for him and amplify the preface, then it is
evident that he did not hesitate to admit *certain kinds* of comedy into
his serious heroic poems. *Paradise Lost,* although its tone and theme
are predominantly tragic, offers examples of several kinds of comedy:
innocent pleasure, the elephant writhing his lithe proboscis, or God
joking with Adam about his need of a mate; grim satire, mostly at
the expense of Satan; and divine comedy, the vision of an ultimately
happy ending.

Each of these kinds of comedy has its proper place in the poem.
There is no room for innocent pleasure in Hell, or in Paradise after
the fall. As for satire in *Paradise Lost,* it is always at the expense of
pretension or pride. It is directed at man's efforts to scale the heavens
by building a tower, or at Satan's vain boasts of equality with an
omnipotent God. Attacking pride, of course, is the traditional
function and very *raison d'être* of satire. Its fundamental cruelty is
only justifiable when someone deserves it by affectations that demand

[14] See Thomas Kranidas, *The Fierce Equation* (The Hague: Mouton, 1965).
[15] See Chapter 3.

to be punctured, and perhaps corrected. As the Augustan poets constantly remind us, its legitimate target is vanity. This, presumably, is why Milton allows Samson his last grim jibe at Dalila, and why Samson can satirize Harapha's pretentions throughout much of his visit. From the first moment, Harapha reveals an arrogance that demands a fall, and so he gets one.

The comedy in *Samson Agonistes* is limited to varieties of satire, more or less bitter depending on the circumstances. It falls within the boundaries demanded by Milton's preface because it is a comedy whose purpose is essentially serious, because it is one with the play's action and spirit rather than digressive comic relief, and because Harapha its main embodiment and butt is no "trivial and vulgar" person but the champion of Philistia and a worthy antagonist to Samson. The satire in the play is directed solely at pride and self-excusing moral aberration, and its function is to act as a kind of spiritual or emotional medicine. In the preface, Milton speaks of purging other emotions or excesses beyond Aristotle's pity and fear, in order to "temper and reduce them to just measure." These emotions are purged by means of the skillful application of their like, as in homeopathic medicine. "For so in Physic things of melancholic hue and quality are us'd against melancholy, sowr against sowr, salt to remove salt humours." In this remark, Milton appears to blend together the theories of Galen and Paracelsus, who thought respectively that man's constitution is made up of the traditional four humors, or else of three elements, sulphur, mercury, and salt. It should be noted that Milton speaks only of three remedies used by the physician, and not necessarily by the playwright. Yet Milton's prose writings show that he thought of satire or mockery as a valuable means for curing self-centered sins. One might speculate — and receive support from the actual practice in the play — that while pity and fear are being purged and set in right order by the main tragic events, pride and such salt or sour humors are at times and in part corrected by the use of satire and comic irony. This irony, which Samson turns against Dalila and Harapha (though as noted in Chapter 5, sparingly, and not before attempting more direct communication), he also turns against himself, thus helping to purge as it were by means of salt or sour his former prideful and ridiculous behavior.

One example is his half-bitter, half-comic recapitulation of his fall
to Dalila's blandishments:

> Full of divine instinct, after some proof
> Of acts indeed heroic, far beyond
> The sons of *Anac,* famous now and blaz'd,
> Fearless of danger, like a petty God
> I walk'd about admir'd of all and dreaded
> On hostile ground, none daring my affront.
> Then swoll'n with pride into the snare I fell
> Of fair fallacious looks, venereal trains,
> Softn'd with pleasure and voluptuous life;
> At length to lay my head and hallow'd pledge
> Of all my strength in the lascivious lap
> Of a deceitful Concubine who shore me
> Like a tame Weather, all my precious fleece,
> Then turn'd me out ridiculous, despoil'd,
> Shav'n, and disarm'd among my enemies.
>
> (526-40)

It would be very difficult to say whether the vision here given expression should more properly be termed comic or tragic. The satire
that Samson turns against Dalila and Harapha is no more bitter or
powerful than what he turns against himself. In his own case, it helps
work his cure. Whether it will have that effect on them is in their
hands.

Samson's description of himself, walking about swollen with
pride or *hybris* like a petty god, thinking himself greater than the
giant sons of Anak (among them Harapha), comes very close to the
behavior of Harapha at their meeting. In fact, it is clear that by introducing the giant into the play, Milton provided Samson with a
parallel, a parodic double. By attacking the state of mind and the
moral errors that are embodied in Harapha, Samson is helped to
purge the same faults from his own spiritual system. Both men are
champions of their people; both are physically impressive and
immensely strong; both have done many great and warlike deeds.
Although we spontaneously dislike Harapha's boasting, there is no
question that behind his boasts lie many substantial acts. In the old
days, Samson boasted just as loudly. Harapha represents strength

without wisdom or judgment. Because his strength is without real moral control, it has become vain and destructive. So too with the former Samson. The Chorus says that Samson's "strength, while vertue was her mate" (173) might have subdued the entire earth and crowned him with highest praises. Without virtue or moral judgment, however, his strength became his "bane" (63), and his trust in it helped lead to his fall.[16] Like Harapha, Samson was more concerned with honor and reputation than with the substance or the purpose of his deeds, and like Harapha he was governed by his pride. Having fallen, and beginning to understand the reasons for his fall, Samson can turn bitter humor on himself, at first exacerbating his own pain and suffering, but then finally helping to cure them at their root or prime cause: sinful pride.

Harapha and Samson were never absolutely alike, of course, even before Samson's fall. Samson's strength was a divine gift, while Harapha's is the natural product of his giant stature. Samson was a champion of the chosen people and of the true God, while Harapha represents the brute force of the tyrannical Philistines and their false god Dagon. But by falling into the false belief that his strength was his own, Samson began to undermine it at its very source. Although he began life as a chosen champion of God, he came closer and closer to turning into a mere Harapha, until only the agony of his fall could save him and set him back on the right course. Harapha, then, represents what Samson nearly became, and would have become if he had not had God's chastening help: strong, famous, the greatest warrior of his people, but empty of purpose at the core. Samson forces Harapha to reveal this emptiness during their confrontation. We can well believe that the experience is a totally new one for the giant. Man to man, boasting hero against boasting hero, he would be a formidable opponent indeed; but he is no match for Samson's new, hard-won spiritual strength and wisdom, or for the divine energies that are beginning to manifest themselves in the Hebrew champion.

---

[16] For a broad discussion of this topos, see A. B. Chambers, "Wisdom and Fortitude in *Samson Agonistes*," *PMLA*, 78 (1963).

8

SAMSON: FURTHER OBSERVATIONS

It is difficult to discuss any aspect of *Samson Agonistes* without speaking about Samson, nor can his character be understood apart from the action, the ultimate tragic and religious nature of the drama, its political, autobiographical, or typological significances, or even the nature of the other characters. As the last chapters have shown, one cannot discuss Dalila, Harapha, Manoa, or the Chorus without comparing them with Samson or discussing their relationship with him, and in the process Samson too is delineated. The whole book must be taken as an approach to Samson's character, then — and a partial one at that. A few things remain to be said, however, among them the obvious yet important fact that Samson is at the same time Milton's most human hero and also a specially elected champion of God who may (after somewhat qualifying the term) be called a saint. He is the center of a play which is both a tragedy and a religious drama, or even a saint's legend: facts which are reflected in his character. Or if one wishes to put it still another way, Milton was both a humanist and a puritan, a religious idealist and a lover of aesthetic beauty and the material things of this world, and Samson reflects this duality in his creator: a duality which might on its surface appear to be in conflict, but which Milton successfully resolved in all his important poems.

In *Paradise Lost,* Milton reconciles the universe of physical matter, whose beauty and goodness are a major topic in the epic, with the God who created it, who was in the beginning, and will be in the end, "all in all"; and he accomplishes this reconciliation by means of what amounts to a philosophic monism — that is, through the belief that matter and spirit are continuous, that both are intrinsically good, and that they cannot be separated. For this reason, Milton cannot in all respects be called a Platonist. In the *Christian Doctrine,* Milton explains these ideas in more detail, notably in his discussion of the impossibility of separating the human soul from the human body, which led in turn to his accepting the doctrine of mortalism, or the death of the whole man, body and soul, until he is resurrected at the Last Judgment.[1] The date of *Samson Agonistes* is not certain. If, as a few Miltonists believe, it was written early in the 1640's, then probably Milton had not yet fully worked out these philosophical matters, or all the sometimes difficult implications which derive from them. Yet although one speaks, for convenience, of body and spirit in *Samson Agonistes* — of spiritual and physical diseases, for example, or of spiritual freedom and physical imprisonment, physical seeing and spiritual blindness, these two realms are not always so easily separated.

It is noticeable that the vehicles and tenors of many of the metaphors in *Samson* are difficult to distinguish from one another, and that many metaphors are so deeply embedded in the language or in description that one is unsure whether or not "metaphor" is the right term. One is led to speak, for example, as if the Philistines were spiritually blind, and indeed there is a moral flaw at the root of their

[1] *Works,* XV, 215-51.

problem: yet it is their inability to see properly what is physically in front of them—at Ramath-lechi or in the temple—or to listen always with proper attention to Samson's words, which leads literally as well as metaphorically to their doom. Except for Samson, who experiences a direct communication from God in his "rouzing motions"—in the words of the Argument, he is *"perswaded inwardly that this was from God"*—everyone in the play must inform himself about spiritual matters through his physical senses. Even Samson receives his culminating enlightenment only after intense interaction with the world and the people around him. One can speak of a Samson who is spiritually enlightened although physically blind—indeed Milton himself insists on this paradox repeatedly—yet in the play spiritual vision, though God's guidance lies behind the events, must come through the senses. The world of seeing, hearing, touching, tasting is the medium through which communication takes place. Samson must return to it out of his fort of silence and hurt despair before he is awarded an inner vision, and even while, in another sense, he is retreating from the world and the comprehension of his friends; while reprobation, on the other hand, is equivalent throughout the play to a lack of contact with physical reality or with actual events—to one or another kind of perceptual insensitivity.

In the same way, easy distinctions can be made between the corpse of Samson and his soul, or between his monument and his spiritual legacy to his people. Yet Samson's physical presence is held constantly before the eyes and touch of our imagination, and his visitors interact with him as much on the level of seeing, feeling, and sensing as they do through conversation or intellect. Even as a victorious saint, Samson addresses those in the future who would emulate him not so much through his words as through bodily action and image. *Samson* is, in sum, a play which constantly operates on a sensory level. Any reading which ignores this, which rises too far into abstraction—noticing the arguments more than the supplementing emotions and perceptions which the characters exchange, or ignoring the blood-covered corpse in the very midst of Manoa's exultations—will do it small justice. Avoiding the example of Harapha, one must taste and touch Samson and not merely listen to the discursive meanings of his words. Such is the invitation and the challenge which the play lays down: a challenge which the reader, much like the characters in the play, must respond to either one way or another.

These matters might be pursued further: to the fact that evil in Milton's poetry is seldom only a neoplatonic descent into matter like the downward-bending sensuality and gluttony toward which Comus leads his victims, or the lust into which Adam and Eve fall after attempting to climb up to godhood; but that it is more fundamentally a denial of reality, a *non serviam* and *non credo* spoken not only to the Creator but to the facts of his creation: symbolized in the plight of Satan, who condemns himself by his revolt to endless reasoning from false premises, and to a state of mind that prevents him from looking at even the good things of the world with love. So Dalila and Harapha argue endlessly from false axioms, unable to grasp the truth which is before them; so the Philistines shut their eyes and go down into darkness. The blind Samson, on the other hand, is given to see, and in the end is in touch with reality itself. In the rest of this chapter several specific aspects of Samson's character will be discussed: his inward growth or spiritual regeneration, his embodiment of the classical ideal of heroism, and his role as a specially elected champion of God or saint.

2

Since 1920, when James Waddell Tupper published an essay agreeing with Samuel Johnson's view that *Samson Agonistes* has no middle, a large portion of the studies written about *Samson* have been devoted to a refutation of Johnson's position. Johnson said that the play has no proper chain of causation, since none of the visits lead directly to each other or to the catastrophe, and therefore that it is deficient in the most basic way possible. The answer to this objection, which modern critics for the most part agree on, is that Milton has internalized the causation, which basically consists of Samson's spiritual development.[2] I have earlier assumed this point of view, but the matter is sufficiently important to deserve closer scrutiny.

In an earlier chapter it was suggested that the action of *Samson* is double, though the two aspects are not in conflict with each other. First, Samson is prepared spiritually to suffer and to die with patience and with faith, restored in spirit to his communion with God. At the same time, however, he is strengthened and given new courage and spiritual energy so that he can confront the Philistines and defeat them through heroic action. In order to prepare for action, Samson must first of all refuse the alternatives offered by each of his visitors. If he lets himself become a passive object for pity or scorn, retires to his father's or his wife's house and gives up the struggle, allows himself to be patronized or used by the Philistines or by their representatives, then he will fail in his mission. Samson begins the play in a state of self-pity and of spiritual lethargy, which is indicated by his careless posture. His arguments with the Chorus and his father appear at first to discourage him even more, but they actually engage his attention and help arouse his mental energies. During his debate with Dalila, the growth of Samson's energy and confidence is evident. He is then able to turn his new-found powers against the blustering Harapha. This encounter concludes with a Samson whose confidence is strengthened even further, who by now is on his feet, physically and mentally alert. He shows absolute confidence and self-control in his interviews with the Public Officer. At his exit, and in the temple, he is himself once more — indeed greater, more confident, and more energetic than he had ever been before. This gradual process, which prepares Samson for action, consists mainly in reacting *against* each of the characters who visit him, and refusing what they

[2]Two recent objections to the regeneration theory are G. A. Wilkes, "The Interpretation of *Samson Agonistes*," *Huntington Library Quarterly*, 26 (1963), 363–79; and Stanley Fish, "Question and Answer in *Samson Agonistes*," *Critical Quarterly*, 9 (1969). Articles on Samson's spiritual growth are legion. The earliest response to Johnson's critique with a theory of interior growth was Richard Cumberland, *The Observer*, No. 76 (1788). Two useful modern studies are Arnold Stein, *Heroic Knowledge* (Minneapolis: Univ. of Minnesota Press, 1957); and Ann Gossman, "Milton's Samson as the Tragic Hero Purified by Trial," *JEGP*, 61 (1962).

demand of him, no matter whether with friendly or unfriendly intentions.

Samson's inner growth in patience, and the ability to suffer is also the result of his reaction against his visitors. Several of them can be said to externalize his own faults or weaknesses. By facing these weaknesses and rising above them, Samson is enabled to grow spiritually. In the interview with the Chorus, Samson is freed from accepting guilt for several things for which he cannot be held responsible: he did not break the law by marrying the woman of Timna, because he was directed to by God; he is not solely responsible for the Philistine victory and the continuing bondage of Israel, because in the past the Jews have failed to follow his lead. In the interview with Manoa, Samson's earlier complaints about the fickleness of Providence are externalized, and, hearing his father repeat his own words, Samson is now able to see their foolishness and to disown them. In this interview Samson also faces for the first time the true nature of his guilt, a step that he must take before he can be truly penitent. The interview with Dalila which follows repeats the temptations which once led to his fall. By successfully resisting her, Samson undoes the effeminating effects of his earlier weakness. At the same time, he is made to realize clearly the difference between true and false repentance, true and false love, the nature and relationship of sin and of weakness, and the choice which he must still make himself between serving Philistia or Israel. In Harapha, Samson confronts and defeats his own double or inferior self: a boaster, a man of strength without wisdom, who trusts not in spiritual but in carnal weapons. The Public Officer is the servant of the Philistine State, as the next chapter will show: he is the instrument of the world's power and tyranny, of force without true authority. Samson's successful resistance to this threat is followed immediately by the rousing motions, a supernatural culmination and confirmation of his spiritual progress. He is now ready to suffer death willingly and patiently, not because he now craves death, and not with a stoic lack of emotion, but because he is willing to martyr himself in the service of truth.

Samson's inward progress, as many critics have noted, is not an even one; it has its setbacks, and it moves by waves and by turns. Moreover, there are two basic movements: a steady, upward spiritual progress, and a psychological movement that first travels downward into near despair and lethargy, reaching its low point at the end of the interview with Manoa, in Samson's second great lament of the play, a passionate outburst which concludes in a near-despairing expression of the death-wish:

> Sleep hath forsook and giv'n me o're
> To deaths benumming Opium as my only cure.
> Thence faintings, swounings of despair,
> And sense of Heav'ns desertion.
> . . . .
> Nor am I in the list of them that hope;
> Hopeless are all my evils, all remediless;
> This one prayer yet remains, might I be heard,
> No long petition, speedy death,
> The close of all my miseries, and the balm.
>   (629-32, 647-51)

From this point on, Samson's psychological movement is all upward, and takes the same direction as his spiritual progress.

The different courses taken by Samson's emotional state and his spiritual health can be partly explained by a theological interpretation of the play. When Samson is led in from the prison, he is in what amounts to a state of spiritual death, into which he has fallen as a result of his betrayal of God's trust. He laments his blindness and captivity, he feels a bewildered sense of spiritual malaise and guilt, but before he can make any progress toward recovery he must first learn to understand and to confront his sin. This he does, undergoing the process known as conversion (that is, a turning of the soul from evil to good) and regeneration (spiritual rebirth or renewal). In Milton's view, regeneration is impossible without the assistance of God's grace, since man in a fallen state cannot satisfy God's justice or merit his help. At the same time, however, the individual must freely choose to cooperate with grace and with the opportunities for spiritual renovation that providence offers him. In *Paradise Lost*, Milton tells us that the repentance of Adam and Eve was only made possible by God's gift of "Prevenient Grace" (XI.3), an initial grace that must precede any action on man's part, even the request for grace. But Milton withholds this information from the reader until

Adam and Eve have confessed their guilt to each other and fallen on their knees to confess their fault to God and ask his forgiveness. The result of presenting the events in this order is that most of the stress falls on the human progress of Adam and Eve and on their free will. The same is true in *Samson Agonistes:* God intervenes openly only toward the end of the play, when it appears that Samson has merited a reconciliation. At the same time, however, God and God's providence are constantly talked about during the play, so that the reader is led to presume by hindsight that it was the secret providence of God which arranged the arrival of all Samson's visitors at the proper time, in order to test and develop Samson's character systematically.

Virtue, Milton believed, is gained by trial or by adversity. Samson is tried first in the fire of suffering, and refined — in the biblical image — like gold. In addition, he is tried by the temptations to alternative action which each of the visitors offers him. Finally, he is tried by the opposition of wills, sharpened by argument and debate, so that he is enabled to define, both emotionally and intellectually, what his course must be. Like an athlete or the *agonist* of the title, he strengthens his spiritual muscles by undergoing an *agon* or struggle of some five or six stages, each stage preparing him for the next, each *antagonist* for the next. In religious terms, the process may be called a *psychomachia,* a contest of the soul. Not all of his opponents are evil, yet (like the angel with whom Jacob wrestled) all must be resisted. Temptations, Milton believed, can be either good or evil, depending on how they are responded to. Plainly the visits of the other characters prove good temptations for Samson, sent by God for his spiritual benefit. Their effect on him is exactly what Milton describes in the *Christian Doctrine:*

A good temptation is that whereby God tempts even the righteous for the purpose of proving them, not as though he were ignorant of the disposition of their hearts, but for the purpose of exercising or manifesting their faith or patience, as in the case of Abraham and Job; or of lessening their self-confidence, and reproving their weakness, that both they themselves may become wiser by experience, and others may profit by their example.[3]

[3]*Works,* XV, 87–89.

Abraham is the traditional exemplar of "faith" in God, Job of "patience." Samson must acquire both these virtues through his trials. He abandons both his former "self-confidence" and his "weakness" of spirit. He "exercises" himself in virtue like an athlete, he becomes "wiser," and he "manifests" his virtue so that "others may profit" from his "example."

Man's spiritual transformation from a fallen to a virtuous state is called regeneration. The definition of regeneration in the *Christian Doctrine,* like that of good and bad temptations, helps to illuminate the action of *Samson Agonistes:* "Regeneration is that change operated by the Word and the Spirit, whereby the old man being destroyed, the inward man is regenerated by God after his own image, in all the faculties of his mind, insomuch that he becomes as it were a new creature, and the whole man is sanctified both in body and soul, for the service of God, and the performance of good works."[4] The old man or the old Adam in Samson is purged away by his suffering. He is made anew. In the phrase first used in Genesis to describe man's creation, he is restored "in God's image" — so that Samson becomes the Image of God in this sense as well as others that were discussed earlier. He is sanctified both in soul and in body: which perhaps is suggested in the play by his recovery of physical as well as spiritual strength. His mental faculties are all rejuvenated. Having been made anew, he then acts in the "service of God," and performs a last "good work," for which his renewed faith has given him strength and will-power.

The effects of regeneration, as we have already seen in the negative case of Dalila, are "repentance and faith." Through repentance, "the regenerate man perceiving with sorrow that he has offended God by sin, detests and avoids it, humbly turning to God through a sense of the divine mercy, and heartily striving to follow righteousness."[5] That Samson is penitent and throws himself on God's mercy is quite obvious. Much of the process can only be assumed, because it takes place inwardly and is reflected only indirectly by Samson's outward behavior and conversation; but that it occurs is clear. Samson's re-

[4]*Works,* XV, 367; small capitals removed.

[5]*Works,* XV, 379; small capitals removed.

pentance is instrumentally brought about by chastisement,[6] the suffering which God's providence causes him to undergo, but which he has also brought on himself by his own free acts. Samson confesses his sin to his father and to his fellow tribesmen, and this helps to prepare the way for his confession to God.[7] Finally, Samson follows the "progressive steps" of repentance: "conviction of sin, contrition, confession, departure from evil, conversion to good."[8] It would be wrong, I believe, to associate these steps too closely or schematically with the structure of the play, even though one is tempted to do so by the fact that there are five steps of repentance and the play consists of five episodes or acts. One may say roughly, however, that Samson is convicted of sin, becomes contrite, and confesses his guilt in the first part of the play — including his soliloquy and the interviews with the Chorus and Manoa. Although these three steps each might be said to begin at some indefinite point in the first part of the play, all of tnem plainly culminate in the interview with Manoa. In his interview with Dalila, Samson can be said to depart from evil — and also, perhaps, in his interview with Harapha, when he dismisses much of what he has formerly been. His final conversion to good takes place between the two visits of the Public Officer.

Neither the pattern of Samson's spiritual development, nor Milton's discussion of the matter in the *Christian Doctrine*, was his own invention. Milton conforms to what had become a well-developed tradition of Puritan spirituality during the seventeenth century. In numerous tracts as well as literary works, one can find similar analyses of the soul's regeneration. The most familiar example is *Pilgrim's Progress*. Two works more unlike in many respects than *Pilgrim's Progress* and *Samson Agonistes* could hardly be found: yet their two heroes follow almost identical paths in their journeys from sin to salvation. The first step for Christian, for example, is conviction of sin; and while this is a great spiritual advance over his former state, and marks the beginning of his pilgrimage, it leads him first into

[6]*Works*, XV, 387.

[7]See *Works*, XV, 385: "Confession of sin is made sometimes to God . . . Sometimes to men."

[8]*Works*, XV, 385.

mental turmoil and soon nearly sinks him in the Slough of Despond. There are similar correspondences in the remaining stages of the journey. Bunyan, of course, makes the stages of his hero's growth extremely plain, for the benefit of his unlettered readers, and frequently pauses for a theological commentary on the action, while Milton works a great deal more subtly, and by example, not precept. Yet their methods and intentions are not entirely dissimilar.

If the pattern of Samson's regeneration, with its various technical stages, were simply the invention of certain seventeenth-century Puritans, developed by them into a science so as to provide their beliefs with a framework, then it would have small meaning for readers today. The theological underpinnings of *Samson*, like many of the esoteric patterns in Joyce's *Ulysses*, would be of greater interest to specialists than to ordinary readers—who indeed would do better to forget the whole matter and to focus on the more human and accessible meanings in the play. The Puritans did not invent this scheme arbitrarily, however. They found it by their own practical experience, and by analysis of their own human natures. The same pattern, with minor variations, can be found in the encounter of Spenser's Red Cross Knight with Despair, or in the Catholic *Everyman*, whose hero must confront Death and—like Samson or Bunyan's Christian—make a descent into the regions of despair before he can go onward. Dante goes through Hell and Purgatory before he reaches Heaven. So too with the Psalmist in the valley of the shadow, or the biblical prophet Jonah, who must go down under the sea in the belly of a whale before he can work out his salvation. Or with Beowulf, who finds victory by pursuing Grendel's mother into the depths of a mysterious lake, or Aeneas, who founds Rome by way of the underworld. The course of the tragic hero does not always follow the entire pattern, but it does in many of the greatest tragedies: Job, *Lear,* and the *Oedipus* cycle. If we had the completed Prometheus cycle of Aeschylus, one assumes that the same curve would emerge as Prometheus is unbound.

If Samson's spiritual progress is understood too narrowly, and if each step is merely equated with its Puritan or Miltonic label, then the whole development will mean relatively little. Milton's handling of regeneration in *Samson* does not encourage us to take this approach, however, for too rigid a pattern can only be imposed on the play with some violence. It is evident that the whole pattern of spiritual growth is absolutely basic; that (for example) the realization that something is wrong must precede any significant renovation — whether personal or political, whether in the case of an individual or of a whole people. Plainly, too, conversion to "good" must imply abandonment of "evil." The path of Samson is like the path of the fallen Adam in *Paradise Lost:* not just because Milton is following a set formula, but because any significantly different path would be contrary to the facts of human nature. The journey of mankind as a whole, as traced in Milton's three major poems, is essentially similar. So would be the path of the Jewish nation — or of the English during the Commonwealth — if only they would seize hold of the proffered opportunity. It certainly is possible to see the pattern in political terms, a dimension that is suggested by the play itself. One remembers Milton's pledge in *The Reason of Church Government* to celebrate at some future time "the deeds and triumphs of just and pious Nations doing valiantly through faith against the enemies of Christ," and to "deplore the general relapses of Kingdoms and States from justice and Gods true worship."[9] At a deeper level, however, the regeneration motif is best seen as a psychological, an archetypal, and a religious process: all realms of human experience that are difficult to separate and which, in the case of *Samson Agonistes,* ought not to be separated.

3

Although Samson's character as Milton portrayed it cannot be finally understood without considering the Christian implications, one should not forget other influences, including the classical. This is especially important if Samson's tragic and human dimensions are not to be lost sight of. One of the major conclusions arrived at by William Riley Parker was that *Samson Agonistes* is not indebted to any specific Greek play or playwright, and that Samson is modeled

[9]*Works,* III, 238.

on no single Greek hero.[10] Certainly this is true: Milton always
preferred networks of complex allusion to any specific imitation or
indebtedness. On the other hand, Parker's authority may have dis-
couraged other critics from pursuing single sources and parallels
and thus illuminating some of the strands which go into making up
the whole. In earlier chapters we have noticed Samson's resemblance
to the most prominent suffering heroes of several traditions: to
Christ, to Job and Isaiah's Suffering Servant, and to Philoctetes,
Oedipus at Colonus, and Prometheus. Another significant parallel,
however, has thus far only been glanced at by critics: that is, the
parallel to Hercules, Samson's traditional pagan counterpart and
analogue.[11] Hercules was perhaps the single classical hero who made
the deepest impression on later ages and on western heroic ideals,
especially in the Renaissance. Some critics have suggested that for
the Renaissance Hercules was *the* classical hero. While the literary
influences on Milton's Samson are many, Hercules is certainly a
major one. A closer examination of the parallel will help suggest
the relationship of Milton's hero to an important classical ideal.

In an early article arguing that the essential spirit of *Samson Agonistes* is Hebraic, R. C. Jebb was mainly concerned to show how Samson
and his classical counterpart Hercules differ. But he points out some
of the obvious parallels with which we may begin. Both heroes are
personifications of strength; both are champions and deliverers who
rid the world of monstrous evils; both suffer imprisonment during
their careers; Hercules is enslaved by Omphale and destroyed by
Deianeira, while Samson is plotted against and betrayed by the
woman of Timna and by Dalila; both come to violent ends.[12] There

---

[10]Parker, *Milton's Debt to Greek Tragedy in Samson Agonistes* (Baltimore:
Johns Hopkins, 1937) especially pp. 75–76, 248–50.

[11]On this subject Parker says almost nothing. See R. C. Jebb, "*Samson
Agonistes* and the Hellenic Drama," *Proceedings of the British Academy,* III
(1908), 341–48; F. Michael Krouse, *Milton's Samson and the Christian Tradition* (Princeton: Princeton Univ. Press, 1949); John M. Steadman, *Milton's
Epic Characters* (Chapel Hill: Univ. of North Carolina Press, 1968); J. C.
Maxwell, "Milton's Samson and Sophocles' Heracles," *Philological Quarterly,* 33 (1954). The fullest discussion is Jebb's.

[12]Jebb, pp. 345–48.

are other obvious parallels. Both heroes scorn armor in favor of simple clothing, and gentlemanly arms for ignoble weapons, Hercules a club or bow, Samson bare hands or an ass's jawbone. Like Samson, Hercules is an object of scorn, mocked by his antagonist Lycus for having made his reputation fighting beasts with ineligible weapons. Milton emphasizes that Samson is a life-long opponent of tyranny, in his last deed a tyrannicide. The main human antagonist of Hercules as portrayed by Euripides and Seneca is the tyrant Lycus; when he kills him, Hercules performs his last benefaction for mankind.

There are other more subtle resemblances between the two heroes. Eugene M. Waith comments on the characteristic isolation of Hercules in the classical dramas, his essential separation from the other characters on account of his greatness, a quality he shares with Samson. According to Waith, in Seneca's *Hercules Furens* "the separation of Hercules not only from Lycus but from all other men is given an almost schematic clarity."[13] Samson is violent and unrestrained in expressing his griefs; for this characteristic Milton might have had as a model not only Job, but also Hercules. As Waith notes, the Hercules of Sophocles' *Trachiniae* makes no effort to conceal or repress his feelings, grievances, and tremendous complaints. And like Samson, Hercules is especially devastated because he has been vanquished by a woman, himself reduced to effeminate weakness, made to seem an ignominious fool, in danger of losing the invincible reputation which his strength had gained him.

In Euripides' *The Women of Trachis,* Hercules is driven mad by Hera, and in this state murders his wife Megara and their children whom he has just succeeded in rescuing from Lycus. Then he comes to his senses again. Like Milton's hero, the chief suffering of the Euripidean Hercules is not physical — the burning robe of Nessus — but consists of mental anguish on account of his own guilty deeds. When Euripides' Hercules first learns what terrible crimes he has committed, he is tempted to commit suicide. But he is persuaded to

[13]Waith, *The Herculean Hero in Marlow, Chapman, Shakespeare and Dryden* (New York: Columbia Univ. Press, 1962), pp. 24–32. I am indebted to Waith's pioneering work in much of this discussion.

live by Theseus who counsels him to acceptance of life. Hitherto Hercules has been mainly an active, deed-accomplishing hero, but now he must learn the chief virtues of the passive hero: patience and endurance of suffering. Thus Hercules is shown surmounting despair and gaining a new inner fortitude. The parallel with Milton's Samson is obvious, and like Milton, Euripides is extensively concerned with the inner development of his character — in a sense, the extension of heroism from outward deeds to inner spiritual growth.

In Sophocles' *Trachiniae,* Hercules is presented mainly as a victim and a sufferer. His active deeds are in the past, a subject for nostalgic reminiscence. In Euripides, Hercules' gradual acceptance of suffering as an essential aspect of heroism is a matter of central concern. "The man who cannot bear up under fate / could never face the weapons of a man" (ll. 1349-50).[14] In Seneca's two plays, influenced by Stoic philosophy, the playwright develops the theme of patient forebearance under trial beyond anything recognizable in the earlier versions. Here is a forerunner of the Renaissance Hercules, portrayed again and again in literature and iconography at the crossroads choosing duty over pleasure. Milton could not follow Seneca's Stoic views (which indeed are not consistently or systematically developed), but he may well have been influenced by his portrayal of a formerly active hero who in the end must learn patience and human limitation through the suffering of pain, adversity, and the pangs of guilt.

One final parallel between *Samson* and the classical dramas about Hercules may be recalled: the presence in Sophocles' *Trachiniae* of the irony of alternatives: either that Hercules will die, or that he will achieve his task and have rest. That the two plays share this unusual device suggests a possible influence. Indebtedness, however, which while possible is not conclusive in any one of the parallels that have been mentioned, is a matter of secondary concern. It is more important to emphasize that Milton found a more complex ideal of heroism in the classics than has sometimes been suggested, a heroism that can suffer and include spiritual growth as well as

[14]Euripides, *Heracles,* trans. William Arrowsmith, *Euripides,* II (Chicago: Univ. of Chicago Press, 1956).

martial prowess or active accomplishments. Even Hercules, who was the greatest of active heroes and the most prolific doer of great deeds, illustrates this. The lesson which irresistible Hercules must learn is also the lesson of Milton's Samson: that not all evils can be conquered through physical strength alone. When they have learned this lesson, both heroes transcend their former greatness: Samson rising like the Phoenix from its ashes, Hercules ascending from the funeral pyre on Mount Oeta to become one of the gods. The essence of the Herculean hero is greatness in all things, a kind of exuberant, superhuman energy, exhibited not only in action but in suffering, and even in the power of vent feelings and complaints. Clearly in this most basic sense Samson may properly be called a Herculean hero.

4

As Michael Krouse points out in his study of the Samson tradition from biblical times to the seventeenth century, many writers had come to consider him a saint by the time Milton wrote his play.[15] The concept of Samson's sainthood could, however, be understood with greater or lesser degrees of sophistication. The process actually began with the Jews, who included Samson among the Judges of Israel, leaders of the nation against external enemies or internal backslidings. The judges came in time between the patriarchs and the later kings and prophets of Israel. The proper roles of all of these figures are essentially the same: to lead their people, and especially to guide them along the paths of true religion.

In the Epistle to the Hebrews, St. Paul adopted Samson into the Christian perspective, including him — together with other notable patriarchs, judges, kings, and prophets — among the Old-Testament exemplars of faith:

And what shall I more say? for the time would fail me to tell of Gedeon, and of Barak, and of Samson, and of Jephthae; of David also, and Samuel, and of the Prophets: Who through

[15]Krouse, *Milton's Samson and the Christian Tradition*.

faith subdued kingdoms, wrought righteousness, obtained promises, stopped the mouths of lions, Quenched the violence of fire,
escaped the edge of the sword, out of weakness were made
strong, waxed valiant in fight, turned to flight the armies of the
aliens. . . . And others had trial of cruel mockings and scourgings,
yea, moreover of bonds and imprisonment: They were stoned,
they were sawn asunder, were tempted, were slain with the
sword: they wandered about in sheepskins and goatskins; being
destitute, afflicted, tormented; (Of whom the world was not
worthy:) they wandered in deserts, and in mountains, and in
dens and caves of the earth. (Heb. xi.32-38)

Clearly Milton had absorbed both the meaning and the tone of this
passage before he wrote *Samson*. He conceived his hero in Pauline
terms, as one of the great ancient forerunners of Christianity, who
wrought wonders by his faith. It is even noticeable that, although
Milton could have found them elsewhere among the epic and tragic
heroes, St. Paul's panegyric is structured on the alternatives of active
warrior and suffering martyr: the two major elements in Samson's
character. A man of faith might be either a great warrior, subduing
kingdoms, establishing righteousness, stopping the mouths of lions,
made strong out of weakness, valiant in fight, driving off armies of
aliens—all deeds of Milton's Samson; or else he might suffer cruel
mockings, bonds, imprisonment; be tempted, be dressed in skins,
destitute, afflicted, tormented, finally killed—also like Milton's
Samson.

The remaining stages in the development of the Samson myth,
between Paul's time and Milton's, are less important. Suffice it to
say that St. Paul's lead was followed and extended by biblical com-
mentators and poets alike, and that Samson became a mighty proto-
Christian or even a Christian warrior and saint, and that all of his
deeds were given typological and allegorical explanations. The ass's
jawbone, for example, stood for the Gospel, a weak instrument that
nevertheless converted thousands. The incident of Samson's lying
with a prostitute, not mentioned in Milton's play, became Christ's
descent into hell; while Samson's subsequent escape, carrying off
the town gates with him, was Christ's harrowing of hell. Needless
to say, Samson's death, with his arms stretched out to a pillar on

either side of him, typifies the crucifixion. Undoubtedly, Milton was familiar with these traditions, and may occasionally make some use of them; as, for example, he seems to have made use of the commentary in the Geneva Bible.[16] Nevertheless, most of them are strained and highly allegorical interpretations which are foreign both to the spirit of Milton (who like many Protestants mistrusted biblical allegory) and of *Samson Agonistes*. It is extremely unlikely, for example, that Milton thought that Samson's night with a prostitute — an incident which could have been accounted for as a manifestation of his sinfulness but which he preferred to omit — was an apt type of Christ's descent into hell (itself an extra-biblical tradition), or that Samson's carrying off of the gates of Azza (146-50), mentioned by the Chorus after it praises him for his victory at Ramath-lechi, is meant to suggest anything more than his heroic strength before his fall. Samson does become a type of Christ in the play, and in this respect Milton relies to some extent on previous writers and exegetes; but the relationship is much more subtle than Milton could have achieved by using such comparatively crude parallels.

Saint Paul, after recounting all the famous deeds of the Old-Testament heroes, and after rising to an emotional crescendo of admiration and praise, concludes thus: "And these all, having obtained a good report through faith, received not the promise: God having provided some better thing for us, that they without us should not be made perfect" (Heb. xi.39-40). Even these great men could not benefit from the covenant of grace, in spite of all their faith and valor. Only with the coming of Christ, Paul goes on, was the promise of their faith fulfilled. Neither Paul nor Milton thought that Samson was a Christian saint. The merits of Christ might be extended back in time, as Milton suggests in the *Christian Doctrine:*

> It ought not to appear wonderful if many, both Jews and others, who lived before Christ, and many also who have lived since his time, but to whom he has never been revealed, should be saved by faith in God alone; still however through the sole merits of Christ, inasmuch as he was given and slain from the

[16]See George W. Whiting, "*Samson Agonistes* and the Geneva Bible," *The Rice Institute Pamphlets,* 18 (1951), 18-35.

beginning of the world, even for those to whom he was not known, provided they believed in God the Father. Hence honorable testimony is borne to the faith of the illustrious patriarchs who lived under the law, Able, Enoch, Noah, &c.[17]

Samson dies with faith in God the Father, and so can be presumed to have received the grace earned by the "sole merits" of the Son; but he dies a Hebrew, "under the law," and in ignorance of his reward. Milton, like St. Paul, takes what might be called a Christianized view of Samson, but that does not mean he thought him a Christian.

That Samson dies a saint is not directly suggested in the play. The Chorus speaks of patience and suffering as "the exercise / Of Saints" (1287-88)—a prophecy which Samson appears to fulfill. Manoa promises that his deeds will be memorialized "In copious Legend, or sweet Lyric Song" (1737), and a "Legend" generally is a saint's life, told for purposes of imitation. Manoa also promises to plant Samson's monument with laurel, an evergreen plant awarded as a prize for great accomplishments, and with palm, which came to be a symbol for the victorious attainment of heaven by a saint—like the palm branches carried by "palmers" or pilgrims who had reached Jerusalem. It is only from our viewpoint outside the play, however, and as presumed Christians, that we are able to call Samson a saint. He is a saint only in a limited sense.

In his works, Milton uses the word "saint" to mean several different things. He is naturally suspicious of Catholic saints (as of all other Catholic practices and beliefs), nor did he believe in earthly processes of canonization. He is particularly scandalized, or pretends to be scandalized, by those Royalists who call Charles I a saint.[18] In *Paradise Lost* (V.247), he refers to Raphael as a saint, presumably because, although he is not human, he is blessed like the human saints with the beatific vision. Usually, however, as in the "Epitaph on the Marchioness of Winchester," or in the Piedmontese Sonnet, or in the sonnet on his "late espoused Saint," he uses the word to refer to someone who has died, and is presumed to have won a heavenly reward. In this sense, the term applies to Samson after his death in the temple. Milton also calls the living Moses a saint (*Paradise Lost*

[17]*Works*, xv, 403–05.

[18]*Eikonoklastes; Works*, v, 90.

XII.200), and in this sense the word can also be applied to Samson before his death. Samson is neither a Christian nor a Christian saint, however. He is a saint of God, by virtue of his faith and his martyrdom; and even before his death, because he is one of the chosen leaders of the Jews.[19]

Samson is Milton's most human hero, and that sometimes has distracted critics from the often-stated fact of his special election by God. There are few points made more often in the play. The effect of his election is somewhat moderated, since most of the time Samson and the other characters speak only of his having *lost* his special relationship to God; but, of course, that loss proves only temporary or illusory, and at the end of the play Samson has gained God's favor back again. In the *Christian Doctrine,* Milton distinguishes between men who are ordinarily elected — that is, all men — and those few who are specially elected.[20] In *Paradise Lost,* God the Father, while discussing with the Son his providential plans for men, speaks of a special group of leaders who will receive a different kind of election from that offered to the others. The rest will all "hear me call, and oft be warnd," and they will receive sufficient grace to "soft'n stonie hearts"; but these special men, because they will serve as leaders or examples, will be set apart:

> Some I have chosen of peculiar grace
> Elect above the rest; so is my will. (III.183-84)

These chosen leaders of men are seen again in the last two books of *Paradise Lost,* acting out their parts in human history. They are Abel, Enoch, Noah, Abraham, Jacob, Joseph, Moses, and Joshua. Milton's list is almost identical with St. Paul's list of faithful men, down to the time of the Judges (Heb. xi.4-30).[21] Milton then passes quickly over the rest of Hebrew history, mentioning only David by name,

---

[19]See also Samuel S. Stollman, "Milton's Samson and the Jewish Tradition," *Milton Studies,* 3 (1971), 185–200. Stollman finds that Milton did not make any significant use of later Jewish or Rabbinic traditions concerning Samson.

[20]*Works,* XV, 349–53.

[21]For reasons of space I have quoted only the end of St. Paul's list of heroes, but the whole chapter is relevant. In *Paradise Lost,* Milton adds Aaron to Paul's list and omits Sara and Rahab, but it is not unlikely that his selection of exemplars from the Old Testament was guided by Hebrews xi.

until he arrives at *"Joshua* whom the Gentiles *Jesus* call" (XII.310). In *Samson Agonistes,* however, Milton has given us the story of another of these forerunners of Christ, one of the specially elected men of faith. Samson's role can only be inferred from *Paradise Lost,* because history in the epic becomes more and more telescoped and rapid as the promise draws near. He belongs, however, in the chaotic period

> when sins
> National interrupt thir public peace,
> Provoking God to raise them enemies:
> From whom as oft he saves them penitent
> By Judges first, then under Kings. . . .
> (XII.316-20)

In the grand sweep of the epic, Samson is not even mentioned by name (except elsewhere in a metaphor). He is simply one of the unnamed judges who temporarily saves his people and leads them for a time to repent their national sins. Nevertheless, Samson, in spite of his earlier lapse into sin, can be said to take his place by the close of *Samson Agonistes* in Milton's roll of single just men, those who like Abdiel stand fast when all around them men are falling away, and who thus pass on the faith from generation to generation until the coming of "one greater Man" (I.4), who will finally fulfill their faith and give new point to their deeds.

9

VENGEANCE, JUSTICE, AND AUTHORITY

Few aspects of *Samson Agonistes* have more disturbed the modern reader than its apparent insistence on the theme of vengeance. Because critics in recent times have been more concerned with esthetics, historical background, or interpretation of various kinds than with morality as such, they have not dwelt on the matter at any great length. But there is little doubt that E. M. W. Tillyard expresses the reaction of many readers when he writes that *Samson* represents a development of Milton's mind which he finds "depressing," because in the drama "there appears a settled ferocity, not very lovely." Tillyard further argues, in common with several other critics, that Milton is personally involved in Samson's vengeance, and suggests that the pleasure Manoa feels at the destruction of the Philistines is not unlike the "savage jubilation" Milton himself would feel at the destruction of Charles II together with his court.[1] Kenneth Fell, in "From Myth to Martyrdom," argues that *Samson Agonistes* occupies a middle position between the unreconstructed barbarism of the Samson myth in Judges and the truly Christian treatment of martyrdom in T. S. Eliot's *Murder in the Cathedral*.[2] Again many readers would doubtless agree.

Certainly the story as it appears in the Old Testament emphasizes vengeance as a reason for Samson's action. Indeed, depending on how one reads the story, it can even be called the only explicit reason:

> Now the house was full of men and women; and all the lords of the Philistines were there; and there were upon the roof about three thousand men and women, that beheld while Samson made sport. And Samson called unto the Lord, and said, O Lord God, remember me, I pray thee, and strengthen me, I pray thee, only this once, O God, that I may be at once avenged of the Philistines for my two eyes.
>
> (Judg. xvi.27-28)

The Samson story in Judges is much shorter than Milton's version, and consists mainly of outward actions, with little description of inward psychological or spiritual states. In this respect, it is similar to most Old Testament narrative. One must often infer emotions or motives from the action, without expecting to have them directly described. For example, Samson's inward suffering, depicted so vividly by Milton, is left by Judges largely to the reader's imagination: "But the Philistines took him, and put out his eyes, and brought him down to Gaza, and bound him with fetters of brass; and he did grind in the prison house" (xvi.21). That is all; yet for a sensitive reader it is enough. It can, therefore, be argued that Samson's prayer is described with similar reticence. While he mentions only what

---

[1]Tillyard, *Milton* (London: Chatto & Windus, 1930; rev. ed. 1966), pp. 283–84.

[2]Fell, *English Studies,* 34 (1953), 145–55. That Samson is tragically mistaken in his vengeance is argued by Irene Samuel, *"Samson Agonistes* as Tragedy," *Calm of Mind,* ed. Joseph A. Wittreich, Jr. (Cleveland: Press of Case Western Reserve Univ., 1971), pp. 235–57.

appears to be a desire for personal vengeance, a higher spiritual motivation cannot be ruled out. The placement of the story in the whole context of Judges, as discussed in the previous chapter, suggests that Samson is to be understood as one of the leaders of Israel whom God has chosen to defeat her enemies and to bring her back from idols to the worship of the true God. There is little doubt that the Jews read the story this way long before Samson was numbered by St. Paul among the heroes of faith.

Vengeance is not mentioned as a motive in *Samson Agonistes* until after Samson's death. Manoa and the Chorus then speak of it several times. Manoa's first reaction, after the Messenger has explained that both the Philistine rulers and Samson are dead, is to exclaim:

> O lastly over-strong against thy self!
> A dreadful way thou took'st to thy revenge.
> (1590-91)

After the Messenger finishes describing how Samson pulled down the temple, the Chorus exclaims, "O dearly-bought revenge, yet glorious!" (1660). And Manoa concludes, during his final speech:

> Come, come, no time for lamentation now,
> Nor much more cause, *Samson* hath quit himself
> Like *Samson,* and heroicly hath finish'd
> A life Heroic, on his Enemies
> Fully reveng'd, hath left them years of mourning,
> And lamentation to the Sons of *Caphtor*
> Through all *Philistian* bounds. . . . (1708-14)

On the surface at least, it does not appear that Milton has diminished the emphasis that Judges puts on the theme of revenge, although no one speaks of vengeance for Samson's eyes, or even mentions the law of an eye for an eye; and Milton has elsewhere added other religious and national motivations not explicitly put forward in his source. Of the three references to revenge, Manoa's first remark may well be thought an initial, overhasty reaction; but the Chorus' statement and Manoa's conclusion are woven into the play's summing up, and as I argue in Chapter 6 must be thought a part of its final vision.

In the *Christian Doctrine,* Milton mentions two courses of conduct which he considers proper toward an enemy. First, he states that

"Even our enemies are not to be excluded from the exercise of our charity," and he quotes a number of the familiar injunctions to this effect in the New Testament. Shortly afterward, however, he writes: "Hatred, however, is in some cases a religious duty; as when we hate the enemies of God or the church.... We are to hate even our dearest connections, if they endeavor to seduce or deter us from the love of God and true religion."[3] The distinction is that one has a duty to love or to turn the other cheek toward merely personal enemies — to "bless them that curse you, do good to them that hate you" (Mat. v.44) — but that conduct toward enemies of God or religion is another matter. What this conduct should be, Milton does not specifically say, beyond citing a few Old and New Testament references of varying import. It might possibly involve resort to the sword; or it might involve such an act as Bunyan portrays in *Pilgrim's Progress,* when Christian must leave his beloved wife and children because they attempt to dissuade him from going on his pilgrimage. This, in effect, is what Samson must do when confronted by the still unrepentant Dalila. On the basis of what Milton does say, however, Samson would be wrong to kill the Philistines for injuries done personally to him — and there is no indication in the play that this is his motive. It might be allowable for Samson to kill them, or for Manoa and the Chorus to approve of his action, because the Philistines are religious persecutors and "seducers" of the Jews, and because there is no other way of escaping their influence.

Tillyard is mistaken, however, in asserting that anyone displays "savage jubilation" at the destruction of the Philistines. When Manoa and the Chorus hear the "universal groan" from the temple, the alternatives appear to them to be either that the Philistines have slain Samson, or that he is slaying them. Either of these possibilities, Manoa concludes, would be a "dismal accident" (1519). Similarly, the Messenger, although he is a Jew, enters speaking of a "horrid spectacle," a "place of horrour," and a "sad event" (1542-51). When the Messenger tells Manoa that the Philistines have been killed, their conversation is as follows:

> *Mess.* Gaza yet stands, but all her Sons are fall'n,
> All in a moment overwhelm'd and fall'n.

[3] *Works,* XVII, 257, 259.

Man. Sad, but thou knowst to *Israelites* not saddest
The desolation of a Hostile City.
    Mess. Feed on that first, there may in grief be surfet.
    Man. Relate by whom. *Mess.* By *Samson. Man.* That still lessens
The sorrow, and converts it nigh to joy.

(1558-64)

Manoa, speaking honestly, admits that the deaths of enemies and oppressors of Israel is not the "saddest" of news. It is, nevertheless, "sad," and even the news that Samson has been the instrument of their destruction, and therefore apparently lives and has recovered his former powers, only *"lessens* | The sorrow, and converts it *nigh* to joy." Surely this is a very restrained reaction from a father who, at this point, is able to think only in terms of alternatives: either Samson is dead, or the Philistines are dead.[4]

So too, after the event has been made plainer, the Semichoruses rejoice more at the assertion of God's will and the rebirth of Samson's faith and greatness than at the destruction of the Philistines that must inevitably accompany these goods. And Manoa's last speech, after he speaks of Samson's vengeance and the mourning of the Philistines, but without expressing any direct pleasure in their sorrow, goes on to mention more important reasons for rejoicing: that Israel now has honor and freedom, if she can but find "courage to lay hold on this occasion" (1716); that Samson has earned eternal fame both for himself and for his ancestors; and that—"best and happiest yet"—Samson has died

> With God not parted from him, as was feard,
> But favouring and assisting to the end. (1719-20)

The Chorus then concludes the play, asserting that Gaza mourns because it has banded together to resist God's "uncontroulable intent" (1754). Here is no rejoicing at Gaza's sorrow for its own sake, no happiness at the suffering of others: only the statement of what amounts to a kind of natural (or divine) law—that those who

---

[4]Citing this passage, Tillyard speaks of Manoa's "cool, ironical gloating" (*Milton,* p. 283). Manoa cannot be speaking coolly here, however, nor does the Messenger receive his words ironically. He hopes that grief for the Philistines will "surfeit" Manoa, leaving no room for further grief at the news he must announce: the death of his son.

continue to resist God will inevitably suffer for it. If the Chorus feels any satisfaction, it is not on account of the Philistines' suffering; it is because their religious faith, which had been in serious doubt, is now confirmed; because the God of Israel, for a while overshadowed by the presumptuous Dagon, has been vindicated and plainly revealed for what he is; and because Samson has found reconciliation with God, and a noble end.

2

If *Samson Agonistes* does not rejoice in the fate of the Philistines, it does nevertheless end on a note of vengeance. Although Milton was tied to the basic outlines of the Samson story in Judges, there is no sign that he attempted to subordinate this element, as he might very well have done. Milton was, of course, familiar with the saying in the Old Testament law, "To me belongeth vengeance, and recompense" (Deut. xxxii.35), later restated as a Christian doctrine by St. Paul, in the Bible's best-known injunction on the subject: "Dearly beloved, avenge not yourselves, but rather give place unto wrath: for it is written, Vengeance is mine; I will repay, saith the Lord. Therefore if thine enemy hunger, feed him; if he thirst, give him drink: for in so doing thou shalt heap coals of fire on his head. Be not overcome of evil, but overcome evil with good" (Rom. xii.19-21). To avenge oneself is to pay back evil with evil, and so to be "overcome of evil." Nevertheless, vengeance is not entirely dispensed with, but rather is resigned upward to God, who, unlike man, has the attributes of omniscience and perfect righteousness that enable him to see that the debt is correctly paid. To judge is not man's privilege; it is God's. By returning good for evil, a man heaps "coals of fire" on an evildoer's head. Because Milton did not believe in predestinated reprobation, this would not mean in his view that the evildoer would be irretrievably damned. He might be, if he did not avail himself of opportunities to repent; or the troubling of his spirit—of the "Umpire *Conscience*" that God has put in him as an objective guide (*Paradise Lost* III.195)—might actually hasten his repentance.

Vengeance is a constantly reiterated theme in the Old Testament. Whenever vengeance is spoken of with approval, however, it consists of God's judgment on the wicked for their evil deeds, and it is executed either by God or by his appointed human agents. The Deuteronomic code forbids man to avenge himself; yet immediately it speaks with fierce approval of the vengeance of God: "If I whet my glittering sword, and mine hand take hold on judgment; I will render vengeance to mine enemies, and will reward them that hate me. I will make mine arrows drunk with blood, and my sword shall devour flesh; and that with the blood of the slain and the captives, from the beginning of revenges upon the enemy. Rejoice, O ye nations, with his people: for he will avenge the blood of his servants, and will render vengeance to his adversaries, and will be merciful unto his land, and to his people" (xxxii.41-43). Milton calls for such vengeance in the sonnet on the slain Piedmontese, which vividly recaptures the Old Testament's tone of moral outrage and its fierce demands for justice: "Avenge O Lord thy slaughter'd Saints, whose bones / Lie scatter'd on the Alpine mountains cold." Such vengeance is not merely equivalent to the ancient law of an eye for an eye, a life for a life: its deepest motivation is outrage at man's injustice and wickedness, together with the assertion of God's righteousness, that will prevail against those who oppose him and prey upon his flock.

Beginning with the prophet Amos, and culminating with Joel and Daniel, the Old Testament increasingly associates divine retribution with the great and terrible "Day of the Lord," when God will arise and fully assert his righteousness, and purge the world of all sin and iniquity. The New Testament conception of the Last Judgment develops from this line of thought, and in fact takes over much of the same imagery. Just as the New Testament goes beyond the Old in forbidding personal violence, in advocating mercy and forgiveness, so on the other side it pictures an even more terrible ultimate justice: "Fire came down from God out of heaven, and devoured them. And the devil that deceived them was cast into the lake of fire and brimstone, where the beast and the false prophet are, and shall be tormented day and night for ever and ever" (Rev. xx.9-10). There are similar passages in the synoptic gospels. This is the two-handed engine that St. Peter speaks of in *Lycidas,* which need smite only once. It is not merely destructive, however, for such apocalyptic events establish righteousness and peace by the elimination of persecution and injustice. In the Old Testament, after the destruction of evil, the prophets speak of God coming down to rule in righteousness on Mount Sion. In the New Testament, the metaphor is the descent of the heavenly Jerusalem, after heaven and earth are made anew:

> And I John saw the holy city, the new Jerusalem, coming down from God out of heaven, prepared as a bride adorned for her husband. And I heard a great voice out of heaven saying, Behold, the tabernacle of God is with men, and he will dwell with them, and they shall be his people, and God himself shall be with them, and be their God. And God shall wipe away all tears from their eyes; and there shall be no more death, neither sorrow, nor crying, neither shall there be any more pain: for the former things are passed away. And he that sat upon the throne said, Behold, I make all things new. (Rev. xxi.2-5)

The Last Judgment, of which Samson's destruction of the temple is an imperfect and impermanent type, is a two-edged sword, bringing at once "respiration to the just" and "vengeance to the wicked" (*Paradise Lost* XII.540-41).

That God may avenge himself or his people is thus made clear in both the Old and the New Testament, and was accepted as a truism by Milton and the Christians of his time. Moreover, vengeance was seldom thought of merely as something negative: its function was to establish justice for the good as well as to wreak it on the wicked. That man may not take private vengeance was equally clear, though not always so easy to accept. The major area of uncertainty is when God acts through human agents, or on the other hand when men merely claim to act for God. After citing seven biblical passages against taking vengeance in the *Christian Doctrine*, Milton adds this qualification: "To avenge the church, however, or to desire that she be avenged of her enemies, is not forbidden." He then cites sixteen texts that support this contention, concluding with the great cry of the martyrs in Revelation vi.10: "How long, O Lord — ?"[5]

It is not forbidden "to avenge" or "to desire that she be avenged."

[5]*Works*, XVII, 289.

Whether one can take vengeance oneself, or only pray for vengeance, is a matter of political theory, as a passage from *The First Defense* reveals:

> Constantine, after his conversion to Christianity, made war upon Licinius his co-emperor, who oppressed the Eastern Christians, and destroyed him. By this act of his he made it clear that one magistrate might punish another, for he for his subjects' sake put to death Licinius, who was as absolute in the empire as himself, and did not leave the vengeance to God alone; and Licinius might likewise have put to death Constantine if Constantine had likewise crushed the people committed to his government.[6]

Elsewhere in *The First Defense,* the matter is made still clearer:

> In civil affairs God has not enjoined such patience that the state must submit to the cruelties of tyrants, but not the church; nay, rather has he enjoined the contrary; indeed he has left unto the church no arms but patience and innocence, prayer and the teaching of the gospel; but into the hands of the state and its officers altogether he has entrusted not patience, but the sword of the law, avenger of wrong and violence.[7]

Constantine need not leave vengeance to God, because he is a magistrate (*magistratus*); indeed, the vengeance of the law, symbolized by the sword, may properly be wielded by the state or any of its qualified officers (*respublica et magistratus*). Anyone can and should desire and pray for vengeance on the Church's enemies; public officials may carry it out. A man may, therefore, properly exercise vengeance against unrighteousness or tyranny if he has a public commission, and acts neither as a private person, nor for private reasons.

3

As a Judge of Israel, Samson has the right to execute vengeance on any who persecute or tyrannize over his nation, attack its religion,

[6]*Works,* VII, 251.
[7]*Works,* VII, 211.

or seduce the people from their God. He is one of the series of judges, between Joshua and Saul, commissioned by God to execute his will: to drive off the enemies of Israel, and to bring back her people into the right way. Milton does not emphasize Samson's long period of office as a judge and recognized leader of the people (Judg. xv.20), presumably because, as suggested in Chapter 3, he wishes to increase his isolation and his complete rejection by the Jews. But he does make it entirely clear that Samson is specially commissioned by God. His birth has been foretold from Heaven by an angel (23-24); his breeding has been "order'd and prescrib'd / As of a person separate to God, / Design'd for great exploits" (30-32); his purpose in life, ordained by God, is to deliver Israel from the "*Philistian* yoke" (39). God has given him his strength (58); has raised him up "of his special favour" (273); has "solemnly elected" him to "some great work," which will have the double purpose of increasing God's "glory" and the "peoples safety" (678-81). It is by God's specific direction that Samson has married the woman of Timna, in order to "begin *Israel*'s Deliverance" (219-26); it is by his "appointment" that Samson has provoked the Philistines (643). In short, as Samson sums it up, he was God's "nursling once and choice delight, / His destin'd from the womb"; he grew up under God's "special eie"; he was led on to mighty deeds "Above the nerve of mortal arm"; and his promise was confirmed by two appearances of an angel (633-40).

The seventeenth century did not lack for persons who thought they had special commissions from God for their actions. As Hooker wryly remarks: "When they and their Bibles were alone together, what strange fantastical opinion soever at any time entered into their heads, their use was to think the Spirit taught it them."[8] This cannot be said of Milton's Samson, however, although several critics have thus interpreted the references to his election.[9] Samson's elec-

---

[8]Hooker, *Of the Laws of Ecclesiastical Polity* (Preface, viii.7), ed. Christopher Morris (London: J. M. Dent, 1907), I, 135.

[9]William Empson, *Milton's God*, rev. ed. (London: Chatto & Windus, 1965), pp. 211–18; Charles Thomas Samuels, "Milton's *Samson Agonistes* and Rational Christianity," *The Dalhousie Review*, 43 (1963), 495–506.

tion to the office of Judge or redeemer, representative of God and charismatic leader, is revealed not merely by an inner light, but is confirmed by the appearance of an angel; or if that be doubted, by Samson's miraculous strength. Having killed a thousand armed men with nothing but an ass's jawbone, Samson can rightly claim external evidence in support of his inner light; nor are the Philistines or critics in much of a position to question his authority. His commission, although it is bestowed by God directly rather than by the state, is an objective fact in the play. As Calvin points out, the civil magistrates are rightly called "the *higher powers,* not the supreme":[10] above them is God. Samson's authority is not institutional – it is even counter-institutional, which is the case with most of the Old Testament judges and prophets – but Milton does not specially emphasize this distinction. Instead, he emphasizes the difference between private and public action, personal and public revenge.

This theme is briefly referred to early in the play. The Chorus discusses God's right to exempt individuals from "National obstriction" (307-14); Manoa brings up the question of service to an unjust state (577-78); and Dalila in her sophistical arguments attempts to pervert the proper relationships between "public good" and "private respects" (849-69, 886-95, 992-94). The first really important discussion of Samson's commission as an agent of God's vengeance, however, is in his lengthy debate with Harapha, the champion of the Philistine state.

Harapha accuses Samson of being "A Murtherer, a Revolter, and a Robber" (1180), while he speaks of himself as a "noble Warriour" who bears "glorious arms" (1166, 1130). This is not merely chauvinism or conceit – the other side of the coin, as it were, from the Jewish viewpoint. The ground for Harapha's distinction between himself and Samson is his charge that Samson has acted illegally and as a private party in his battles with the Philistines, unsupported by the duly constituted authorities of Israel; while he himself serves under the legitimate authority of the Philistine state. He has a

[10]From Calvin's commentaries on the Epistle to the Romans, in *On God and Political Duty,* ed. John T. McNeil (Indianapolis: Bobbs Merrill, 1956), p. 84. Although Milton was not in all respects a Calvinist, this compendium makes a useful background to the play.

regular commission as Champion, while he contends that Samson
has none. Harapha asks, rhetorically:

> Is not thy Nation subject to our Lords?
> Their Magistrates confest it, when they took thee
> As a League-breaker and deliver'd bound
> Into our hands. . . . (1182-85)

"Magistrates," an unusual word to apply to the Jewish leaders of
this period, indicates the direction of Harapha's argument. The magis-
strates, the officers of the state, who might legally claim the right of
vengeance, warfare, or the execution of justice, have all taken the
Philistine side. They have made a league or covenant with the Philistine rulers, recognizing them as their own proper rulers; and any
claim Samson may have had previously to be a magistrate himself
was invalidated when the Jews surrendered him at Ramath-lechi.
Therefore, by definition all Samson's acts are private, and he is a
league-breaker and a murderer. The laws of Christian nations universally made this distinction. Unless a man was legally enrolled in
the military, or commissioned as a privateer, or otherwise authorized
by the state, he would be technically guilty of murder if he killed
his country's enemies even if he fought alongside commissioned
soldiers. How much more a private person acting alone, and in defiance of his government?

Political theory in seventeenth-century England was based squarely
on St. Paul's letter to the Romans, although Royalists and Puritans
naturally drew different conclusions from this text: "Let every soul
be subject unto the higher powers. For there is no power but of God:
the powers that be are ordained of God. Whosoever therefore resisteth the power, resisteth the ordinance of God: and they that
resist shall receive to themselves damnation" (xiii.1-2). Harapha's
charge is that Samson is resisting the "powers that be"; and therefore
that he is wrong not only legally but morally. Harapha suggests that
not even Samson's God will condone such behavior (1178-80), although this is a somewhat theoretical point in his eyes, since he
must believe that the Jews, accepting Philistine rule, have also
accepted their national god Dagon. The power to legitimize violent
action, however, comes not only from the state, but through it from
God, as Calvin points out in his commentary on this passage. The

constituted authorities are God's deputies only. Therefore, although Paul's injunction can be used to support the "powers that be," it can also be used to justify revolt against those powers if they act improperly and become tyrannous. Milton had argued so in many of his prose tracts, for example *The Tenure of Kings and Magistrates,* and Samson so argues now:

> My Nation was subjected to your Lords.
> It was the force of Conquest; force with force
> Is well ejected when the Conquer'd can. (1205-07)

Leadership under God approximates the harmonious order of the divinely ordained hierarchy within the limitations of human weakness; leadership contrary to God is usurpation and tyranny.[11]

Although the Philistine rule is tyrannical, for Samson to act against it without authority would be for him to execute private vengeance, however good his reasons, which would be against the law and the moral code. Therefore, Samson must respond to Harapha's charge that, because his warfare is unsanctioned by the Jewish leaders, it really has been robbery, revolt, and murder. This he does, in a closely-reasoned, formal response to the charges:

> But I a private person, whom my Countrey
> As a league-breaker gave up bound, presum'd
> Single Rebellion and did Hostile Acts.
> I was no private but a person rais'd
> With strength sufficient and command from Heav'n
> To free my Countrey; if their servile minds
> Me their Deliverer sent would not receive,
> But to thir Masters gave me up for nought,
> Th' unworthier they; whence to this day they serve.
> I was to do my part from Heav'n assign'd,
> And had perform'd it if my known offence
> Had not disabl'd me, not all your force:
> These shifts refuted, answer thy appellant
> Though by his blindness maim'd for high attempts,
> Who now defies thee thrice to single fight,
> As a petty enterprise of small enforce.
>   (1208-23)

---

[11]See *Paradise Lost* XII.64-96.

Samson begins the argument with a review of the charges: "But I a private person. . . ." Charles Samuels, misreading this statement as an admission, writes that "Samson claims . . . the more particular right of private rebellion."[12] Empson, although he does not commit himself explicitly to this error, gives a similar impression. He writes that, because there has been no war of liberation, Samson acts "alone." He then quotes lines 1208-16. He concludes: "The rebel doctrine of the Inner Light . . . gave a dangerous amount of encouragement to any self-righteous fanatic."[13] But, of course, Samson is not admitting to private action; he is summing up Harapha's arguments in order to answer them. He is alone only because the Jews have failed him and failed their God (256-76, 1213-16). He is therefore put in the position of the "one just man" in an unjust situation.

What "disabl'd" Samson (1219), leading to the withdrawal of God's support and capture by the Philistines, was not the Philistine state, which could exert only "force" rather than authority, but his "known offense" (1218)—that is, revealing the secret of his strength to Dalila. As long as Samson served God, he had the power and the authority God gave him. When he put Dalila before God, however, in much the same way that Adam preferred Eve, he put his private desires and lusts before his public commission and so betrayed it. Thus Samson's regeneration, his recovery of the special relationship he once enjoyed with God, though chiefly important for its own sake and as an emblem for imitation, also will enable him to act one last time not as a private person, but as a magistrate and deputy of God, empowered to take, and not merely to wish, violent action against tyranny and wrong. Indeed, Samson has already recovered so far that he concludes his argument by challenging the Philistine champion to a judicial duel, in order to confirm who is in the right.[14] Because what he has argued is true, he is confident that God will uphold his cause. Final confirmation of Samson's argument comes when Harapha, who as the Philistines' champion is not a buffoon

[12]Samuels, pp. 500–501.

[13]Empson, p. 217.

[14]See George R. Waggoner, "The Challenge to Single Combat in *Samson Agonistes*," *Philological Quarterly*, 29 (1960), 82–92.

or an ordinary coward but a soldier and (humanly speaking) a hero, is comically humiliated. Samson thus wins his judicial duel more effectively than if the two had come to physical blows. His fortitude and magnanimity are revealed to be on a higher level than Harapha's; his commission from God as the champion of Israel proves superior to Harapha's as champion of Philistia.

4

In the play's final interview, Samson confronts the Public Officer. This title, given in full in the Argument and in the list of persons, is repeated by the Chorus when he enters (1306). It is difficult not to think that the word "public" in his title refers back to the argument about public and private action that shortly precedes this episode. One may also recall the phrases Milton uses in his prose works to describe those ordinarily authorized to wield authority and the sword of vengeance: *magistratus,* or *respublica et magistratus,* the state and its officers. To underline these associations, Milton adds visual evidence, and provides the Officer with an emblem of public office: "in his hand / A Scepter or quaint staff he bears" (1302-03). The Officer, in other words, has the commission and authority of the state to execute justice or vengeance on Samson. He is the deputy of the Philistine rulers: "to thee our Lords thus bid me say" (1310); "This answer, be assur'd, will not content them" (1322); "Regard thy self, this will offend them highly" (1333); "I am sorry what this stoutness will produce" (1346). Although these remarks have sometimes been interpreted to reveal sympathy for Samson's difficulties if he does not obey, in fact the officer is merely doing his duty to a tyrannical state. His sympathy is, on a small scale, not unlike Satan's pity for Adam and Eve, which must give place to the compelling necessity of "public reason just" (*Paradise Lost* IV.389). If Satan can be called the epitome of the tyrant, then the Public Officer is the epitome of tyranny's servant or instrument.

The entire double interview between Samson and the Public Officer underlines the confrontation between an unjust state, represented by a duly constituted deputy, and an apparently private person who has or will soon have the commission of God himself to take action. When Samson refuses to bow to the force of the state, he passes his final test, for almost immediately thereafter he receives from God the grace necessary to complete his regeneration, confirming in him patience to suffer and courage to act. Between the authority of man and the authority of God there can be no question:

> If I obey them,
> I do it freely; venturing to displease
> God for the fear of Man, and Man prefer,
> Set God behind: which in his jealousie
> Shall never, unrepented, find forgiveness.
> Yet that he may dispense with me or thee
> Present in Temples at Idolatrous Rites
> For some important cause, thou needst not doubt.
> $\qquad\qquad\qquad$ (1372-79)

Although Samson now knows that he need not obey the Mosaic law simply for its own sake, and recognizes how easily God can set it aside for some good cause, he also knows that he cannot dispense with the law himself, on his own judgment, and that no state has the authority to dispense him from it. He will not go to the temple because, unless he is inspired to the contrary, the law represents God's will in the matter, and God's will must come before man's. (Samson also reveals his new understanding of God's mercy: even this sin, if repented, would find forgiveness.)

Having resolved to prefer God before man or the government of man, in contrast with his former conduct, Samson is at once rewarded by feeling again the spirit and authority of God within him:

> Be of good courage, I begin to feel
> Some rouzing motions in me which dispose
> To something extraordinary my thoughts.   (1381-83)

Now Samson's spiritual preparation is complete; now he has permission to violate the letter of the Mosaic law; and now he is authorized to act once more as an instrument of divine retribution.

The Public Officer enters for a second time, and threatens Samson

with the full force of the state—beginning once again with a clear
statement of his own authority:

> *Samson,* this second message from our Lords
> To thee I am bid say. Art thou our Slave,
> Our Captive, at the public Mill our drudge,
> And dar'st thou at our sending and command
> Dispute thy coming? come without delay;
> Or we shall find such Engines to assail
> And hamper thee, as thou shalt come of force,
> Though thou wert firmlier fastn'd then a rock.
>
> (1391-98)

Like Satan, who thinks God rules only by the force of his thunder-
bolts, and who for his own weapon invents the cannon—an evil
parody of divine authority—the unjust state knowingly or unknowingly must replace justice with tyranny. Citizenship in such a state
becomes slavery and captivity; the "public Mill" is a fitting emblem
for the state itself; and "Engines to assail / And hamper" are the
ultimate emblems of authority corrupted to sheer force.

Samson now agrees to go with the Public Officer. His decision has
been brought about by the renewal of God's spiritual guidance, not
by change of mind or of principle. He dissimulates in his reply,
making an ironic statement of the truth which he knows the Officer
must, because of his total subservience to Philistia, misinterpret:

> I am content to go.
> Masters commands come with a power resistless
> To such as owe them absolute subjection;
> And for a life who will not change his purpose?
> (So mutable are all the ways of men)
> Yet this be sure, in nothing to comply
> Scandalous or forbidden in our Law.   (1403-09)

The conflict has been between duty to God and duty to the state. The
Public Officer, secure in his conviction that the Philistine state is all-
powerful, readily believes Samson's protestations that "absolute subjection" to it is only reasonable and probable. Yet the reader has just
heard Samson explain to his friends that human commands are "no
constraints," that if one obeys the state he does so freely. In fact, as

Joseph Summers points out, Samson's true "master" is God.[15] Only he can be said to have "power resistless," only he can demand "absolute subjection," only he, in a final irony that not even Samson can perceive, can offer eternal life. "And for a life who will not change his purpose?"[16]

When he goes to the temple of Dagon, Samson confronts not merely the representative of the state, but the unjust state itself: the Philistine people and all their lords. These are men who, by their sins against God and against Israel, have prepared their own destruction; they have compiled a debt which now must be paid. They are reprobate, insensate to goodness, given over to evil:

> Drunk with Idolatry, drunk with Wine,
> And fat regorg'd of Bulls and Goats,
> Chaunting thir Idol, and preferring
> Before our living Dread who dwells
> In *Silo* his bright sanctuary.   (1670-74)

Although each person in the crowd might repent individually at any moment up to his death, the Philistines have until this occasion rejected the possibility. Now their iniquities are full, in the Old-Testament phrase, and God's judgment is about to come upon them.

---

[15]Summers, "The Movements of the Drama," *The Lyric and Dramatic Milton*, ed. Summers (New York: Columbia Univ. Press, 1965), pp. 171–73. One supposes Milton may have had in mind that well-known injunction: "No man can serve two masters" (Mat. vi.24). The 1671 text reads "Masters"; Summers takes this ambiguous form as a possessive singular, but the more usual modernization of a possessive plural fits his reading better.

[16]The passage in Deuteronomy on God's right to execute vengeance also cites his power over life and death: "See now that I, even I, am he, and there is no god with me: I kill, and I make alive; I wound, and I heal: neither is there any that can deliver out of my hand" (xxxii.39). All of Deuteronomy xxxii.1-43, is relevant background to *Samson*. No citation of individual verses can provide the full context, particularly the important Deuteronomic interpretation of providential history. There are detailed parallels as well, such as the repeated references to God as a rock, which gives ironic meaning to the Officer's threat to drag Samson away "Though thou wert firmlier fastn'd then a rock," or God's threat to hide his face, in a context relevant to *S.A.* 1749.

Indeed, they invite their own ruin on themselves (1684), morally by their sins, literally when they attempt to force Samson to entertain them.

Samson's last speech to the crowd ironically continues what he had told the Public Officer in concealed fashion (that hearing he might not hear): that the strength of the Philistines, which they think irresistible, must bow before the greater strength of God, working through his champion. The Philistines, like their Officer, are unable to see beneath the surface admission of reasonable obedience to the Philistine power; they must be convinced by more than words:

> Hitherto, Lords, what your commands impos'd
> I have perform'd, as reason was, obeying,
> Not without wonder or delight beheld.
> Now of my own accord such other tryal
> I mean to shew you of my strength, yet greater;
> As with amaze shall strike all who behold.
>   (1640-45)

The irony with which Samson comments on the Philistines' lack of perception is no more powerful than the irony with which he addresses them as "Lords," and speaks of his obedience "as reason was" to their commands. For the pragmatic reasonableness of the Philistines is not the right reason of the devout man, and the demonstration Samson is about to give them will show how little real power and lordship they can claim in the face of an angry God. "Lords, Ladies, Captains, Councellors, or Priests, / Thir choice nobility and flower" (1653-54), all are destroyed; "The vulgar only scap'd who stood without" (1659). Samson has apparently submitted to their will, having no other choice; but at the last he acts of his "own accord," freely choosing his end, but supported and directed by God, who sanctions and gives authority to his action.

Although Manoa at first speaks confusedly and perhaps incorrectly of "thy [Samson's] revenge" (1591), the Chorus is more impersonal: "O dearly-bought revenge, yet glorious" (1660), and so finally is Manoa: "*Samson*...heroicly hath finish'd / A life Heroic, on his Enemies / Fully reveng'd" (1710-12). The grammatical construction of the two final statements is ambiguous: it is not clear whether Samson has avenged himself, or whether he has been avenged by God. In fact, both alternatives are true. Samson is avenged for his own blinding, imprisonment, suffering, and humiliation, but that is not the motivation from which he acts; and, moreover, it is unimportant in comparison with his fulfillment of his mission: the vindication and glorification of God, the salvation of Israel, and the destruction of her oppressors. The final cause of the Philistines' fall is God's providence, the efficient cause is Samson's free action cooperating with that providence. In still another sense, the Philistines bring destruction upon themselves, and so bear the moral responsibility for causing the catastrophe. For the evils which they committed against God, against Israel, and against Samson, and because of the blindness which moral evil in the person and the state brings about, they are finally destroyed.

Commissioned by God, Samson has been empowered to execute not private but divine vengeance, not spite but justice. In his deed he is supported and vindicated by God himself, the source of all public power and authority, the dispenser of life and of death, of punishment and of reward:

> Oft he seems to hide his face,
> But unexpectedly returns
> And to his faithful Champion hath in place
> Bore witness gloriously; whence *Gaza* mourns
> And all that band them to resist
> His uncontroulable intent.   (1749-54)

As in the Last Judgment, punishment and reward, destruction and vindication are conjoined. The evildoers and the persecutors receive their reward; the victims and the saints receive theirs. Vengeance is the Lord's; he will repay. In the words of the Son, before driving Satan and his followers over the edge of Heaven: "Vengeance is his, or whose he sole appoints" (VI.808). Samson is not Christ, but he is his type. He combats evil not perfectly, but with the highest heroism, self-sacrificing as well as active, of which man — aided and authorized by God but without the Christian revelation — is capable. Samson is not one of those whose action St. Paul condemns for opposing the powers that be. Instead, he is God's deputy, also described by the same passage from Romans, in words that perfectly fit him: "For he is the minister of God to thee for good. But if thou do that which is evil, be afraid; for he beareth not the sword in vain: for he is the minister of God, a revenger to execute wrath upon him that doeth evil" (xiii.4).

10

ASPECTS OF THE VERSE

Much of the greatness of *Samson Agonistes* lies in Milton's masterful technique: his skillful use of verse and of other poetic devices to help achieve his effects. Several studies have been made of the verse, but there has been as yet no agreement exactly how to scan many of the lines in the play.[1] It is not even certain that regular methods of scansion are always appropriate, although most critics agree that Milton employed variation and counterpoint, sometimes quite extreme, against the background of a more regular notional rhythm. That notional rhythm is generally iambic — the stress pattern into which English naturally falls. There are, however, relatively few com-

---

[1]See Robert Bridges, *Milton's Prosody* (London: Oxford Univ. Press, 1901); F. T. Prince, *The Italian Element in Milton's Verse* (Oxford: Clarendon Press, 1962); M. Whiteley and Prince, "Verse and its Feet," *Review of English Studies,* 9 (1958), 268–79; Edward Weismiller, "The 'Dry' and 'Rugged' Verse," *The Lyric and Dramatic Milton,* ed. Joseph H. Summers (New York: Columbia Univ. Press, 1965), pp. 113–52.

pletely regular lines, so that regularity itself as well as irregularity can
be used for emphasis, as it is in Samson's words to Dalila:

> Ĭ thought whĕre all thy círcling wíles would énd;
> Ĭn féign'd Rĕlígiŏn, smóoth hўpócrĭsíe.   (871-72)

The smoothness of the lines underlines the meaning, as it would not
in a more regular context.

The lines in *Samson* vary extremely in length as well as stress. In
addition, it is evident that Milton's ear was as sensitive to quantity
and duration of the syllables, or of the pauses between them, as it was
to stress. Scansion is inadequate to do more than approximate these
complexities. To take a brief example from Samson's prologue:

> Whý wăs mў breéding ordĕr'd aňd prĕscríb'd
> Ás ŏf ă pérsŏn sépărăte tŏ Gód,
> Dĕsígn'd fŏr gréat explóits; if Ĭ mŭst dýe
> Bĕtráy'd, Cáptĭv'd, aňd bóth mў Eýes pút oút,
> Máde ŏf mў Enĕmĭĕs thĕ scórn aňd gáze;
> Tŏ grínd ĭn Brázĕn Féttĕrs úndĕr tásk
> Wĭth thĭs Heáv'n-gíftĕd strĕngth? . . .
>   (30-36)

There is some uncertainty as to the proper stressing: weak stresses,
for example, might in theory be put on "and" and the last syllable of
"separate" in the first two lines. It would be possible to read the third
line "if Ĭ mŭst dýe." "Enemies" also might have a weak stress on the
last syllable. Quantity enters in: there are two places where three
stresses follow one another, but with quite different effects. In "bóth
mў Eýes pút oút," the word "Eyes" is dwelt on for some time, while
"put" and "out" are stressed but quantitatively short. In "thís Heáv'n-
gíftĕd strĕngth," all the stressed syllables are probably long: "this"
because of its consonants and the syntax leading up to it, "Heav'n" as
an elided word, and "gift-" because of its consonants. The first two
lines reverse the first foot, are almost identical metrically, and depart
but little from the notional pattern. The third line returns to regular
iambic pentameter, preparing the way for the extreme irregularities of
the fourth line with its reversed second foot — much more unusual
than a reversal of the first foot — and its cluster of concluding stresses.
The fifth line makes the transition to an extremely regular sixth line,

"To grind in Brazen Fetters under task," appropriate to the meaning.
Then the seventh line bursts once more into irregularity that emphasizes the paradox of working under task at the mill with a strength
given by God to achieve quite another purpose: "With this Heav'n-
giftĕd strength. . . ."

This passage, though it offers some problems, is relatively amenable
to traditional scansion. In other passages, however, Milton piles irregularity on irregularity until there is some question whether a
notional rhythm still exists. The problem is raised by Edward Weismiller, and presumably will be more fully discussed in his promised
essay on Milton's verse that will round out the Milton Variorum. My
own view is that Milton stretches traditional methods to their limits
(as in other areas) but that without some norm to be departed from or
played upon these very extremes would lose their effect.

Weismiller, in the most recent serious investigation of Milton's
prosody in the play, writes that the verse of *Samson Agonistes* is dry,
rugged, and uncompromisingly severe.[2] It is not a bad generalization
to proceed from; but the description no better fits the whole of *Samson* than the phrase "grand style" characterizes all of *Paradise Lost.*
(Another generally "spare" quality of the poetry in *Samson* is an absence of epic similes and elaborate comparisons, with a few obvious
exceptions. In comparison with *Paradise Lost* the metaphors are generally briefer, more organic, often buried from superficial view. Although this difference may be partly due to the dates of composition,
it more probably reflects the natural differences between the dramatic
and the narrative modes.)

The play, like the epic, is written in verse that is incredibly flexible,
corresponding at all times to the subject or the emotion that is being
expressed. The best term for this is Milton's own: decorum. But more
than a brief discussion of scansion, in a general study like this, is
likely to deter even willing readers. Moreover, it falsifies the reality
to discuss versification apart from such matters as imagery, diction,
tone, effect, meaning, or even intention. They are too interwoven. The
following passage illustrates some of the variety possible to Milton's

[2]Weismiller, p. 113 ff. The phrase is borrowed from John Addington
Symonds.

versification, and also the way it interacts with some of these other factors. It modulates from creeping, bitter, "dry" complaint to full-voiced, elevated lament, without any sense of incongruity; and it accomplishes this largely by means of the rhythms and the sounds of the words:

> They creep, | yet see, || I dark in light expos'd |
> To daily fraud, | contempt, | abuse and wrong, ||
> Within doors, | or without, || still as a fool, ||
> In power of others, | never in my own; ||
> Scarce half I seem to live, || dead more then half. ||
> O dark, | dark, | dark, | amid the blaze of noon, |
> Irrecoverably dark, | total Eclipse |
> Without all hope of day! (75-82)

Part of the contrasting effect resides simply in the meaning and the diction: from creeping, fraud, contempt, abuse, fool, living death, we turn suddenly to absolutes: dark, blaze, noon, total, all. Yet much of the effect also comes from the sense of restriction in the first five lines, verses which allow themselves no ounce of comfort. Frequent, cramping pauses, unpleasant consonant sounds, growing predictability of rhythm lead up to the final balance: "Scarce half I seem to live, dead more then half." In one sense, the next three lines give vent to an even intenser pain: yet at the same time they offer some relief, by permitting the emotion to be expressed at its fullest, and by a more unrestrained rhythm, thus allowing for the moment some sense of purgation. This release quickly begins to ebb away, however, into the flat, despairing rhythms of the last line. The whole speech from which this passage is taken, like Samson's other laments, plays all the permutations on grief and suffering, particularly by means of oscillation between such moods as intense pain amounting almost to exaltation; flat despair; a sense of suffocating restriction; or ironic bitterness. Usually these changes in mood are skillfully supported by the prosody.

Everyone, I think, would agree to the effectiveness of the verse in the passage just examined. There are many passages of similar power, which most readers can appreciate without stopping to examine them critically. Instead, it may prove more useful to look briefly at two other kinds of verse in the play, both of which have left the critics less than unanimously happy. One is the choral verse, especially with regard to the rhymes; the other is abstract or transcendent verse, which makes small use of concrete metaphor or "objective correlatives." As it happens, much of the latter kind of verse is also spoken by the Chorus.

2

The purpose and effect of the rhythms and the rhymes in the choruses have been much debated and discussed.[3] Milton appears to have been influenced by the Italian *canzone* and possibly the Italian choral drama, by the English ode, by the Book of Revelation, by the Psalms, and most directly by the Greek tragedians themselves. Probably Milton used rhyme to give his words a sense of elevation and sublimity, an effect found in several of his possible models. Just as Shakespeare reserves prose in his plays for the less dramatic moments, when emotions are plainly slack or clowns are on the stage, but turns to verse in moments of intensity or elevation, so Milton turns from a relatively looser or dryer kind of verse (though it is never quite prosaic) to a more elevated style, and for much the same reasons. The effect of elevation is quite obvious in such passages as the Chorus'

[3]In addition to Bridges, Prince, and Weismiller, see C. S. Lewis, *A Preface to Paradise Lost*, rev. ed. (New York: Oxford Univ. Press, 1961); Una Ellis-Fermor, *The Frontiers of Drama* (London: Methuen, 1945; rev. 1964); Christopher Ricks, *Milton's Grand Style* (on *P.L.*) (Oxford: Clarendon Press, 1963). For attacks on Milton's style see F. R. Leavis, *Revaluation: Tradition and Development in English Poetry* (London: Chatto & Windus, 1936; 2nd ed., 1956) and *The Common Pursuit* (London: Chatto & Windus, 1953); T. S. Eliot's essays on Milton; Louis Martz, "Chorus and Character in *Samson Agonistes*," *Milton Studies*, 1 (1969), 115–34. The Psalms are proposed as models by Frank Kermode, "*Samson Agonistes* and Hebrew Prosody," *Durham University Journal*, 14 (1953), 59–63; Italian models by Prince; Cowley's odes by Weismiller; Italian musical drama by Gretchen L. Finney, "Chorus in *Samson Agonistes*," *PMLA*, 58 (1943), 649–64. Roberts W. French, "Rhyme and the Chorus of *Samson Agonistes*," *Laurel Review*, 10 (1970), 60–67, suggests that the rhyme undercuts the Chorus; Robert Beum, "The Rhyme in *Samson Agonistes*," *Texas Studies in Literature and Language*, 4 (1962), 177–82, that it heightens and universalizes.

description of the battle of Ramath-lechi (124-50), or the praise of religious heroes (1268-96), or the commentary of the Semichoruses on Samson's last deed (1669-1707). In many respects, however, the most interesting of the choruses are those which have sometimes been thought merely comical, foolish, or bathetic.[4] One such, which may be taken to represent the rest, is the chorus following Samson's meeting with Manoa, which is mainly a response to the great lament with which that meeting ends:

> Many are the sayings of the wise
> In antient and in modern books enroll'd;
> Extolling Patience as the truest fortitude;
> And to the bearing well of all calamities,
> All chances incident to mans frail life
> Consolatories writ
> With studied argument, and much perswasion sought
> Lenient of grief and anxious thought,
> But with th' afflicted in his pangs thir sound
> Little prevails, or rather seems a tune,
> Harsh, and of dissonant mood from his complaint,
> Unless he feel within
> Some sourse of consolation from above;
> Secret refreshings, that repair his strength,
> And fainting spirits uphold.   (652-66)

The passage begins quietly, and reasonably, with the Chorus' references to philosophical wisdom: the appropriate tone to take with this subject. This wisdom is not simply to be dismissed by the reader, for most of it, especially "Patience as the truest fortitude," is central to the play's final meaning. But, as the Chorus goes on to suggest, theoretical wisdom, however wise, is one thing, real grief another. "Little prevails" and "Harsh," with the help of position and pause, stress the natural reaction to proffered advice. There is still a solution, however: the victim may "feel within / Some sourse of consolation from above; / Secret refreshings." The words carry the buried metaphor of grace and divine consolation welling up from within like a spring

[4]See Leavis, Martz, French; also Walter Savage Landor, "Southey and Landor: Second Conversation" (1846).

of water ("sourse"). To sum up, the Chorus offers good advice, knows that it cannot be immediately accepted, and suggests what will prove to be the solution: all reinforced by the verse.

The next lines of this chorus have proved more difficult. Refreshing consolation is for the future. Now the Chorus joins Samson in his lament:

> God of our Fathers, what is man!
> That thou towards him with hand so various,
> Or might I say contrarious,
> Temperst thy providence through his short course,
> Not evenly, as thou rul'st
> The Angelic orders and inferiour creatures mute,
> Irrational and brute.
> Nor do I name of men the common rout,
> That wandring loose about
> Grow up and perish, as the summer flie,
> Heads without name no more rememberd,
> But such as thou hast solemnly elected,
> With gifts and graces eminently adorn'd
> To some great work, thy glory,
> And peoples safety, which in part they effect:
> Yet toward these thus dignifi'd, thou oft
> Amidst thir highth of noon,
> Changest thy countenance, and thy hand with no regard
> Of highest favours past
> From thee on them, or them to thee of service.
>   (667-86)

We may remind ourselves once more about Milton's opinion of stoicism: that it is one of the opposites of true patience. "Sensibility to pain, and even lamentations, are not inconsistent with true patience; as may be seen in Job and the other saints, when under the pressure of affliction."[5] Out of sympathy for Samson's plight, the Chorus has joined his lament.

We must consider the often-raised possibility that these lines are meant to be comic, and that Milton is having some enjoyment at the expense of the Chorus' ignorance. In part, this interpretation rests on

---

[5]*Christian Doctrine; Works,* XVII, 253.

what seems to some critics the foolish meaning of the Chorus' lament. Contrary to their views, Milton thought it legitimate to question providence in circumstances such as these, as long as the questioner adheres to some ultimate trust and faith in God. Job was rebuked for his questions, yet he was also praised and rewarded for his patience and faith, and certainly was preferred to his more rationalistic comforters. The speaker in *Lycidas* calls divine providence "the blind *Fury* with th' abhorred shears" and calls into question God's conduct of the world, yet he receives a correction from Apollo that is less rebuke than comfort. These doubts and griefs are legitimately vented, just as long as the speaker listens to the offered consolations and corrections, and proceeds from questions to eventual assent.

That Milton is secretly laughing at his Chorus and undercutting its remarks by means of bad verse is unlikely for several other reasons. It would make the play primarily not a tragedy but a satire; it would satirize characters who are essentially well-meaning and who are searching for the truth, while satire is normally reserved for presumption, conceit, and pride; it would be unworthy of Milton's stated seriousness of purpose. Such an interpretation, moreover, removes most of our attention from Samson's plight and turns it instead on the psychology of the Chorus, quite unlike what we have learned to expect from the play. One difficulty still remains to be faced, however: it is that most handbooks of poetry tell us that three-syllable rhymes like "various" and "contrarious," or such heavy rhymes as "mute," "brute," "rout," "about," are usually comic.

The solution to this problem is that Milton's sense of decorum is a great deal wider than many critics are willing to admit, even though most of them are aware that he habitually flouted the rules when he saw some reason to do so. In the case of this speech, the poetry dances on a kind of tightrope, just keeping within the emotional bounds, although going well beyond what most poets would dare attempt. Although the context is totally different, I can think of no better image for what Milton accomplishes here than Chesterton's defense of orthodoxy against the charge of dullness:

> People have fallen into a foolish habit of speaking of orthodoxy as something heavy, humdrum, and safe. There never was anything so perilous or so exciting as orthodoxy. . . . It was the equi-

librium of a man behind madly rushing horses, seeming to swoop
this way and to sway that, yet in every attitude having the grace
of statuary and the accuracy of arithmetic.... In my vision the
heavenly chariot flies thundering through the ages, the dull
heresies sprawling and prostrate, the wild truth reeling but erect.[6]

Substitute for Chesterton's orthodoxy Milton's decorum, and the description is extremely apt. The daring rhymes "various" and "contrarious" suggest the Chorus' mood of rebellion, exasperation, and
near insolence in addressing the God whom they feel is responsible
for Samson's plight. The heavy sarcasm at the expense of brutes,
whether animal or human, is motivated by basically the same feelings. Consideration of great men, among them Samson, moves the
Chorus to greater dignity; but with their fall, "Amidst thir highth of
noon," the poetry lapses back into bitter dryness.

The next stanza of the chorus, with its description of carcasses left
out as a prey for dogs and fowls, will hardly seem comic. The Chorus
grows increasingly bitter when it thinks of the fates of great men. The
stanza ends, however, not with such relatively dramatic deaths, but
with "Painful diseases and deform'd, / In crude old age" — an "evil
end" that has not even a modicum of heroism in the ordinary sense to
recommend it. The progression is highly characteristic of Milton's
subtle inflations and deflations.

In the last brief stanza before noticing the approach of Dalila, the
Chorus brings its lament to a close:

> So deal not with this once thy glorious Champion,
> The Image of thy strength, and mighty minister.
> What do I beg? how hast thou dealt already?
> Behold him in this state calamitous, and turn
> His labours, for thou canst, to peaceful end.
>   (705-09)

The Chorus' brief characterization of Samson includes three phrases
that are as accurate and important as any in the play. It then turns to
some last pointed questions and complaints in the Jobean mode, but

[6]Gilbert Keith Chesterton, *Orthodoxy* (New York: Dodd, Mead, 1955), pp.
185–87.

quickly shifts to a concluding prayer that ends on a note of calm and promise for the future: "turn / His labours, for thou canst, to peaceful end." The two last words are charged with ironic, tragic, but ultimately consolatory meaning. The Chorus may complain, it may even address God querulously and almost disrespectfully; but its motivations are fundamentally the admirable ones of human sympathy and love, and it retains even in its exasperation and grief an ultimate faith in God's power and eventual beneficence. There are worse ways of addressing God. Finally, in the small phrase "*thou canst*" is as much understated meaning as the similar phrase Milton addresses to the Holy Spirit in the invocation to *Paradise Lost*: "Instruct me, for *Thou know'st*" (I.19).

One might object that the Chorus has said nothing whatever in this speech about Samson's guilt, which is the major cause of his calamitous downfall. Quite true, and yet irrelevant. It is Samson's responsibility to recognize the nature of his guilt and to repent it. The Chorus, as his friend, has assisted him in this, but now it plays a more sympathetic role. If it tells only a part of the truth, nothing it says is a lie, or is inappropriate to the occasion. The play must work its way to a fuller statement of the truth, and a more fruitful response to the events, as must the Chorus; but this expression of loyalty and venting of emotions is an allowable, probably even a necessary, stage in that psychological and spiritual journey.

It is usually when the Chorus departs from high seriousness or elevation that critics have had most difficulty with the nature of Milton's verse. In the chorus just examined this is due mainly to immoderate sorrow, sympathy for Samson's plight, exasperation and near rebelliousness at his treatment by providence. When one comes to think of it, such daring rhymes as "various" and "contrarious" are exactly appropriate to such a mood. The point is so crucial to a proper understanding of the play that it is worth expanding by a brief examination of part of another critically notorious chorus: the expatiation on the nature of women that follows Samson's interview with Dalila. In this case certainly the critics are right to insist that the reader is not meant to agree with everything the Chorus says. It is driven by partisan feeling to even greater extremes than before. Yet while not accepting as a statement of philosophic truth what is more in the nature of an emotional outpouring, we should nevertheless feel a wry sympathy for the loyalty which this partisanship implies:

> It is not vertue, wisdom, valour, wit,
> Strength, comliness of shape, or amplest merit
> That womans love can win or long inherit;
> But what it is, hard is to say,
> Harder to hit,
> (Whichever way soever men refer it)
> Much like thy riddle, *Samson,* in one day
> Or seven, though one should musing sit;
>   If any of these or all, the *Timnian* bride
> Had not so soon preferr'd
> Thy Paranymph, worthless to thee compar'd,
> Successour in thy bed,
> Nor both so loosly disally'd
> Thir nuptials, nor this last so trecherously
> Had shorn the fatal harvest of thy head.
>   (1010-24)

This generalized misogyny no more represents Milton's considered judgment (or that of the play) than Adam's similarly wild words after his fall but before his reconciliation with Eve — as most Miltonists would agree. But like Adam's speech it is dramatically appropriate. Milton has found for it the right style: except for the last line it is dry, bitter, comic, awkward, and twisted. Once more, and for similar reasons, the Chorus employs rhymes that are extravagant and unusual: "wit," "hit," "it," "sit," interspersed with "merit" and "inherit," which rhyme awkwardly with the others on the weak syllable. (Perhaps "refer it" belongs to this second group.) The effect is somewhat moderated by the lack of stress on many of these rhyme syllables, but at the same time strengthened by a great deal of internal assonance on the same sound: It, is, wisdom, win, inherit, it is, is, whichever, riddle, in, musing, If, *Timnian,* Paranymph, in, disally'd, this. If one includes the rhymes, short *i* appears twenty-four times in this passage. As the verse of *Samson* falls into no single invariant style — though certain styles are more characteristic of the play than others — so there is no single function for all the choral rhymes. Most result in elevation and emotional intensification, but in some exceptional passages such as this, the effect can be the reverse.

The rhyme is not the only sign of comic awkwardness in this passage. Because Milton habitually puts important, emphatic words at the ends of most of his lines (though *Samson* is more flexible in this regard than *Paradise Lost*), one immediately notices the peculiarly anticlimactic structure of these lines, further evidence that the Chorus' bitter mood is getting the best of it:

> But what it is, hard is to say,
> Harder to hit,
> (Whichever way soever men refer it)
> Much like thy riddle, *Samson,* in one day
> Or seven, though one should musing sit. . . .

There are few places in Milton's poetry where five consecutive lines end in similar anticlimax—and for that matter few lines containing such tongue-twisting internal rhymes as these: "Whichever way soever men refer it." The distortions are plainly deliberate—not to undercut the Chorus so much as to embody a moment of near-incoherent exasperation resulting from its sympathy with Samson and because it has been goaded to the limit by Dalila's last speech. This is the general import of the deliberate, comic awkwardness with which Milton has permeated this chorus.

3

The other kind of poetry that I particularly want to discuss might be called abstract, although in some cases a better term is transcendent. This is poetry that makes little or no use of what modern criticism has taught us to be the very essence of poetry: imagery, sensuousness, the concrete, the use of objective correlatives as vehicles for emotion. One can either learn to appreciate this kind of poetry or not, and no amount of rational discussion will do more than suggest that there may be prejudices in our responses to poetry that need clearing away. It may be admitted to begin with that "abstract" poetry is often bad: thin, weak, lacking in body, not poetry but simply statement. This does not prove, however, that all such poetry is bad by its very nature. It may also be admitted that such poetry must be used sparingly, and usually built up to and justified by verse that accommodates itself more directly to the senses. What is certain is that no critical "rule" holds good universally. There can be no rule that all poetry must be sensuous or concrete. Yeats is among the most concrete and powerful of all modern poets, a man who had an instinctive hatred of abstractions, which he thought bloodless: yet he used them in his poetry far more often than he would have liked to admit — often in his best poetry. Even Dante, one of the most concretely metaphoric of poets, used abstraction when it best served his purpose: note the brilliant mixture of imagery and metaphor with abstract language in Canto XXXIII of the *Paradiso*. So too the choruses of the Greek tragedies, which frequently mingle image and abstraction.

It should also be realized that modern criticism is overly concerned with imagery, metaphor, and other tropes. To some extent we have lost touch with many of poetry's other devices, such as rhythm, word-order, grammar, parallelism, and the like — what rhetoricians in Milton's time usually called schemes. These devices too appeal not only to the intellect, but also to the senses, especially the bodily sense of rhythm. Thus a passage of poetry which, as far as its imagery is concerned, seems abstract, may nevertheless speak strongly to deeper, unconscious feelings and bodily processes. Take, for example, the beginning of Manoa's last speech:

> Come, come, no time for lamentation now,
> Nor much more cause, *Samson* hath quit himself
> Like *Samson,* and heroicly hath finish'd
> A life Heroic, on his Enemies
> Fully reveng'd, hath left them years of mourning,
> And lamentation to the Sons of *Caphtor*
> Through all *Philistian* bounds. . . . (1708-14)

This speech seems deliberately to avoid using concrete imagery. Samson has quit himself, not like a lion or a phoenix, but like Samson. He has heroically finished nothing more specific than a heroic life. Any picture we may have in our minds — the lamentation of Manoa and the Chorus, the lamentation of the Philistines, Samson's life and death — is deliberately vague. It is evident, however, that this passage works in several concrete ways on the level of feelings that have nothing to do with vision or the external senses. One way is by means of the rhythm, both the meter as such, and the use of phrases of parallel length, together with heavy mid-line pauses. Another is the use of repetition and a kind of hypnotic circling about: from "lamentation" to "lamentation," *"Samson . . . like Samson,"* "heroicly . . . A life Heroic."

So too, a little later in this same speech, Manoa begins with something concrete — wailing and knocking the breast — but soon progresses to what might be thought the mere naming of emotions. Again, however, rhythms and repetition play their part, so that the feelings are powerfully and bodily transmitted on the poetic level:

> Nothing is here for tears, nothing to wail
> Or knock the breast, no weakness, no contempt,
> Dispraise, or blame, nothing but well and fair,
> And what may quiet us in a death so noble.
>
> (1721-24)

As in *Paradise Lost,* each line ending is marked off with an important word to be dwelt on, while to some extent the phrasing counterpoints the lineation. Considered rhetorically, as a period made up of individual members, we have something like this:

> *Nóthĭng* ĭs hére fŏr teárs,
> *nóthĭng* ⎰tŏ wáil
>   ⎱ŏr knóck thĕ bréast,
> *ñŏ* weáknĕss,
> *ñŏ* cŏntémpt,
> [no] dĭspráise,
> [n]ŏr bláme,
> *nóthĭng* bŭt ⎰wéll
>   ⎱and fáir,
> Ănd whát mǎy quiet ŭs ĭñ ă deáth sŏ nóblĕ.

This speech functions as the traditional *kommos* or dirge at the end of a Greek tragedy, and a large part of its power consists in the fact that it is precisely a dirge, with the rhythms of a dirge. Ostensibly — in fact, in a very real sense — Manoa is saying that there is no need to mourn, because his son has died victoriously and well. At the same time, however, most of his *words* are actually the words of a dirge, and his rhythms the rhythms of a dirge. Here is a consolation made up of such individual terms as tears, wail, knock the breast, weakness, contempt, dispraise, blame. Even the words which grammatically contradict their drift are negative: no and nothing. Thus the speech conveys a strong undercurrent of human grief and lamentation beneath its triumph, an anguish which modulates only in the last line-and-a-half into a more peaceful mood, with the appearance of the passage's first actually tranquil or positive words: well and fair, quiet, and noble. This turn in the emotional current is reinforced by the passage's vowel sounds. The first lines are dominated by long *a* and long *e*: here, tears, wail, weakness, dispraise, blame, sounds which disappear after the change in emotional emphasis. The same effect is accomplished by the repetition of grammatical negatives in the first lines: nothing, nothing, no, no; then a third nothing, which habit leads us to expect will be followed by still more sorrowful words, thus increasing the sense of surprise and relief at the appearance of the phrase "well and fair." At the end of the passage there is only one negative word, the ultimate one toward which Manoa's grief has been leading: death. But it has been reduced by its context to manageability (which ordering or attempted management of death is the main function of elegiac poetry). It is surrounded by quietness and by nobility, preceded by well and fair, and unobtrusively placed in the weak antepenult position so the last stress can fall on "noble." Thus Manoa recognizes and celebrates his son's victory, but comes to the recognition through human grief and difficulty: precisely the effect which Milton wishes to enforce at the close of his play.

The last passage in the play is the most difficult and also the greatest of Milton's essays in transcendent poetry. It is deeply understated, totally under control, but as full of emotion as any other passage the play can offer, including the great outbursts. Because of what has gone before, Milton has reached a point where "peace" *means* peace, and doesn't simply state it; "calm" transmits calmness; the windings and rhythms of the two sentences perfectly follow the development of feeling; while short, simple monosyllables play off against polysyllables. To cite a specific instance, note how the two-syllable word "passion" stands out from, and in a sense is rejected by, the monosyllables of the last line. The rhymes are formal and regular, bringing the play to an ordered, harmonious close. In the whole passage, the only words that might seem extraneous are the phrase "in place." They are accounted for, however, by Douglas Bush's gloss: "at the right place and *time*."[7] Few instincts in Milton are stronger than his consciousness that something has come too soon or is not yet ripe, as in the first lines of *Lycidas*. At the same time the sonnets on his twenty-third year and on his blindness bear witness to his strong faith in the ripeness and inevitability of God's time as opposed to man's. The concluding lines, although they remind us of the passions and sorrows that have been raised in the play, end with a sense of consolation, peace, and fulfillment.

> All is best, though we oft doubt,
> What th' unsearchable dispose
> Of highest wisdom brings about,
> And ever best found in the close.
> Oft he seems to hide his face,
> But unexpectedly returns
> And to his faithful Champion hath in place
> Bore witness gloriously; whence *Gaza* mourns
> And all that band them to resist
> His uncontroulable intent,
> His servants he with new acquist
> Of true experience from this great event
> With peace and consolation hath dismist,
> And calm of mind all passion spent.

[7] *The Complete Poetical Works* (my italics).

11

CONCLUSIONS

Not all the findings in this study were anticipated when it was begun. One unexpected development was the growing evidence of close compatibility between *Samson Agonistes* and the *Christian Doctrine.* The other prose works could have been more often cited, for they provide numerous parallels to certain special areas of concern in the poem, such as freedom of spirit, the right to depose tyrants, the slavish behavior of nations under tyranny, even the right to separate from an incompatible wife. No other single prose work, however, or even perhaps all of them together, proves as widely relevant to understanding the play as the *Christian Doctrine.* In fact, many more passages from this work could have been cited, on a variety of subjects, were it not for fear of overballasting this book.

What is one to make of this close correspondence between the two works? Critics now generally accept Maurice Kelley's theory, in *This Great Argument* (Princeton: Princeton Univ. Press, 1941), that Milton wrote the *Christian Doctrine* partly to set his thoughts in order in preparation for writing *Paradise Lost,* and that the theological framework of the epic and the theology of the prose treatise often coincide. The two works are not, of course, the same. One is a poem, with all that that implies, while the other is written in discursive prose; one moves the senses and emotions, the other addresses chiefly the reader's reason; one is more universal, deliberately reticent about Milton's individual or heretical beliefs, while the other is relentless in working them out. Nevertheless, the prose work is often most helpful in understanding the poem. William Riley Parker has this to say about the *Christian Doctrine:*

> The first part, involving thirty-three chapters, Milton subdivided to give adequate attention to God's nature, God's internal efficiency as revealed in general decrees and in the special decree of predestination, and God's external efficiency as revealed in generation, creation, and the divine government of all things including man before and after the Fall. (*Here was the theology basic to any epic poem concerned with the Creation and Fall.*) The second part, involving seventeen chapters, he subdivided to treat of man's various duties, towards God, towards himself, and towards his neighbour. (*Here was possible material for another, shorter poem.*)[1]

[1]Parker, *Milton: A Biography* (Oxford: Clarendon Press, 1968), I, 481, Parker's italics. In this book Parker also sums up his reasons for dating the play early, pp. 903–17. Other arguments for an early date are Parker, "The Date of *Samson Agonistes,*" *Philological Quarterly,* 28 (1949), 145–66; "The Date of 'Samson Agonistes': A Postscript," *Notes & Queries,* 203 (1958), 201–02; "The Date of *Samson Agonistes* Again," *Calm of Mind,* ed. Joseph A. Wittreich, Jr. (Cleveland: Press of Case Western Reserve Univ., 1971), pp. 163–74 (published posthumously and edited by J. T. Shawcross); Allan H. Gilbert, "Is *Samson Agonistes* Unfinished?" *Philological Quarterly,* 28 (1949), 98–106; John T. Shawcross, "The Chronology of Milton's Major Poems," *PMLA,* 76 (1961), 345–58. In favor of the traditional dating, see Ants Oras, "Milton's Blank Verse and the Chronology of His Major Poems," *SAMLA Studies in Milton,* ed. J. Max Patrick (Gainesville: Univ. of Florida Press, 1953), pp. 128–97; Oras, *Blank Verse and Chronology in Milton* (Gainesville: Univ. of Florida Press, 1966); Ernest Sirluck, "Some Recent Changes in the Chronology of Milton's Poems," *JEGP,* 60 (1961) 749–85. An article whose findings could support a late dating is Seymour Chatman, "Milton's Participial Style," *PMLA,* 83 (1968), 1386–99; and see the review of Oras' 1966 monograph by J. Max Patrick, *Seventeenth-Century News,* 25 (Summer 1967), item 3. The extremely complicated arguments from internal evidence are so far incon-

Since Parker believed, though without offering any definite proof, that *Samson Agonistes* was composed earlier than the *Christian Doctrine,* the shorter poem he refers to is presumably *Paradise Regained.* His statement may be slightly modified, since *Paradise Lost* makes some use of the second book of the *Christian Doctrine,* and *Paradise Regained* extensive use of the first. More important, however, *Samson Agonistes* makes just as full a use of what Milton assembled in the *Christian Doctrine* as either of the epics. Further, it uses not merely the same material, but also a great many theological points to which the other works refer scantly or not at all.

One example of this is the process of conversion and regeneration, which is given in far greater detail than in *Paradise Lost.* Another is the matter of vengeance: when it is justified, and who may take it. Yet another is the question of whether—and when—it is legitimate to conceal the truth. Still another is spiritual blindness and hardening of the heart, together with the very specialized matter of refusing to respond to a miracle. Or one may mention the matter of Samson's obligation to obey the law unless divinely exempted, in spite of the Chorus' persuasive appeals to the Miltonic principle of spiritual freedom, which he had expressed so widely in his earlier works, notably *Tetrachordon.* The logic of Milton's beliefs forced him in the *Christian Doctrine* to recognize that the Jews were bound to obey the Mosaic law, arbitrary and unsatisfactory as it was, unless specifically exempted from it by God, for as long as the covenant was in force. That is the position which Samson takes. Also significant is Samson's presumed salvation through faith in the Father alone, a point that was far from settled among Milton's contemporaries.[2]

---

clusive. Since the only real argument for dating the play early is the lack of incontrovertible evidence for dating it late, the traditional dating, supported by most scholars and best fitting the known facts of Milton's life and intellectual development, must be preferred. This is aside from any additional evidence presented here.

[2]For example, although Sir Thomas Browne was deeply concerned about the fate of virtuous pagans, he could see no theological way of rescuing them from hell (*Religio Medici* I.liv). Lactantius is among the few authorities Milton could cite in support of his views on this point; but see Donne, "Satyre III," ll. 9–15.

The lack of references to Samson's being taken directly into heaven may also be relevant. Direct references are kept out by historical probability and poetic purpose, but plainer indirect references could easily have been provided through the imagery, or through unconscious irony. As late as 1646, as Sonnet XIV reveals, Milton was orthodox on this point, but by the time he wrote the *Christian Doctrine,* very possibly while writing it and working his theories out to their logical conclusions, he became a mortalist. If the play was written after about 1658, then Milton would have assumed the death of Samson's soul along with his body, until he received eternal life at the Last Judgment. Connected with this is the fact that the play makes no easy distinctions between body and soul. The characters avoid mentioning the soul, which would be an anachronism, but they also fail to mention even the going-out of Samson's life's-breath, or *ruach.* It would have been easy for Milton to suggest a distinction between soul and body indirectly, but he does not. The play, in its imagery and the very texture of its language, posits an indissoluble connection between soul and body — just as in *Paradise Lost* or the *Christian Doctrine.*

None of these points can be said to constitute proof in itself. Taken together, however, along with the rest of the parallels turned up during the course of this study, their total effect is impressive. Milton first considered Samson as a subject for a play about 1639-42, when he wrote down his ideas for possible dramas in the Trinity College Manuscript. Samson is only one among dozens of other possible subjects, however, nor is it by any means the most prominent. Milton had gone through the Bible and British history and jotted down nearly every major figure or heroic action that might be of use to him. During his public years, Milton may have thought about the matter further, or even done some preliminary work on it, but no evidence for this exists.

There is one further piece of evidence against dating *Samson* earlier than the Restoration, as I attempt to show elsewhere.[3] Indeed, this evidence argues against *Samson* having been a serious project during the 1640's even in Milton's mind. In the Preface,

[3]There is a fuller discussion in my "Milton's *Samson* and the Stage, With Implications for Dating the Play," just completed.

Milton writes: "Division into Act and Scene referring chiefly to the Stage (to which this work never was intended) is here omitted." But *Samson* does divide naturally into acts; they are only unindicated in the text by act or scene divisions. Evidence from Milton's prose writings, especially the statement of his literary plans in *The Reason of Church Government*, shows that in the 1640's Milton hoped to write public drama that could be staged. He was planning to write moral or religious tragedies for the edification of the English people, to be performed outdoors or in public theaters. Milton knew the traditional as well as the contemporary Puritan objections to staging plays, but he thought them mistaken. The plays outlined in the Trinity Manuscript contain several stage directions: indications that he hoped to see them performed. Yet their structure and their use of conventions are similar to *Samson Agonistes*. *Samson* thus resembles plays Milton intended for acting, and is moreover intrinsically an actable play. Probably it was kept from the stage by extrinsic events — in particular, the downfall of the Commonwealth and the loss of Milton's hoped-for national audience. But Milton wrote in his preface that *Samson* was "never" intended for the stage. This word, taken with what we know of his earlier hopes and plans, shows that — except for the inconsequential notes in the Trinity Manuscript — *Samson* could not have been a serious project even in Milton's mind during the 1640's, when he was thinking in terms of staging his projected dramas, and probably was not begun before his time was taken up with writing the *Christian Doctrine* and *Paradise Lost*.

One cannot be certain about *Samson*'s dating solely on the basis of the obvious technical mastery it shows, since Milton might have been capable of equal achievements as early as 1637. But the subject, the complex spirit, the handling of the action, all tend to support a view of late composition. Probably, Milton wrote the *Christian Doctrine* and began serious work on *Paradise Lost* (which had a partial earlier existence as a play) in the late 1650's. When the full-scale epic was finished, he then went on to write the chaster and more difficult *Paradise Regained*. Finally, having considered in their broadest aspects happiness lost and regained, and the triumph of goodness over temptation, evil, and mortality, he turned to a more human situation: an example of what the larger combat might mean for an individual man. He chose one of the many heroes of faith between Adam and Christ, one of those who helped to prepare the way. He had passed over Samson in the sweeping history of *Paradise Lost,* but now he focused on him both as a specially-elected exemplary hero and as a representative of everyman. Samson is man, struggling with the problems of mortality, with only a dimly realized faith with which to combat them: yet that faith is sufficient. The mood of the play, as this study attempts to describe it, is consistent neither with Milton's political optimism in the 1640's, nor with his growing sense of discouragement and defeat—still clinging, however, to the last possibilities for political action—in the 1650's. All the sufferings of the commonwealth period and its aftermath went into this play, but they are confronted and subsumed, so that in the end *Samson* is a paean to man's triumph in spite of, in fact because of, his mortality.

2

To sum up everything that has been said thus far would point too much attention at the criticism itself, when it is better to direct it back toward the play. If the criticism has been worthwhile, it must be allowed to speak for itself. A few conclusions do emerge, however, and it will do small harm to mention some of them briefly. First, the more one looks at various aspects of *Samson Agonistes,* the more clearly it appears how well Milton has succeeded in writing a play that is both a tragedy and a story of religious regeneration and triumph. At nearly every point, in nearly every respect, everything comes together to contribute both to tragic experience and to religious enlightenment. At first glance, it might appear that Samson dies an active hero's tragic death, and suffers at the same time the religious death of a martyr, but even that is too simple: for Samson's action is that of a religious champion and redeemer, while his passive suffering is a part of his tragedy. Or it might be thought that the Chorus' closing words, "All is best," refer principally to Samson's religious triumph, and his reconciliation with God; but they can equally well recall his sublime death as a tragic hero, as a man who has died well and proven himself larger than common humanity.

A second conclusion is that while Milton adheres closely to the examples set him by the Greek tragedians, the spirit of *Samson* is not simply Greek. It is a complex mixture of Hebrew story, Greek technique, and Christian purpose: but its spirit can only be said to be an inextricable mixture of all three.[4] Its tragic effect, its sense of inevitability, its pervasive use of irony, its wide use of rational argument, its choral solemnity, are mainly but not exclusively Greek. Its concern with Law, with national destiny, with the purifying power of suffering, with providential guidance, with vengeance and justice, are characteristically but not exclusively Hebrew. Its efforts to rise out of law into spirit, its theme of vicarious sacrifice, its sense of dignity emerging from suffering and degradation, its shadowing-forth of the Messiah, are typically but not exclusively Christian. To mention only a few of the qualifications one must make to these statements: Judaism has its own spirit of irony and tragedy, the Greek tragedies are often concerned with the conflict between law and the individual, Christianity and the Greeks are concerned with justice and vengeance, and the purifying power of suffering is of major concern to all three traditions.

As far as the religious meaning is concerned, not that the tragic can really be separated from the religious, Samson dies a Hebrew hero. Yet his example suggests to Manoa and the Chorus that there is something more — at the very least, that God is above the Law. At the same time it suggests to the presumptively Christian reader both man's inadequacy without full revelation of the Savior (who though not mentioned in the play is known to the reader), and at the same time the sufficiency of a partly blind faith in God, that will save

---

[4]The problem of spirit has been complicated because many Miltonists agree that the Greek tragedies and Greek gods are somehow essentially rational, while Hebrew spirit and God are irrational. Nothing could be more misleading. We now recognize better than the earlier classicists the large irrational element in the Greek spirit, nor is the Old Testament as wholly irrational as some nineteenth-century critics once thought. Discussions of the spirit of *Samson* in terms of Matthew Arnold's "Hellenism" and "Hebraism," often without mention of Arnold, are illuminating but somewhat disingenuous.

Samson eternally in spite of his partial ignorance. In the deepest sense, *Samson* is a Christian play, addressed to Christian readers, or those willing to suspend disbelief; but it remains human and tragic, it engages man's experience in the world, and it confronts problems of shame, suffering, and death that no faith can entirely dispense with—all by means of its masterly indirection. Milton has therefore written a play that is Christian in no simple sense.

One should stress again the play's deep humanity. Although Samson is a tragic hero of no ordinary stature, and a great religious hero and exemplar as well, throughout the whole course of the drama he remains very much a man. His humanity is a part of his greatness—indeed, a vital and essential part of it. His humanity is not really separable from his role as a hero, nor is his psychological development really distinct from his religious growth or his acquist of tragic experience. Even after the rousing motions have confirmed his reunion with God and strengthened him to confront with perfect resolution whatever extraordinary events providence has in store for him, no sensitive reader can fail to notice and sympathize with his still human feelings that are revealed during these last moments of his life.

A last conclusion, or perhaps better a last caution, is that none of the patterns that have been discussed are simply imposed on the play. They grow out of its deeply human interactions, and they are, for the most part, more subtle and complex than criticism can well do justice to. Yet as in all Milton's poems, this complexity is seldom in tension or conflict with itself. *Samson Agonistes,* like *Lycidas* or *Paradise Lost,* can be almost endlessly glossed and commented on, and more and more facets of it can thus be brought to light (until the reader's patience may sometimes be tried): yet *Samson* remains an organic whole for a reader who draws back and approaches it afresh: its action, its purpose, its emotional effect unified and natural and (using the word in roughly its theological sense) ultimately simple.

INDEX TO PRINCIPAL PASSAGES
FROM *SAMSON AGONISTES*

GENERAL INDEX

BOSTON PUBLIC LIBRARY

3 9999 00121 148 9

Boston Public Library

Copley Square

General Library

PR3566
.L6
1974
2633466409

The Date Due Card in the pocket indicates the date on or before which this
book should be returned to the Library.
Please do not remove cards from this
pocket.